The Doctrine of
Responsible Party Government

The Doctrine of Responsible Party Government

Its Origins and Present State

AUSTIN RANNEY

THE UNIVERSITY OF ILLINOIS PRESS, URBANA, 1962

For my parents,

FRANK ADDISON *and* FLORENCE EDITH RANNEY

Preface

This study was first presented as a doctoral dissertation to the Graduate Faculty of Yale University in 1948. At that time the only major recent discussions of the doctrine of responsible party government available were E. Pendleton Herring's *The Politics of Democracy* (1940) and E. E. Schattschneider's *Party Government* (1942). Since 1948, however, this point of view has emerged from relative obscurity to occupy the center of the stage for those political scientists who are concerned with the proper organization and function of political parties in the American system. Perhaps the most important single cause for the party-government doctrine's current prominence was the publication, in 1950, of the report of the Committee on Political Parties of the American Political Science Association—an event which has evoked a considerable and ever-growing volume of literature on these important and difficult problems.

The present study has therefore been considerably revised in order to take into account this new literature on American political parties; and it is the author's hope that his analysis of the original advocates and critics of the doctrine of responsible party government will not only make clear the sources and origins of that doctrine, but will also make a useful contribution to the current debate about its validity.

The author is deeply grateful to Professor E. E. Schattschneider of Wesleyan University, who suggested the subject of this study, and to Professor Emeritus Francis W. Coker of Yale University, who directed its initial phases. For reading all or portions of the original manuscript and making many valuable suggestions, he also wishes to thank Professor Robert A. Dahl and Cecil H. Driver of Yale, and Dr. E. M. Kirkpatrick and Dr. Charles B. Hagan of the Department of State. For making many useful contributions to the preparation and revision of the manuscript for publication, he is indebted to Professors Clarence A. Berdahl, D. Philip Locklin, Jack W. Peltason, Raymond P. Stearns, and Francis G. Wilson, all of the University of Illinois. The author also wishes to acknowledge his particular debt to Dr. Howard R. Penniman of the Psychological Strategy Board for directing the research for the study and for providing its orientation in the problem of democracy and political parties, and to Professor Willmoore Kendall of Yale, who, by his careful guidance of its organization and writing, converted the chore of writing a doctoral dissertation into an exciting process of learning. Finally, for so well fulfilling her classic wifely function of restoring morale and lifting spirits, the author's wife, Elizabeth M. Ranney, is offered this brief acknowledgment of her invaluable help.

AUSTIN RANNEY

University of Illinois
December 1, 1953

Acknowledgments

The author gratefully acknowledges the permissions granted by the following publishers and authors to reprint certain passages from the works listed below:

The American Political Science Association, through its executive director, Edward H. Litchfield, for use of my article, "Toward a More Responsible Two-party System: A Commentary."

The *Southwestern Social Science Quarterly,* through its editor, Oliver Benson, for use of my article, "Goodnow's Theory of Politics."

Doubleday, Page and Company, for use of R. S. Baker, *Woodrow Wilson: Life and Letters.*

Henry Holt and Company, for use of Herman Finer, *Theory and Practice of Modern Government,* revised edition.

Professor Sidney Hook, for use of his *Reason, Social Myths and Democracy.*

The Macmillan Company, for use of R. M. MacIver, *The Web of Government.*

The Oxford University Press, for use of Ernest Barker, *Reflections on Government.*

Rinehart and Company, for use of E. E. Schattschneider, *Party Government;* and for use of *Toward a More Responsible Two-party System* (Copyright, 1950, by the American Political Science Association).

The University of Illinois Press, for use of Willmoore Kendall, *John Locke and the Doctrine of Majority Rule.*

The University of Pennsylvania Press, for use of A. D. Lindsay, *Essentials of Democracy.*

Mrs. Edith Bolling Wilson, for use of R. S. Baker and W. E. Dodd, editors, *The Public Papers of Woodrow Wilson,* Volume I.

Contents

CONTENTS

Part One

Preliminary Considerations

CHAPTER ONE

The Problem

Concern with the kind of institutions necessary for translating the popular will into governmental action is a relatively recent development among democratic political theorists. Although many political thinkers beginning with Plato have discussed the merits of democracy, discussion has centered for the most part about such issues as that of the people's right and fitness to rule. The question of *how* the people might rule or whether it is even possible for them to rule have not, until recently, concerned either the opponents or defenders of democracy. As Professor E. E. Schattschneider observes:

So certain were the philosophers that the people would in fact use their new powers that the whole controversy has been concentrated on the competence of the masses to direct public affairs. At this point oceans of ink have been wasted. In the manufacture of this breach in the theory of the subject, the admirers and critics of democracy have collaborated with a singular unanimity of opinion. The enemies of democracy assumed, as unquestionably as did its friends, that popular sovereignty would be effective automatically. The fact that both sides agreed upon a definition produced an interesting debate. It is unfortunate, however, that the definition agreed upon had little relation to the facts of a working democratic system of government.[1]

Thus John Locke, to take only one leading example, disposed of the question with his doctrine of the "right of revolution." Though he nowhere bothered to state it explicitly, "[Locke] must have supposed (1) that independently of institutional midwifery of any kind, there will at all moments exist such a thing as a majority-will with which governmental law and policy can be made to coincide, (2) that the majority will in fact revolt when the governmental act does not coincide with its will, and (3) that revolutionary movements enjoying majority support can be counted upon to succeed." [2] None of these three propositions would command support from modern students of politics; but

[1] *Party Government* (New York: Farrar and Rinehart, 1942), pp. 14-15. Schattschneider suggests that the explanation for this omission lies in the fact that until recently political thinkers had no actual democratic government to observe in action, and could therefore not be expected to realize the problems involved in keeping governmental action responsive to the popular will. *Ibid.*, pp. 13-14.

[2] Willmoore Kendall, *John Locke and the Doctrine of Majority Rule* (Urbana: The University of Illinois Press, 1941), pp. 128-29. Kendall goes on to point out that Locke's failure to consider seriously the problem of *how* the majority will control the government is his gravest deficiency as a theorist of majority-rule democracy. *Ibid.*, pp. 124-29.

3

for Locke, reputedly one of our greatest democratic philosophers, they constituted an adequate conception of the machinery necessary for keeping the government amenable to the majority-will.

The classical theorists' slighting of this question has left modern democratic thinkers a big job to do. To define democracy as "government by the people," or "government by consent of the governed," or even "government based upon political equality, popular sovereignty, popular consultation and majority-rule" [3] is to state where ultimate political power in the community is located. One learns little from such definitions, however, about how this power is to be made effective, although this question surely becomes crucial, at some point, in any discussion of the merits of democracy. If, for example, we should discover that there is no machinery capable of converting the popular will into governmental action, and that the people in fact *cannot* rule, then insistence upon their *right* to rule would be idle. It is for this reason that most modern theorists of democracy would agree with Ernest Barker that one of the democrat's biggest jobs is to search for the best kind of "conduit or sluice by which the waters of social thought and discussion are brought to the wheels of political machinery and set to turn those wheels." [4]

In the American system, as in most systems professing to be democratic, political parties have historically been the most important agency for bringing the popular will to bear upon the government. [5] The study of party and its function would therefore seem to be quite as important as the study of the more formal aspects of American government; and one might suppose that American political scientists would have undertaken such a study long ago. Curiously enough, however, political parties were hardly mentioned, let alone carefully investigated, by American scholars until after the Civil War. [6] The

---

[3] This is the definition given by Kendall. *Ibid.*, pp. 31-32. The author prefers this definition of democracy, and will use it throughout this study.

[4] *Reflections on Government* (London: Oxford University Press, 1942), p. 39.

[5] Cf. James Bryce, *The American Commonwealth* (2 vols.; London: Macmillan and Company, 1889), I, 639; Herman Finer, *The Theory and Practice of Modern Government* (2 vols.; London: Methuen and Company, 1932), I, 395-97, 539-46; R. M. MacIver, *The Web of Government* (New York: The Macmillan Company, 1947), pp. 210-15; Schattschneider, *Party Government*, pp. 2-3; and Barker, *Reflections on Government*, pp. 37-39.

[6] Cf. Austin Ranney, "The Reception of Political Parties into American Political Science," *Southwestern Social Science Quarterly*, XXXII (December, 1951), 183-91. Although such writers as Madison, Jefferson, Taylor, Kent, and Story mentioned parties, they did so only fragmentarily and unsystematically. Only Francis Lieber, in his *Manual of Political Ethics* (2 vols.; Boston: Charles C. Little and James Brown, 1838), I, 413-68, examined parties at any length, and even he abandoned the subject in his later works. Theodore Dwight Woolsey's *Political Science* . . . (New York: Scribner, Armstrong and Company, 1877) devoted an entire chapter to an analysis of the American party system, and from then on American studies of parties appeared with rapidly increasing frequency. For an explanation of the pre-Civil War scholars' silence on parties and the reception of parties after 1870, see Ranney's article cited above.

particular period covered by this study has been selected for two reasons: First, because in it American political scientists first began to publish systematic analyses of the function of parties in the American system; and, second, because much of the present-day literature on this question has advanced remarkably little beyond the pioneer writers of the 1870-1915 period.[7]

In order to understand the general nature of the period's literature on parties, however, it is first necessary to observe the points at which its major agreements and disagreements took place. It should be noted, for one thing, that almost all of the writers in the period professed a belief in democracy and conceived of themselves as searching for the best means of establishing popular control over the formal government, although there was no definition of democracy or conception of what constituted "popular control" agreed upon among them. In the second place, they all agreed that political parties had played and were playing an important role in the American system; but they disagreed upon the nature and desirability of that role as well as upon the broader question of whether in "a truly democratic America" either the parties they knew or any possible future variant of them could have a place. Finally, they all agreed that the American parties they observed were not translating the popular will into governmental action as faithfully as was desirable; but they disagreed upon the reasons for this failure as well as upon what should be done about it.

This study has two major purposes. The first of these is to summarize and analyze the ideas of certain writers in this period, 1870-1915, about the function of political parties in the American system. The writers to be considered are: Woodrow Wilson, A. Lawrence Lowell, Henry Jones Ford, Frank J. Goodnow, M. I. Ostrogorski, and Herbert Croly. They have been selected because, in the author's opinion, their inquiries into the problem were more thorough and more systematic than those of their contemporaries, and because one or another of them represents each major view expressed in the period on the issues outlined above.

In attempting to accomplish this first purpose, the author proposes to summarize and examine critically each writer's views upon the following key questions:

1. What is the nature of democracy? What is meant by "popular control of government?"

[7] For a brief but helpful general history of ideas about the nature and function of party, see F. G. Wilson, *Elements of Modern Politics* (New York: McGraw-Hill Book Company, 1936), pp. 321-31. For a brief account of the sudden increase in American studies of party after 1870, see C. E. Merriam and H. F. Gosnell, *The American Party System* (rev. ed.; New York: The Macmillan Company, 1933), pp. 409-13. For a brief summary of some interpretations of party made in this period, see C. E. Merriam, *American Political Ideas* (New York: The Macmillan Company, 1920), pp. 289-309. The author's own survey indicates that from 1870 to 1889 only six works by American authors dealing with parties were published; from 1890 to 1900 seventeen more appeared, and since 1900 they have been printed in great profusion.

2. What is a political party? Who are its members? What is and/or should be the nature of leadership within a party, and what sort of control should the party members have over their leaders?

3. What functions should political parties perform in a democratic system? What additional functions, if any, should they perform in the American system in particular? [8]

4. Which of these functions are being performed and which are not performed by the actual American parties observed? Are the existing parties on the whole doing more good than harm?

5. Why do the existing parties fail to do a better job?

6. What should be done in order to secure a more accurate expression of the popular will and its more faithful translation into governmental action?

The second purpose of this study is to determine what contribution these writers can make to the present-day discussion of the function of political parties in the American system. Most of that discussion today centers about a set of answers to the above questions which, taken together, may conveniently be labeled the doctrine of responsible party government. This point of view first gained the spotlight in 1942 with the publication of Professor Schattschneider's provocative and widely read *Party Government* and has held it ever since.[9] The full measure of its present acceptance by a considerable number of American political scientists is shown by the fact that in 1950 the Committee on Political Parties of the American Political Science Association published a report of its recommendations for improving our party system; and most of these recommendations were based squarely upon the doctrine of responsible party government.[10] The report touched off a debate over the proper organization and function of American parties that is far greater in both volume and intensity than in any period since 1915.[11]

Judging from the content of the present controversy, however, few of its

---

[8] It must here be made clear that some of the writers to be considered took no explicit position upon this question. Henry Jones Ford, for example, professed to be describing *only* the functions American parties were performing. Like all the others, however, he made certain judgments of the existing parties, praising them in some places and criticizing them in others. These judgments were based upon a conception of how parties *should* behave in a democratic system which was no less important to his position because he did not state it explicitly. The author will therefore attempt to infer Ford's views on this question from the explicit judgments he made of the existing party system.

[9] See also Professor Schattschneider's *The Struggle for Party Government* (College Park, Md.: The University of Maryland Press, 1948).

[10] "Toward a More Responsible Two-party System," *American Political Science Review*, XLIV, Supplement (September, 1950). This report was also published between boards by Rinehart and Company in the same year.

[11] See, for example, such critical analyses of the report as Julius Turner, "Responsible Parties: A Dissent from the Floor," *American Political Science Review*, XLV (March, 1951), 143-52; and Austin Ranney, "Toward a More Responsible Two-party System: A Commentary," *American Political Science Review*, XLV (June, 1951), 488-99.

participants, whether attackers or defenders of the report, are aware that the political scientists at the turn of the century had so thoroughly explored these crucial and difficult questions. So the present study is offered, not simply as a study in the history of American political ideas, but rather in the hope that a rediscovery and re-examination of the writings of Wilson, Lowell, Croly, and the rest may help us today in our effort to understand and evaluate both the doctrine of responsible party government and the role that our parties actually *do* perform in the American system.

Before we can judge the value of this contribution, however, it is first necessary to summarize in some detail the current doctrine of responsible party government. And that is the task of the next chapter.

CHAPTER TWO

The Case for Responsible
Party Government

In explicating the doctrine of responsible party government, it is first necessary to recognize, in order that we may avoid it, a kind of confusion that runs
through much of the present-day literature about the function of political parties
in the American system. The confusion arises because frequently the terms
"function" and "parties" are each used in two interchangeable but quite
different senses. "Parties" often refers in one place to (a) the existing organizations, and in another to (b) some possible future variant of them. "Function"
sometimes means (1) the role the parties are observably performing, and sometimes (2) the role they *should* perform.

Most contemporary political scientists, including those who take the party-
government position, agree that American parties, in sense (a), have in fact
performed a number of valuable functions, in sense (1), in the American
system. The points are often made, for example, that parties have reduced the
conflict between legislative and executive agencies sufficiently to minimize the
crippling effects of separation of powers and thereby enabled the formal governments to act more effectively; that parties have been great unifying, nationalizing forces; and that they have made American government more amenable
to the popular will than it would have been in their absence.[1]

The doctrine of responsible party government, however, is primarily concerned with parties in sense (b) and with the functions in sense (2). Yet its
advocates are often guilty of confusing the meanings of "party" in precisely
the fashion described above. As a leading example of this kind of confusion,
consider the opening argument of the Parties Committee report. The Committee, to their credit, recognized the necessity of making their model party
system—in sense (b)—explicit: "There is little point to talking about the
American party system in terms of its deficiencies and potentialities except

---

[1] Cf. Schattschneider, *Party Government*, pp. 1-3; MacIver, *The Web of Government*,
p. 213; H. R. Penniman, *Sait's American Parties and Elections* (4th ed.; New York:
Appleton-Century-Crofts, 1948), pp. 177-81; V. O. Key, *Politics, Parties and Pressure
Groups* (2d ed.; New York: Thomas Y. Crowell Company, 1947), pp. 666-75, 698-700;
and C. E. Merriam and H. F. Gosnell, *The American Party System* (3d ed.; New York:
The Macmillan Company, 1947), pp. 426-37.

8

against a picture of what the parties ought to be. Our report would be lacking in exactness without an indication of the sort of model we have in mind." [2] They then proceed to outline the leading characteristics of what they regard as a model party system: It must be effective, in that it must have parties that are "able to bring forth programs to which they commit themselves . . . [and that possess] . . . sufficient internal cohesion to carry out these programs." And such a system must also have an effective opposition party which "acts as the critic of the party in power, developing, defining and presenting the policy alternatives which are necessary for a true choice in reaching public decisions." [3]

Having outlined the nature of their model party system, the Committee next faced the task of convincing their readers that this is a desirable model—that this is indeed what American parties *should* be like. Their report, however, makes no such attempt to defend the desirability of their model. In place of such a defense the reader is given this curious statement: "Beyond that, the case for the American two-party system need not be restated here. The two-party system is so strongly rooted in the political traditions of this country and public preference for it is so well established that consideration of other possibilities seems entirely academic." [4] After absorbing this statement the reader cannot be sure just what the Committee means by the term "the American two-party system"; for, in its foreword, the report previously described it as consisting of "two loose associations of state and local organizations, with very little national machinery and very little internal cohesion . . . [both of which are] . . . ill-equipped to organize [their] members in the legislative and the executive branches into a government held together and guided by the party program.[5]

It therefore becomes evident that the Committee used the term, "the American two-party system," in not the usual two, but in no less than *three*, different senses: (a) the party system that exists now, (b) the model party system, and (c) the present monopoly of public support and governmental offices in the United States by the two major parties, in contradistinction to the dispersion of public support and governmental offices among many parties, as in certain European countries—in short, a "two-party system" as opposed to a "multi-party system." And the argument apparently is this: The Committee thinks (a) should be made more like (b) and sees no reason to defend (b) as a desirable model, because the American people are so deeply committed to (c) that any other model is impracticable!

This kind of confusion runs through much of the present-day party-government literature, and we shall observe it again in some of the older

[2] "Toward a More Responsible Two-party System," p. 17.
[3] *Ibid.*, pp. 17-18.
[4] *Ibid.*, p. 18.
[5] *Ibid.*, p. v.

writers to be considered in subsequent chapters of this study. It is not, however, an inherent characteristic of the doctrine of responsible party government. And the remainder of this chapter will be devoted to the explication of the party-government model, the reasons why its advocates believe it to be a desirable model, their assessment of the existing American party system in the light of the model, and their proposals for making the existing system more like the model. Their case begins with a certain conception of the nature of democracy.[6]

THE NATURE OF DEMOCRACY

The doctrine of party government rests upon the belief that, in a modern, thickly populated society like that of the United States, democracy should be conceived of as popular *control* over government, and not as popular *participation* in the day-to-day activities of government. In such a society, the argument runs, governmental problems are so complex that the great bulk of the people can have neither the leisure nor the special training required to formulate specific and workable measures for their solution. It does not follow, however, as a number of critics of democracy have argued, that popular government is therefore impossible.[7] It follows only that the democrat must be sure what sort of a contribution the people must make to the governmental process in order to satisfy the requirements of "government by popular sovereignty, political equality, popular consultation and majority-rule." The answer to that question is provided by Professor Finer:

The general body of the electorate does not, and cannot, under present conditions, contribute more to politics than some a smoldering, some a flaming, sensibility of their wants and passions. Even these are not clearly focused to themselves, and are hardly articulate without use of the jargon of propaganda. This holds good not

---

[6] The full case for the doctrine of responsible party government which occupies the rest of this chapter cannot be found, in the present writer's opinion, in any other single place. What follows, then, is his own collection of the various leading party-government arguments and their assembly in what seems to him the most logical order. There are three main sources of these arguments: first and most important, the writings of Professor Schattschneider already cited; second, "Toward a More Responsible Two-party System"; and third, Chapters 12, 13, and 14 of Finer's *Theory and Practice of Modern Government*.

[7] Two such criticisms of democracy by contemporary American writers may be found in H. L. Mencken, *Notes on Democracy* (New York: Alfred A. Knopf, 1926); and James Burnham, *The Machiavellians, Defenders of Freedom* (New York: The John Day Company, 1943). Its most famous expositions, however, are by Gaetano Mosca, *The Ruling Class,* translated by Hannah D. Kahn, edited and revised by Arthur Livingston (New York: The McGraw-Hill Book Company, 1939); Vilfredo Pareto, *The Mind and Society,* translated by Andrew Bongiorno and Arthur Livingston, edited by Arthur Livingston (New York: Harcourt, Brace and Company, 1935): and Robert Michels, *Political Parties: A Sociological Study of the Oligarchical Tendencies of Modern Democracy,* translated by Eden and Cedar Paul (London: Jarrold and Sons, 1915).

only of the poor; it is just as true of the middle and upper classes who have not had a special training in the social sciences. A consciousness of wants is the independent contribution of the electorate to representation: but not a knowledge of what is possible.[8]

In a democratic society, therefore, the people, through some kind of "institutional midwifery," make known their wants to the government's rulers, i.e., those who at the moment are carrying on its day-to-day activities. They also exercise *control* over the government in this sense: If half-plus-one of the people feel their wants are not being satisfied, they can, in peaceful and orderly elections coming at frequent intervals, replace the set of rulers in power with an alternate set, an "opposition," which all along has been "keeping its ear to the ground" to learn and anticipate the people's wants, pointing out the errors and deficiencies of the rulers in power, and which now stands ready itself to assume power. Thus the people control the government by determining who shall carry on its activities. [9] There is plenty of popular participation in government, but not in the delusive sense of participation in the specific work of governmental agencies. For, as Sidney Hook points out: "The effective working of democracy demands the presence of a number of . . . conditions. Among these, the active participation of the governed in the processes of government is primary. By active participation is meant not the attempt to do the specific work of officials but free discussion and consultation on public policies, and voluntary cooperation in the execution of mandates reached through the democratic process." [10]

It should be pointed out that this conception of democracy, unlike some of those to be encountered in subsequent chapters of this study, is a purely political one. It is concerned only with the location of ultimate political power in the community and with the processes by which that power is made effective. The nature of the particular decisions made by such a government do not make it more or less democratic so long as the framework within which they are made exhibits the above characteristics. In short, party government is a proposal for implementing majority-rule, no matter what the majority may decide to do with its power. Any decision made in accord with the majority's wishes is, by definition, a "democratic" decision. The problem to which the proponent of party government feels he has a special answer is: How can majority-control of the government be made effective?

[8] *Theory and Practice of Modern Government*, p. 274.

[9] Cf. Professor Finer's view that "the desire for responsible government is paramount: people wish not merely to represent their views, but actually to make and unmake governments." *Ibid.*, p. 219.

[10] *Reason, Social Myths and Democracy* (New York: The John Day Company, 1940), p. 287.

THE NATURE AND CONDITIONS OF PARTY GOVERNMENT

The second major contention of the doctrine of party government is that the popular control over government which is the essence of democracy can best be established by the popular choice between and control over alternate responsible political parties; for only such parties can provide the coherent, unified sets of rulers who will assume collective responsibility to the people for the manner in which government is carried on. Only in the alternation in office of such parties can the popular will be translated into governmental action.[11]

Party government in its most ideal form, according to its proponents, should work in the following manner: There must exist at least two (and preferably only two) unified, disciplined political parties. Each has its conception of what the people want and a program of various measures designed to satisfy those wants. In a pre-election campaign each attempts to convince a majority of the people that its program will best do what the people want done. In the election each voter votes for a particular candidate in his district, primarily because that candidate is a member of the party which the voter wants to take power, and only secondarily because he prefers the individual qualities of one candidate to those of the other. The party which secures a majority of the offices of government in the election then takes over the entire power of the government and the entire responsibility for what the government does. It then proceeds to put its program into effect. Or perhaps unforeseen circumstances arise which make the party decide to alter or even abandon its program. In any event, at the next election the people decide whether, on the whole, they approve of the general direction that the party in power has been taking—in short, whether their wants are being satisfied. If the answer is yes, they return that party to power; if the answer is no, they replace it with the opposition party.

This is what is meant by "responsible party government." Such a government, its proponents argue, would perform at least three indispensable functions in a truly democratic society. In the first place, by selecting from the myriad public issues the particular ones upon which elections are to be fought, parties would enable the people to express themselves effectively upon those issues. This function Schattschneider terms the "simplification of alternatives"; and he argues its importance thus:

The immobility and inertia of large masses are to politics what the law of gravity is to physics. This characteristic compels people to submit to a great channelization of the expression of their will, and is due to *numbers,* not to want of intelligence. An electorate of sixty million Aristotles would be equally restricted. In other words, the parties take from the people powers that are merely theoretical. Nature, having first made numbers what they are, limits the effective powers of the people,

---

[11] Cf. Schattschneider, *Party Government,* pp. 13-14; MacIver, *The Web of Government,* pp. 210-15; and Barker, *Reflections on Government,* pp. 37-39.

and the parties merely take advantage of the fact. The people are a sovereign whose vocabulary is limited to two words, "Yes" and "No." This sovereign, moreover, can speak only when spoken to.[12]

To be sure, parties, by choosing only certain issues to debate, deprive the people of the chance to express their will on other issues. This point, however, involves a less severe criticism of the party-government system than one may think; for it is highly doubtful whether, in the absence of parties and their channelizing function, there would often exist anything approaching a majority-opinion on the issues which parties leave alone. In any event, party government would enable the people to choose effectively a general program, a general direction for government to take, as embodied in a set of leaders committed to that program. It might limit the people's theoretical (but, in the absence of any organizing agency, meaningless) freedom of choice among the almost infinite number of possible specific measures; but it would give them the *effective* choice between alternative general programs.

In the second place, the advocates of responsible party government argue that it would accomplish the important function of energizing and activating public opinion. How this function might be accomplished did not concern the classical theorists of democracy. The antidemocrats seem to have believed that under any conditions the people were incapable of displaying the concern with public affairs required by democracy; and the democrats apparently assumed that, if given the power, the people would automatically take up the responsibility for their government. As Schattschneider comments:

The fact that this assumption involves a colossal over-simplification of the democratic process was not and probably could not have been understood by the pre-democratic theorists. They made the very natural mistake of under-estimating the difficulties arising from the numbers, preoccupation, immobility, and indifference of the people. Everyone took it for granted that the people themselves would assume responsibility for the expression of their own will as a matter of course without so much as dreaming of the intervention of syndicates of self-appointed political managers and manipulators who for reasons of their own might organize the electorate and channelize the expression of the popular will.[13]

The experience of some two-hundred years of popular government, maintain the party-government theorists, has indicated that some sort of extra-governmental agency is needed to energize and activate public opinion. Party government, they believe, would provide such an agency: "The party educates the public while seeking merely to influence it, for it must appeal on grounds of

[12] *Party Government*, p. 52. A. D. Lindsay makes the same point when he writes: "Strictly speaking, phrases such as the 'the will of the people' or 'the voice of the people' are mere mythology. The great mass of the people can only consent to what government or some other organized group of people proposes to do." *The Essentials of Democracy* (Philadelphia: University of Pennsylvania Press, 1929), p. 32.

[13] *Party Government*, pp. 13-14.

policy. For the same reason it helps to remove the inertia of the public and thus to broaden the range of public opinion. In short, the party, in its endeavors to win the public to its side, however unscrupulous it may be in its modes of appeal, is making the democratic system workable. It is the agency by which public opinion is translated into public policy." [14]

Finally, its friends believe, party government would establish popular control over government by making the group of rulers in power *collectively* responsible to the people. A considerable group of American writers, on the other hand, have maintained that the *individual* responsibility of the various public officers to their particular constituents is more easily understood, more clearly establishable, and, therefore, more effective than the collective responsibility of an organized and unified group of public officials to the entire electorate.[15] Some have even argued that such individual responsibility is the only conceivable kind, and that no such thing as "group" or "party" responsibility can exist. Thus William Graham Sumner wrote:

I cannot trust a party; I can trust a man. I cannot hold a party responsible; I can hold a man responsible. I cannot get an expression of opinion which is single and simple from a party; I can get that only from a man. A party cannot have character, or conscience, or reputation; it cannot repent, nor [sic] endure punishment or disgrace. I know very well that we are in the habit of predicating all these things of party, but I should think our experience had offered the fullest proof that we cannot properly predicate any of these things of a party, except in a broad, half-metaphorical sense, under which all the sharpness and efficiency necessary to practical politics are lost. The proof is, at any rate, satisfactory to me.[16]

These writers do not see any problem in making the government as a whole responsible to the entire electorate. After all, they point out, each member of the national representative assembly is responsible to his constituency, and the constituencies added together make up the entire national electorate. Since every whole is self-evidently the sum of its parts, the national assembly must be responsible to the entire electorate.

From the party-government point of view, however, it must be said that the evidence of our actual experience with representative government makes this latter proposition considerably less self-evident than it appeared to Sumner and his cohorts. The Congress of the United States, point out the party-government writers, throughout most of its existence has been a good example

---

[14] MacIver, *The Web of Government*, p. 213.

[15] Cf. C. F. Dole, *The Spirit of Democracy* (New York: Thomas Y. Crowell Company, 1906), pp. 212-13; Joseph Alden, *The Science of Government in Connection with American Institutions* (New York: Sheldon and Company, 1876), p. 30; Albert Stickney, *Democratic Government* (New York: Harper and Brothers, 1885), pp. 6-7; Woolsey, *Political Science*, II, 57-58.

[16] *The Challenge of Facts and Other Essays*, edited by A. G. Keller (New Haven: Yale University Press, 1914), p. 367.

of a representative assembly based largely on individual rather than group responsibility. That is to say, congressmen have depended for re-election solely upon their relation to their particular constituencies, and their connection with or independence of the program of the party whose label they bore has been a factor of relatively little importance.[17] How, the proponents of party government ask, has this system of largely individual responsibility worked out?

Its general effect, they reply, has been not only to destroy the responsibility of the government as a whole to the people at large, but also to obscure even the responsibility of the individual representative to his constituents. To take up the latter point first, it is necessary always to remember, they advise, that responsibility is a concomitant of power, in the sense that no man can or will assume full responsibility for something over which he is denied full control. The individual congressman has very little power over what Congress does or does not do, and he can hardly be held responsible for anything save how he votes. Even this responsibility, however, is less clearly established than it may seem, they argue; for the congressman usually has little power over *what* he is given the opportunity to vote on. If his constituents accuse him of not voting for the measures he promised to vote for in his campaign, he can usually reply quite truthfully that he had little chance to do so: his particular measures were never reported out of committee, someone else got a rule where he was denied one, someone else added crippling amendments he was unable to block, etc. The fact is, the party-government writers argue, that power in Congress is so fragmented and the whole legislative process so complex and confusing that the bewildered voter usually has great difficulty in deciding whether his representative should be blamed or rewarded—since he seems to have so little effect on what Congress has done or has not done. In short, they conclude, under this system of individual responsibility and fragmentation of power, the responsibility even of the representative to his constituents is muddled, vague, and confused, while Sumner and his associates assumed it would be defined and clear.[18]

The party-government writers argue, in the second place, that the system of individual responsibility in America has made almost impossible the responsibility of the government as a whole to the people in general. In such a system there really is no government as a whole, no individual or set of individuals possessing control of the government and capable of being effectively blamed or rewarded for what it does. If the sum of the individual representatives is, in this sense, less than a government as a whole, then the sum of the individual responsibilities, themselves obscured and confused, is considerably less than a

---

[17] Cf. Roland Young, *This is Congress* (New York: Alfred A. Knopf, 1943), pp. 18-19. See also James M. Burns, *Congress on Trial* (New York: Harper and Brothers, 1949), pp. 8-13.

[18] Cf. Young, *This is Congress*, pp. 18-19, 27-28.

general responsibility of the whole government to the people at large. We have learned instead, they contend, that a system of individual responsibility places a premium upon the dominance of local, sectional matters over national questions. Most congressmen have felt that their chances of re-election rest upon "doing something for their constituencies"—getting public money spent in their districts; obtaining tariff schedules favorable to their local industries; blocking legislation which, while it may help the rest of the nation, hurts their constituencies; etc. The "record," upon which almost every congressman has stood, has had little to do with his position on national issues.[19]

That the system of group responsibility provided by party government avoids these difficulties, its proponents argue, is shown by English experience. In England, they point out, there exists at all times a real government as a whole, a set of representatives who really control the government and who are, therefore, clearly responsible for what it does. In such a system the voter votes primarily for a *party*, through the medium of voting for its representative in his particular district. The relative qualities of the individual candidates involved are of small importance.[20] There is thus a premium on the consideration of national instead of purely local problems, since a party *and its individual representatives* know that they will win or lose on the basis of their national program and record as a group.[21] In this manner, the party-government argument concludes, the responsibility of the whole government to a majority of the whole electorate is established, and even the relationship between the individual representative and his constituency is more clearly defined and, therefore, more responsible. The establishment of group responsibility in this sense is the unique and important contribution of party government.

To complete the picture of what is involved in the doctrine of party government, it must be observed that its proponents warn that several conditions must be fulfilled if it is to exist. In the absence of any of these conditions, parties cannot be expected to do their job. First and foremost, they say, party government requires the existence of parties which have sufficient coherence and discipline for their members to display solidarity on all great questions of public policy. After all, party government is based upon the substitution of *party* for individual responsibility. If the members of each party frequently desert their party's line on questions of public policy, then the people cannot effectively either blame or reward either party, *as a party,* for what it does or does not do.

[19] Cf. T. K. Finletter, *Can Representative Government Do the Job?* (New York: Reynal and Hitchcock, 1945), p. 119; G. B. Galloway, *Congress at the Crossroads* (New York: Thomas Y. Crowell Company, 1946), pp. 284-88; P. H. Appleby, *Big Democracy* (New York: Alfred A. Knopf, 1945), pp. 287-88; and Young, *This is Congress,* pp. 60-71.

[20] Cf. W. I. Jennings, *Cabinet Government* (Cambridge: Cambridge University Press, 1936), pp. 16-17, 362.

[21] Cf. *ibid.,* pp. 361-62.

Party responsibility, upon which party government depends, cannot exist in such a situation.[22]

The problem then becomes: How do we go about getting parties whose members *will* stick together on public questions? And that, in turn, leads to the examination of the further questions: What should constitute party membership? Just who should be considered as the party members from whom we may expect this solidarity and discipline? At this point in the argument the first great split in the party-government ranks appears. For some of them advocate one conception of party membership, and others advocate quite a different one. These may be called respectively the "ticket-voter" and the "party-worker" conceptions of party membership. Let us briefly examine the content of each.

The ticket-voter conception holds that parties are composed of all those who more or less regularly vote (or have voted, or declare that they will vote) for the party ticket. This position is certainly current in the propaganda of the parties themselves, useful in their attempts to create the illusion that they are "huge associations of partisan voters." [23] That it is apparently also the dominant position among the academic advocates of responsible party government is clearly shown by the position of the Committee on Political Parties on the matter of "intraparty responsibility": They argue that party responsibility includes not only "the responsibility of both parties to the general public, as enforced in elections" but also "the responsibility of party leaders to the party membership, as enforced in primaries, caucuses and conventions." [24] In order to achieve this "intraparty democracy," the Committee proposes, among other things, the general adoption of the closed primary, and various ways and means for the rank and file of the party members to discuss and formulate party policies.[25] Their commitment to the ticket-voter notion of party membership is most clearly shown, however, in their proposals for making the national conventions more representative of the party members: The present conventions are unrepresentative, they argue, because there is such a great variation from delegation to delegation *in the number of party voters represented by each delegate.* So quite evidently they believe that the party leaders in each convention *should* represent the voters who vote for that party's ticket.[26]

This belief in the ticket-voter notion of party membership is certainly shared by those who have written our direct primary laws; for, despite the considerable

---

[22] Cf. the Parties Committee's judgment that "an effective party system requires, first, that the parties are able to bring forth programs to which they commit themselves and, second, that the parties possess sufficient internal cohesion to carry out these programs," "Toward a More Responsible Two-party System," pp. 17-18. See also *ibid.*, pp. 20-24.

[23] Schattschneider, *Party Government*, p. 54.

[24] "Toward a More Responsible Two-party System," pp. 22-23.

[25] *Ibid.*, pp. 65-69, 70-73.

[26] *Ibid.*, pp. 28-29.

variation from state to state in such laws, the most stringent requirement of party membership (and its consequent right of voting in the party's primary) is the voter's own declaration that he is a member of the party.[27] The ticket-voter conception is certainly the foundation of one of the most widely circulated charges against the existing American parties: that they are oligarchically organized, boss-controlled, and therefore undemocratic in their internal organization. And this has led a number of their critics to conclude that our parties are too hopelessly undemocratic internally ever to act as proper agencies for carrying on democratic government.[28] The majority of the present party-government writers differ from these critics, not in their judgment of the undemocratic character of the parties' internal organization, but only in their greater optimism about the possibilities (through such mechanisms as we have noted above) for making the party leaders more responsible to the rank-and-file party members.

A minority of the current party-government writers, however, take the position that this is a false and misleading conception of party membership, and that its widespread acceptance constitutes a serious barrier to the achievement of responsible parties in the United States. Led by Professor Schattschneider,[29] they argue that, for one thing, the ticket-voter notion exposes parties to criticism they do not deserve. If one defines a party as made up of the twenty-seven million voters who support its national ticket, it is obvious that the party can be run by only a very small percentage of its members. Michels' "Iron Law of Oligarchy"—that parties are always run by small elites and never democratically by all their members—becomes unanswerable; and it leads many to conclude, as pointed out above, that parties are therefore antidemocratic or even wicked. The real harm of this conception, however, lies in the fact that it tends to make the parties unable to exercise real control over their members and requires the

---

[27] See Professor Clarence A. Berdahl's useful summary of the party-membership requirements in the forty-seven direct primary states, "Party Membership in the United States," *American Political Science Review*, XXXVI (February and April, 1942), pp. 16-50, 241-62.

[28] Much American criticism of parties has centered about these charges. For samples of such criticism, see D. G. Thompson, *Politics in a Democracy* (New York: Longmans, Green and Company, 1893), pp. 45-50; W. G. Sumner, *Folkways* (New York: Ginn and Company, 1906), p. 230; James Schouler, *Ideals of the Republic* (Boston: Little, Brown and Company, 1908), pp. 209-10; and A. M. Kales, *Unpopular Government in the United States* (Chicago: The University of Chicago Press, 1914), pp. 67-68.

[29] It is interesting to note that Professor Schattschneider, who is certainly the leading exponent of the party-worker view of party membership, was also the chairman of the Committee on Political Parties, whose report, as we have seen, is so wedded to the ticket-voter conception. This fact might indicate that he simply changed his mind, but the present writer is more inclined to believe that Schattschneider was outvoted on this point in the Committee's deliberations, and, being, as he is, a good majoritarian-democrat, went along with the Committee majority.

members to accept no real obligation to the party—two characteristics of "membership," they point out, that are not to be found in any other association. Thus any Byrd or McKellar, they argue, can explain his many votes against his party's program by announcing that he refuses to be "dictated to" by the party "oligarchy," that he reserves the same right of "independence" that any other member (i.e., ticket voter) has, and that he nevertheless is as good or better a party member and public servant than the congressman who slavishly sticks to his party's line.

In order to develop party government in the United States, its proponents believe, it will be necessary to gain public acceptance of a definition of parties which more nearly fits the facts and which makes for party unity behind a program. As Schattschneider suggests: "A more realistic theory, closer to the facts, can relieve us of the nightmarish necessity of doing the impossible. Let us suppose that the concept of the party membership of the partisans is abandoned altogether. If the party is described as a political enterprise conducted by a group of working politicians *supported* by partisan voters who approve of the party but are merely partisans (not members of a fictitious association), the parties would seem less wicked." [30] Without attempting a complete or final definition, these party-government writers suggest that party members be thought of as *party workers*—people who devote energy to party activities by ringing doorbells, making speeches, writing campaign literature, etc.; people who, by voting in party caucuses and conventions, participate in making party decisions; people who, by agreeing to abide by the decisions of party caucuses and conventions, assume some obligation to the party; and people over whom, by its ability effectively to bestow or withhold the party label, the party has some real control. Parties made up of such members, they believe, should be capable of achieving the unity behind programs of public policy that is fundamental to responsible party government.

This, then, is the nature of party government proposed as a model by which to judge the existing party system and as a goal for which we should strive. It remains only to discover the extent to which, in the opinion of those who advocate this model, the *existing* American parties fail to measure up to it.

AMERICAN PARTIES AND PARTY GOVERNMENT

Those who advance the party-government position agree, although some stress this point much more than others, that the existing political parties are performing a significant and valuable role in the American system, and that the nation is notably better off with them than it would be with no parties at all. They also agree, however, that measured by the standard outlined above, American parties do not provide anything like "responsible party government."

[30] *Party Government*, p. 59.

They document this judgment by pointing to certain characteristics of the existing party system.[31]

In the first place, they point out, American major parties do not have any real programs—they do not "stand" for anything. Their platforms are for the most part merely collections of generalities designed primarily with an eye to offending as few people as possible. It is standard practice for them either to equivocate on or to ignore completely the pressing and divisive issues of the day. Almost never is there any important difference between the programs of the two parties. In consequence their propaganda beclouds the issues and befuddles the voters. Seldom does it clarify or educate, as the doctrine of party government says it should.

In the second place, the party-government writers charge that American parties seldom display unity upon matters of public policy. Legislative votes or any other governmental action is very rarely along strict party lines. Thus, in terms of who does what, it is often very difficult for the voter to determine what *the* position of either party on such questions is. Since party lines break down so easily, one party is about as "responsible" as the other for what the government does or does not do, regardless of which party is in "power." This means that the people can for the most part vote negatively: They can turn the party in power out of office as a punishment for its failure to satisfy their wants, but they cannot reasonably expect the opposition party to stand behind its announced program, nor can they reasonably expect a significant change in the way things are going. This, in turn, means that the people are deprived of the chance to make a clear and effective choice at the polls. It means that the American party system is not doing the job of translating the popular will into governmental action.

These writers conclude that the deficiencies of the existing American party system, when measured by the standard of responsible party government, add up to this: In a system of party government the parties seek power, not as an end in itself, but in order that they may put their programs into governmental action. They therefore conceive of their job as having two aspects: winning elections in order to get power and using the power they win to carry out their programs. Thus each party organizes its forces with the unity and discipline

---

[31] In what follows, the author will make no attempt to cite specific evidence for the various observations made about the nature of the existing party system. The generalizations made can be found in any of the standard texts, and particularly in those of H. R. Penniman and V. O. Key, previously cited. They are eloquently articulated in the works of Professors Schattschneider and Finer, and the report of the Committee on Political Parties contains a full and convenient summary of them. The disagreements among present-day students of the American party system, whether they adhere to the party-government school or not, are not so much over the characteristics of the system as over the questions of *why* those characteristics exist, to what extent they are desirable or undesirable, and what, if anything, should be done about them.

necessary *before* elections in the campaigning activities necessary to win power and *after* elections in the governmental activities necessary to put their programs into law.

In the American system, on the other hand, the parties consider winning power to be their sole end. When power is won, their job is completed. Thus each party demonstrates a considerable measure of unity and discipline in the campaigning activities necessary to elect the party ticket; but neither demonstrates (or apparently feels under any real obligation to demonstrate) such unity and discipline *after* winning power as it would need to put its program into law. In their capacity as agencies for organizing and conducting elections, they are highly developed; and in their capacity as agencies for carrying on government, they are underdeveloped. Yet no political party, these writers argue, can deny its obligations as an agency for carrying on government; and the result of the deficiencies of American parties is not that they completely fail to fulfill these obligations, but only that they fulfill them inadequately and with a minimum of responsibility.

The present-day exponents of the doctrine of party government devote less attention to the question of *why* American parties are as they are than to the other aspects of the problem. They do not, however, ignore it completely. Schattschneider, for example, suggests that the formal governmental structure within which the parties must operate is the fundamental explanation for their deficiencies. That structure, he points out, is based upon such institutions as separation of powers, fixed and staggered terms of office, and federalism, none of which is "well suited to the needs of party government. . . . One is tempted to say that these provisions have made real party government impossible in the United States; what we have instead is an abortive attempt at party government." [32] Finer makes essentially the same point from another angle when he contends that the explanation for the ability of British parties to provide party government where American parties cannot lies mainly in the fact that the British parties come into possession of the whole plenitude of sovereignty if they attain a majority, whereas American parties, even if they obtain a majority of the offices, succeed to no such command of the government.[33] Beyond this, the party-government writers have little to offer as an explanation of why American parties are the way they are.

The question of what can be done to achieve party government in the American system has received somewhat more attention. There is general agreement among them that, even though the constitutional system may be inappropriate for responsible party government, there is little point in pressing for its amendment. Schattschneider, for example, argues that since parties have in the past

[32] *Party Government*, pp. 124-26.
[33] *The Theory and Practice of Modern Government*, p. 356.

shown such great capacity for changing the Constitution without formal amend-ments—as in their reshaping of the Electoral College system for electing the President—that there are no "grounds for excessive pessimism about the possi-bilities of integrating party government with the constitutional system. The greatest difficulties in the way of the development of party government in the United States have been intellectual, not legal. It is not unreasonable to suppose that once a respectable section of the public understands the issue, ways of promoting party government through the Constitution can be found." [34]

The Committee on Political Parties takes substantially the same position. There is little point, they say, in attempting to amend the Constitution so as to substitute a cabinet system for our present presidential system. It is unlikely that such an amendment could be adopted; in any case responsible parties are a precondition for the successful operation of a cabinet system and, if we can achieve such parties, they can provide us with fully effective democratic govern-ment within the present constitutional arrangements. [35] The final section of their report, entitled "The Prospect for Action," concludes that there is con-siderable reason to believe that the pressure groups, the party leaders, the bureaucracy, the Congress, and the President will all discover that each of them will gain by the advent of a more responsible party system—and that we need not expect irrevocable opposition to such a system from any of them. [36] In any case, they avow, the electorate is the most powerful of all our political agencies; and if we can convince its members of the benefits of more responsible parties and show them the serious dangers of inaction on this problem, the battle will be largely won. The doctrine of responsible party government will then become a fundamental part of every American's thinking about how his government should be run. [37]

This, then, is the doctrine of responsible party government as it is being expounded today. We now turn to the examination of the writers from 1870 to 1915 and to their ideas upon the proper organization and function of political parties in the American system.

---

[34] *Party Government*, pp. 209-10.
[35] "Toward a More Responsible Two-party System," pp. 35-36.
[36] *Ibid.*, pp. 85-90.
[37] *Ibid.*, pp. 90-96.

Part Two

Party as the Instrument of Democracy

CHAPTER THREE

Woodrow Wilson

Woodrow Wilson was one of the first American writers after the Civil War to consider seriously the function of political parties in the American system. He was the first to advance the doctrine that responsible party government would be the best way of organizing democracy in the United States. As early as 1879, while still an undergraduate at Princeton, he published an article on "Cabinet Government in the United States" defending this point of view.[1] Throughout the rest of his academic career, he recurred again and again to his fundamental conviction that party government is the necessary prerequisite for the establishment of effective popular control of government in America.[2]

Wilson's concern with the problem of party and its place grew out of his belief that the most rewarding way to study politics is to examine the forces that actually make government behave as it does. He strongly disapproved of the legalistic, formalistic approach which dominated the American political science of his time, and which was typified by the works of such men as John W. Burgess.[3] To study public law as though it were the only—or even the basic—aspect of political science seemed to him a profound mistake:

Public law is the formal basis of the political life of society, but it is not always an expression of its vital principle. We are inclined, oftentimes, to take laws and constitutions too seriously, to put implicit faith in their professions without examining their conduct. . . . In other words, statute books and legal commentaries are all very well in the study of politics, if only you quite thoroughly understand that

[1] *International Review*, VII (August, 1879), 146-63.

[2] Wilson's views on the function of political parties are to be found primarily in "Cabinet Government in the United States"; "Committee or Cabinet Government?" in *The Public Papers of Woodrow Wilson: College and State*, edited by R. S. Baker and W. E. Dodd (New York: Harper and Brothers, 1925), I, 95-129; *Congressional Government* (Boston: Houghton Mifflin Company, 1885); "Leaderless Government," an address before the Virginia Bar Association, August 4, 1897, in *Public Papers*, I, 336-59; *Constitutional Government in the United States* (New York: Columbia University Press, 1908); and *The New Freedom* (Garden City, N. Y.: Doubleday, Page and Company, 1913).

[3] J. W. Burgess, *Political Science and Comparative Constitutional Law* (2 vols.; Boston: Ginn and Company, 1891). For Wilson's sharply critical review of this work and of the conception of political science underlying it, see the *Atlantic Monthly*, LXVII (May, 1891), 692-99.

they furnish only the crude body-colors for your picture of the State's life, upon which all your finer luminous and atmospheric effects are afterwards to be worked.[4]

Wilson's avowed ambition was to write about the philosophy that lies behind American institutions. In a letter written even before he had begun formal graduate work in political science at Johns Hopkins, he wrote:

I want to contribute to our literature what no American has ever contributed, studies in the philosophy of our institutions, not the abstract and occult, but the practical and suggestive philosophy which is at the core of our governmental methods; their use, their meaning, "the spirit that makes them workable." I want to divest them of the theory that obscures them and present their weakness and their strength without disguise, and with such skill and plenitude of proof that it shall be seen that I have succeeded and that I have added something to the resources of knowledge upon which statecraft must depend.[5]

In setting this as his goal, Wilson was consciously following the path laid out by the English writer, Walter Bagehot, in his famous study of the English constitution.[6] Bagehot's analysis of the real character of the English constitution, as opposed to what he called the "literary theory" of its nature, caused a considerable stir in the United States as well as in England. His essays were, Wilson's biographer tells us, the first thing to excite Wilson about the study of politics. Wilson read them over and over, marked them carefully, and quoted them the rest of his life. Clearly Bagehot was one of the most important influences in shaping both Wilson's approach to politics and, as will be pointed out below, many of his conclusions.[7]

At least in the early stages of his career, Wilson quite consciously modeled his approach upon Bagehot's, as one of his letters indicates:

I've planned a set of four or five essays on "The Government of the Union," in which it is my purpose to show, as well as I can, our constitutional system as it looks in operation. My desire and ambition are to treat the American constitution as Mr. Bagehot . . . has treated the English constitution. His book has inspired my whole study of our government. He brings to the work a fresh and original method which has made the British system much more intelligible to ordinary men than it ever was before, and which, if it could be successfully applied to the exposition of our Federal Constitution, would result in something like a revelation to those who are still reading the *Federalist* as an authoritative constitutional manual.[8]

Throughout his academic career, therefore, Wilson was striving to go behind

---

[4] "The Study of Politics," in *An Old Master, and Other Political Essays* (New York: Charles Scribner's Sons, 1893), pp. 51-52.

[5] Wilson to Ellen Axson, October 30, 1883, in R. S. Baker, *Woodrow Wilson: Life and Letters* (4 vols.; Garden City, N. Y.: Doubleday, Page and Company, 1927), I, 213.

[6] *The English Constitution, and Other Political Essays* (rev. American ed.; New York: D. Appleton and Company, 1877).

[7] Cf. Baker, *Woodrow Wilson: Life and Letters*, I, 86-87, 210-11.

[8] Wilson to Ellen Axson, January 1, 1884, in *Ibid.*, I, 213-14.

the legal façade of our governmental structure in order to understand the forces
that made it work the way it does. From the beginning he accepted Bagehot's
contention that political parties play a determinative role in representative
government.[9] He was aware that the American scholarship of his time had
little to say about what function parties perform in the American system and
even less about what function they should perform. He was determined to fill
that gap, and presented in his various works the first systematic American
exposition and defense of the doctrine of party government.

THE NATURE OF DEMOCRACY

As Wilson's political ideas matured, he became more and more a convinced
majority-rule democrat. It is true that in his earlier writings one can find several
statements with an unmistakably antidemocratic coloring. For example, in
"Cabinet Government in the United States," Wilson began by pointing out
that there was widespread concern with the low state to which, in the opinion
of many observers, American government had sunk. Universal suffrage, he
noted, was one of the things to which many of those observers pointed as the
cause of the trouble. "But," he continued, "while it is indisputably true that
universal suffrage is a constant element of weakness, and exposes us to many
dangers which we might otherwise escape, its operation does not suffice alone
to explain existing evils." [10] In *Congressional Government* he did not conceal
his opinion that the American Senate is undemocratic in constitution and effect,
and that that fact has several advantages: "The fact that [the Senate] is less
quickly sensitive to the hasty or impulsive movements of public opinion constitutes its value as a check, a steadying weight, in our very democratic system.
. . . This is the most conspicuous, and will prove to be the most lasting, use
of the Senate in our system. It is valuable in our democracy in proportion as it
is undemocratic . . . the Senate saves us often from headlong popular tyranny." [11]

To assess the significance of these statements, however, it is necessary to
remember that Wilson wrote both of these passages in the full flush of his
enthusiasm for Bagehot, who was certainly no majority-rule democrat. On the
contrary, Bagehot stressed his belief that party government in England depended
upon a restricted franchise; for under a system of universal suffrage, he said,
Parliament would not be composed of moderate men, and the consensus upon
which party government depends could no longer exist.[12]

Whatever the reason for his early antidemocratic tendencies, Wilson became

---

[9] Cf. Bagehot, *The English Constitution*, pp. 209-10.
[10] "Cabinet Government in the United States," pp. 146-47.
[11] *Congressional Government*, pp. 226-27.
[12] *The English Constitution*, pp. 214-16.

increasingly committed to majority-rule democracy as he matured. Thus in *The New Freedom* he said:

I believe, as I believe in nothing else, in the average integrity and the average intelligence of the American people, and I do not believe that the intelligence of America can be put into commission anywhere. I do not believe that there is any group of men of any kind to whom we can afford to give that kind of trusteeship. I will not live under trustees if I can help it. No group of men less than the majority has a right to tell me how I have got to live in America. I will submit to the majority, because I have been trained to do it,—though I may sometimes have my private opinion even of the majority. I do not care how wise, how patriotic, the trustees may be, I have never heard of any group of men in whose hands I am willing to lodge the liberties of America in trust.[13]

Wilson never forgot Bagehot's injunction that consensus—an "agreement to disagree"—is the basis of party government. In his more mature years, however, he departed from Bagehot's position by maintaining that such a consensus can be achieved in a democracy founded on universal suffrage and majority-rule.[14]

Wilson did not believe, however, that the definition of democracy as majority-control of the government tells the democrat all he needs to know about how that control is to be organized and made effective. He regarded the problem of democratic organization as crucial, and felt that democratic theorists had unduly neglected it: "Though democrats by long inheritance and repeated choice, we are still rather crude democrats. Old as democracy is, its organization on a basis of modern ideas and conditions is still an unaccomplished work. The democratic state has yet to be equipped for carrying those enormous burdens of administration which the needs of this industrial and trading age are so fast accumulating." [15]

He therefore determined to explore for himself the whole question of what institutional machinery would best establish popular control over government.

It is important to note that Wilson always conceived of democracy as popular control over government, never as popular participation in the day-to-day processes of government. It must also be observed that he never thoroughly examined other conceptions of democracy, but simply assumed that his idea was the proper one. Thus, in his essay on "The Character of Democracy in the United States," he wrote:

This vast and miscellaneous democracy of ours must be led; its giant faculties must be schooled and directed. Leadership cannot belong to the multitude; masses of men cannot be self-directed, neither can groups of communities. We speak of

---

[13] *The New Freedom*, pp. 64-65. See also *Constitutional Government in the United States*, p. 14.

[14] *Constitutional Government in the United States*, pp. 51-52.

[15] "The Study of Administration," *Political Science Quarterly*, II, (June, 1887), 217-18.

the sovereignty of the people, but that sovereignty, we know very well, is of a peculiar sort, quite unlike the sovereignty of a king or of a small, easily concerting group of confident men. It is judicial merely, not creative. It passes judgment or gives sanctions, but it cannot direct or suggest. It furnishes standards, not policies.[16]

If democracy means popular control of government, continued Wilson, the indispensable characteristic of democratic government must be its *responsibility* to the people. "Responsibility," indeed, was the keyword in his whole philosophy of government; for the fundamental purpose of all his political writings was to discover the best method for making American government truly responsible to the people. To establish such responsibility, he continually pointed out, Americans will have to understand its nature: They will have to realize that responsibility is the concomitant of power, in the sense that only he who has full power over an instrument can reasonably be held responsible for its use.

If there be one principle clearer than another, it is this: that in any business, whether of government or of mere merchandising, *somebody must be trusted,* in order that when things go wrong it may be quite plain who should be punished. . . . *Power and strict accountability for its use* are the essential constituents of good government. A sense of highest responsibility, a dignifying and elevating sense of being trusted, together with a consciousness of being in an official station so conspicuous that no faithful discharge of duty can go unacknowledged and unrewarded, and no breach of trust undiscovered and unpunished,—these are the influences, the only influences, which foster practical, energetic, and trustworthy statesmanship.[17]

The kind of responsibility Wilson wanted to see established is *collective*: that of a group of governmental rulers to the entire electorate. To him the sort of purely individual responsibility of each individual congressman to his constituents is so unsatisfactory in its results as to be no responsibility at all. His primary objection to it was that it cannot possibly provide for any responsibility of the government as a whole to the people at large.

The average citizen may be excused for esteeming government at best but a haphazard affair, upon which his vote and all of his influence can have but little effect. How is his choice of a representative in Congress to affect the policy of the country as regards the questions in which he is most interested, if the man for whom he votes has no chance of getting on the Standing Committee which has virtual charge of these questions? . . . It seems almost a thing of despair to get any assurance that any vote he may cast will even in an infinitesimal degree affect the essential course of administration. There are so many cooks mixing their ingredients in the national broth that it seems hopeless, this thing of changing one cook at a time.[18]

---

[16] In *An Old Master,* pp. 129-30. See also "Political Sovereignty" in *Ibid.,* pp. 73-74; and "The Study of Administration," pp. 214-15.

[17] *Congressional Government,* pp. 283-84. The emphasis is Wilson's. See also "The Study of Administration," pp. 213-14.

[18] *Ibid.,* pp. 331-32.

There is only one way to establish the responsibility of the whole government to the people, Wilson maintained. It is to concentrate the power of the government in one group of governmental leaders and to hold that group to strict account for how it uses its power. He referred constantly to a proposition that seemed to him axiomatic: "The more power is divided, the more irresponsible it becomes. . . . It is ever the little foxes that spoil the grapes." [19]

The foundation of Woodrow Wilson's doctrine of party government, then, was his conception of democracy as popular control of, rather than participation in, the activities of government. Popular control of government can be made effective, he believed, only by holding the government's rulers *collectively* responsible to the people. One of democracy's greatest problems is therefore to find the machinery that will most effectively establish that responsibility. The essence of any such machinery, Wilson was convinced, must be the concentration of governmental power in the hands of a unified ruling group, and the holding of that group strictly accountable for how the government is carried on.

THE FUNCTION OF POLITICAL PARTIES IN THE AMERICAN SYSTEM

Woodrow Wilson believed that the primary function of political parties in any democratic system is to establish effective popular control over the government. If it is true, he argued, that democracy consists essentially in the popular choice of and control over alternate groups of collectively responsible public officials, then there is a very real sense in which "party government is inseparable from representative government. Representative government is, indeed, only another name for government by partisan majorities. Majorities rule in municipal, in State, and in national affairs alike. Representative government is government by majorities, and government by majorities is party government, which up to the present date is the only known means of self-government." [20]

Responsible party government is an essential institutional mechanism for democracy, Wilson was convinced, because only such a system can provide the concentrated, unified, and collectively responsible leadership which democracy demands. The "individual" responsibility of each public official in which many of his contemporaries placed their hopes was to him no real responsibility at all:

It seems to be unquestionably and in a high degree desirable that all legislation should distinctly represent the action of the parties as parties. . . . Plainly this cannot be effected by punishing here and there a member of Congress who has voted for a flagrantly dishonest appropriation bill, or an obnoxious measure relating to the tariff. Unless the punishment can be extended to the party—if any such be recognizable—with which these members have voted, no advantage has been won for self-government, and no triumph has been gained by public opinion. [21]

---

[19] *Ibid.*, p. 93.

[20] "Committee or Cabinet Government?", p. 108. See also "Leaderless Government," p. 339.

[21] *Congressional Government*, pp. 97-98. See also *ibid.*, pp. 85, 101-02, 116-20.

In addition to this primary function, Wilson believed that political parties should accomplish several other important jobs in any democratic system. For one thing, their struggles in the various legislative bodies, particularly on the national level, should produce a high order of debate and thereby both encourage popular interest in public affairs and educate public opinion upon the issues of the day. These functions seemed to Wilson of the greatest importance, for he believed that the people must be interested in and familiar with the activities and debates in their government. Only if they know what it is doing can they effectively hold it responsible; and by becoming familiar with legislative debates on matters of public policy the people will be informed on such matters. Party government, as exemplified by the English system, Wilson declared, well satisfies both of these needs. In England the fate of a minister or of a whole party frequently depends upon the outcome of parliamentary debates. If a party's fortunes rest upon how well its leaders conduct themselves in such debates, he said, it is likely that the party will devote every energy to making its arguments as persuasive and its public leaders as able as possible. With such stakes of power involved, the people become interested in the debates. With popular interest comes popular familiarity with them; and thus public opinion in England is at once focused upon the government and informed about the leading issues.[22] In a system of party government the parties will also encourage the nation's ablest men to serve in public office, he said, because the party leaders will be the governmental leaders. The only pathway to high place will lie through service to a party in defending its program. Thus the nation's most able men will be drawn into politics, since only through party activities can they achieve their goal of public office and power.[23]

These are the major functions which, in Wilson's opinion, political parties should perform in any democratic system. In the American system in particular, he added, the nature of the formal governmental structure is such as to require them to assume additional jobs. Of these by far the most important, in his opinion, is that of breaking down the operation of separation of powers between the executive and legislative branches of government sufficiently to permit the swift, unified, and purposive governmental action necessary to solve the pressing problems of our complex society.[24] Parties, he believed, are the only conceivable agency for accomplishing this important job:

The degree of separation now maintained between the executive and legislative branches of our government cannot long be preserved without very serious inconvenience resulting. Congress and the President now treat with one another almost

[22] *Ibid*, pp. 85, 101-02, 116-20.

[23] *Ibid.*, p. 214.

[24] Wilson believed that, in urging cooperation between the two branches, he was returning to the founding fathers' intentions and not violating them. *Constitutional Government in the United States*, pp. 204-11.

like separate governments, so jealous is each of its prerogatives. The Houses find out only piecemeal and with difficulty what is going on at the other end of the Avenue, in bureaus which have been created by statute. . . . We risk every degree of friction and disharmony rather than hazard the independence of branches of the government which are helpless without each other. What we need is harmonious, consistent, responsible party government, instead of a wide dispersion of function and responsibility; and we can get it only by connecting the President as closely as may be with his party in Congress.[25]

Wilson had a deep sense of the urgency of the problem. Perhaps, he said, there was a time when America could afford deadlock, inaction, and confusion in its government. Perhaps there was even a time when the people actually wanted it that way, when it was appropriate to the kind of society in which they lived. If so, he was convinced, that time is long since past:

The grave social and economic problems that now thrust themselves forward, as the result of the tremendous growth and concentration of our population, and the consequent sharp competition for means of livelihood, indicate that our system is already aging, and that any clumsiness, looseness, or irresponsibility in governmental action must prove a source of grave and increasing peril. . . . Instead of the present arrangements for compromise, piecemeal legislation, we must have coherent plans from recognized party leaders and means for holding those leaders to a faithful execution of their plans in clear-cut Acts of Congress.[26]

Thus responsible party government represented for Wilson an ideal which must be achieved if the American system is to become truly democratic. He also believed that its achievement is a matter of urgent necessity, since without it American government is unable to meet its considerable obligations.

EVALUATION OF AMERICAN PARTIES

Wilson had no illusions about the ability of the American party system he knew to fulfill the requirements of responsible party government. He was convinced that, judged by the standards he had set, the existing American parties are woefully inadequate. There were several aspects to that inadequacy, he believed, but they could all be summed up in this one indictment: American parties are irresponsible in the sense that the people cannot justly reward or effectively punish them for what they do or do not do while they are in power. Neither party, he said, has any real principles or program. Neither party takes

---

[25] "Mr. Cleveland's Cabinet," in *Public Papers*, I, 221-22. The obvious question arises at this point: If the basic difficulty lies in the constitutional structure, why not change the Constitution itself so as to eliminate separation of powers instead of depending upon the indirect and devious effects of parties? Wilson's several (and somewhat inconsistent) answers to this question will be discussed in connection with his proposals for achieving party government in the American system.

[26] "Government Under the Constitution," in *An Old Master*, pp. 180-81. It is interesting to note that, despite the passage of fifty-odd years since Wilson wrote these lines, the same note of urgency appears in much of the present-day party-government writing. Cf. "Toward a More Responsible Two-party System," pp. 31-33, 91-96.

a clear and distinct position *as a party* on matters of public policy. Therefore, he concluded, the voters can reasonably hold neither party responsible for what happens to public policy while it is in office:

Provided with parties in abundance, and entertained with many nice professions of political principle, we lack party responsibility. American parties are seldom called to account for any breach of their engagements, how solemnly soever those engagements may have been entered into. . . . "Platforms" are built only for conventions to sit on, and fall into decay as of course when conventions adjourn. Such parties as we have, parties with worn-out principles and without definite policies, are unmitigated nuisances.[27]

In consequence, Wilson continued, the individual voter is deprived of his chance to express a meaningful choice at the polls:

I, for my part, when I vote at a critical election, should like to be able to vote for a definite line of policy with regard to the great questions of the day—not for platforms, which Heaven knows, mean little enough—but for *men* known and tried in public service; with records open to be scrutinized with reference to these very matters; and pledged to do this or that particular thing, to take definite course of action. As it is, I vote for nobody I can depend upon to do anything—no, not if I were to vote for myself.[28]

This confusion and bewilderment of the voter, in turn, has the effect of making the people distrust Congress and look with suspicion upon our representative institutions.[29] Alarming though such a development is, Wilson argued, it is unavoidable so long as

the constituencies can hardly tell whether the works of any particular Congress have been good or bad. . . . During its brief lifetime both parties may have vacillated and gone astray, policies may have shifted and wandered, and untold mischief, together with some good, may have been done; but when all is reviewed, it is next to impossible oftentimes to distribute justly the blame and the praise. A few stubborn committee-men may be at the bottom of much of the harm that has been wrought, but they do not represent their party, and it cannot be clear to the voter how his ballot is to change the habits of Congress for the better. He distrusts Congress because he feels that he cannot control it.[30]

Perhaps the most striking symptom of our party system's inadequacy, Wilson pointed out, is the paradoxical fact that the same parties which cannot muster sufficient discipline and organization *inside* the government to stand together on matters of public policy nevertheless display an abundance of organization and discipline *outside* the government in the activities necessary to winning elections. As he put it:

[27] "Committee or Cabinet Government?", p. 109.
[28] "Leaderless Government," p. 355.
[29] *Congressional Government*, pp. 188-89.
[30] *Ibid.*, p. 189.

Outside of Congress the organization of the national parties is exceedingly well-defined and tangible; no one could wish it, and few could imagine it, more so; but within Congress it is obscure and intangible. Our parties marshal their adherents with the strictest possible discipline for the purpose of carrying elections, but their discipline is very slack and indefinite in dealing with legislation. The only bond of cohesion is the caucus, which occasionally whips a party together for cooperative action against the time for casting its vote upon some critical question.[31]

This, then, was to Wilson the great paradox of the existing American parties: Disciplined and unified outside the formal government, they are anarchic and torn with dissension inside it. So long as this basic dualism in their nature persists, Wilson was convinced, responsible party government cannot be achieved in the United States. It was therefore of the greatest importance to him to discover *why* the parties are the way they are. Only when he had answered that question could he deal with the problem of how party government might be achieved in the American system.

EXPLANATION OF AMERICAN PARTIES

Wilson agreed with most of his contemporaries upon the immediate explanation for the dual nature of American parties. Their real leaders are the local bosses, he said, not the national party "leaders"; and their real centers of power are the local machines, not the national committees or congressional caucuses. Since the bosses are concerned only with private gain and not with public policy, they exercise their power only for election- and patronage-winning purposes. In matters of public policy they simply are not interested, and permit their underlings in the formal government to do as they wish on such matters.[32]

When he dealt with the further question of why American parties are controlled by local bosses, however, Wilson had an answer that differed sharply from the explanation offered by most of his contemporaries. They tended to explain the situation largely in terms of the "ignorance" and "sloth" of the people, the reluctance of "good" citizens to soil themselves by going into politics, and the consequent domination of politics by venal and power-hungry bosses.[33] To Wilson this was a facile and inadequate answer. He believed instead that the fundamental cause of the bossism and consequent irresponsibility of American parties lies in the nature of our formal government structure—a conclusion which he reached through the following line of reasoning.

In the first place, he said, any government has to have some kind of effective

---

[31] *Ibid.*, pp. 98-99.

[32] S. K. Padover, ed., *Wilson's Ideals* (Washington, D. C.: American Council on Public Affairs, 1942), pp. 56-57.

[33] For some sample explanations of American parties in these terms, see: C. F. Dole, *The Spirit of Democracy* (New York: Thomas Y. Crowell Company, 1906); A. T. Hadley, *Standards of Public Morality* (New York: The Macmillan Company, 1907); and J. H. Hyslop, *Democracy: A Study of Government* (New York: Charles Scribner's Sons, 1899).

leadership if it is to produce a consistent line of policy and provide a coherent ruling group which the people can hold responsible for how the government is run. American government is certainly no exception; for "our government is a living, organic thing, and must, like every other government, work out a close synthesis of active parts which can exist only when leadership is lodged in some one man or group of men. *You cannot compound a successful government out of antagonisms.*" [34]

In the second place, such leadership, he said, simply did not exist in the formal structure of American government. No official agency of that government can possibly provide it. The nation could not expect any real leadership from the President, for example, because congressional aggression had shorn him of all his real power, and he had become at best a mere supervisor of administration—a sort of chief clerk.[35] Then, too, the replacement of the congressional caucus with the national nominating conventions had resulted in a predominance of "dark horse" compromise Presidents. Rarely, said Wilson, were the great party leaders nominated for the Presidency; and even more rarely were they elected. There was therefore no reason to believe, he concluded, that the President would ever be a real leader of either the government or his party.[36]

One might hope, continued Wilson, that since Congress had grabbed all the power inside the government it would provide the necessary leadership. But Congress, he pointed out, was so organized that it could not provide any unified, coherent, responsible leadership within itself let alone within the entire government. Its work was carried on by the various standing committees, and its power was fragmented among them. Yet they worked in jealous independence and mutual suspicion of each other, and so the government and the nation got no real leadership from any one of them or from all of them together:

There are in Congress no authoritative leaders who are the recognized spokesmen of their parties. Power is nowhere concentrated; it is rather deliberately and of set policy scattered amongst many small chiefs. It is divided up, as it were, into forty-seven seignories, in each of which a Standing Committee is the court-baron and its chairman lord-proprietor . . . both their mutual jealousies and their brief and restricted opportunities forbid their combining, and each is very far from the office of common leader.[37]

---

[34] *Constitutional Government in the United States,* p. 60. The emphasis is added.

[35] *Congressional Government,* pp. 5-31, 42-47; "Cabinet Government in the United States," pp. 146-47.

[36] "Leaderless Government," pp. 343-46; "Mr. Cleveland's Cabinet," pp. 217-18. Wilson, as will be pointed out below, later changed his mind about the possibilities for leadership contained in the Presidency. This change, however, did not materially affect his general position on the matters discussed here, but only his ideas on the question of what should be done about it.

[37] *Congressional Government,* pp. 91-92. See also "Government Under the Constitution," pp. 168-89; and "Leaderless Government," pp. 346-51.

Furthermore, the committees for the most part did their work in complete secrecy, he observed, and this made it impossible for them to become genuinely responsible leaders.[38]

Wilson saw the whole problem of leadership as immensely complicated by the operation of separation of powers. That institution, he said, was designed by the founding fathers to fragment power and splinter leadership; and, unhappily for the welfare of the American system, it had worked all too successfully.[39] The result has been that

a strong party administration . . . must often be impossible. We are thus shut out in part from real party government such as we desire, and such as it is unquestionably desirable to set up in every system like ours. Party government can exist only when the absolute control of administration, the appointment of its officers as well as the direction of its means and policy, is given immediately into the hands of that branch of the government whose power is paramount, the representative body.[40]

In the third place, Wilson continued, leadership from some source is the only alternative to chaos; and since the formal government cannot provide it, leadership in the American system has, by default, devolved upon an agency entirely outside the official governmental structure—namely, the party system. In this, Wilson said, the United States is unique: only here is the party system entirely outside of and distinct from the formal government.

Under every other system of government which is representative in character and which attempts to adjust the action of government to the wishes and interests of the people, the organization of parties is, in a sense, indistinguishable from the organs of the government itself. Party finds its organic lodgment in the national legislature and executive themselves. The several active parts of the government are closely united in organization for a common purpose, because they are under a common direction and themselves constitute the machinery of party control. Parties do not have to supply themselves with separate organs of their own outside the government and intended to dictate its policy, because such separate organs are unnecessary. The responsible organs of government are also the avowed organs of party. The action upon them is open and direct, not circuitous and secret.[41]

Wilson believed, for reasons to be pointed out below, that this complete separation in the United States of party agencies and leaders from the official governmental agencies and leaders is the fundamental cause of the nature of American parties.

In the fourth place, he pointed out, American parties cannot afford to be

---

[38] *Congressional Government,* pp. 60-61; "Committee or Cabinet Government?", pp. 97-104.

[39] Wilson was perhaps the first American scholar in this period to attack the principle and deplore the effects of separation of powers, and to consider methods for by-passing it.

[40] *Congressional Government,* pp. 267-68.

[41] *Constitutional Government in the United States,* pp. 211-12.

as leaderless as the formal government. In order to accomplish the herculean
tasks thrust upon them by the governmental structure they must have the fullest
measure of leadership and discipline. Running those parties is a full-time job,
if for no other reason than because there are so many nominations to be made
and so many elections to be organized and campaigns to be fought.[42] Therefore,
the real party leaders, Wilson argued, are inevitably the men who devote themselves to doing party work, such as organizing, campaigning, etc. Most of them
do not themselves bother to hold public office or carry on the activities of the
official government. Their time is consumed by purely party activities. In
America, therefore, the real party leaders are private, unofficial, usually obscure
individuals, called "bosses." The official leaders of the government, said
Wilson, are merely "phantom leaders"—men with no real power over either
the government or the parties which they nominally control:

We are without official leaders—without leaders who can be held immediately
responsible for the action and policy of the government, alike upon its legislative
and upon its administrative side. Leaders of some sort we, of course, always have;
but they come and go like phantoms, put forward as if by accident, withdrawn,
not by our choice, but as if upon some secret turn of fortune which we neither
anticipate nor as a nation control—some local quarrel, some obscure movement of
politics within a single district, some manipulation of a primary or some mis-
carriage in a convention.[43]

In the fifth place, the consequences of this separation of the real party leaders
(the bosses) from the nominal, official leaders (the holders of public office)
Wilson regarded as very grave. For one thing, it produces the uniquely American
distinction between the "politician" and the "statesman," which is a significant
factor in producing the general popular distrust of representative institutions.[44]
The most serious consequence of this differentiation, however, is the fact that
the real leaders of American parties work all the time in obscurity and secrecy.
The people can therefore know little or nothing of their activities, and can
hardly hold them responsible for the manner in which the government is carried
on: "One of the worst features of the boss system is this fact, that it works
secretly. I would a great deal rather live under a king whom I should at least
know, than under a boss whom I don't know. A boss is a much more formidable
master than a king, because a king is an obvious master, whereas the hands of
the boss are always where you least expect them to be." [45]

Finally, since the bosses work always in secrecy and therefore cannot effectively
be held responsible by the people, they are not only able to concentrate upon

---

[42] "Political Reform," an address before the City Club of Philadelphia, November 18,
1909, in *Public Papers*, II, 188-92.

[43] "Leaderless Government," pp. 339-40.

[44] *Constitutional Government in the United States*, pp. 212-13.

[45] *The New Freedom*, pp. 225-26. See also *ibid.*, pp. 119-20.

rewarding themselves with patronage and graft—they are actually *encouraged* to do so, Wilson said. Under a political system calculated to make its real leaders concentrate upon private gain instead of public policy, he concluded, the parties can hardly be expected to unite behind programs of public policy.

Wilson, then, saw in the governmental structure of the United States the basic cause of the irresponsibility of American parties. His conviction on this score was considerably strengthened when, as was frequently his practice, he compared American government and parties to their English counterparts. In England, he pointed out, the formal governmental structure, in the form which was called "cabinet government," makes for centralized and effective leadership *within* its own agencies. As his master, Bagehot, had described it: "The principle of Parliament is obedience to leaders. Change your leader if you will, take another if you will, but obey No. 1 while you serve No. 1, and obey No. 2 when you have gone over to No. 2. . . . If everybody does what he thinks right, there will be 657 amendments to every motion, and none of them will be carried or the motion either." [46] In England, that is to say, political parties are encouraged to operate *inside* the formal government because that government contains a point of power—a majority in the House of Commons—the possession of which enables a party to wield the full power of the entire government. As a consequence, said Wilson, the party leaders are identical with the governmental leaders.[47] Party operations are thus carried on in full view of the people, and the parties are forced to concentrate upon defending their programs of public policy and putting them into effect—since it is largely by such activities that they hope to win elections. It was in this sense, said Wilson, that the formal structure of English government enables responsible party government to flourish there.

In the United States, on the other hand, the governmental structure makes impossible the development of any kind of effective *official* leadership. As a result, Wilson argued, political parties have arisen outside the constitutional structure to provide at least a measure of the leadership so desperately needed; and for their services in making the government work after a fashion, parties deserve the nation's gratitude. Yet American parties, like any other, cannot entirely escape the consequences of the kind of formal government within which they are forced to operate. Driven entirely outside the official structure, they inevitably produce a sharp differentiation in both function and personnel between party leaders and official leaders. This, in turn, means that the party leaders work in obscurity and therefore cannot be held responsible by the people. The result, said Wilson, is that the leaders with the real power con-

---

[46] *The English Constitution*, p. 209.
[47] Cf. *ibid.*, pp. 209-10.

centrate on making money, and responsible party action on matters of public policy simply does not exist in the United States.

It was in this sense, Wilson concluded, that the existing American parties are as they are because of the hostile constitutional system within which they have to operate. Responsible party government is possible only where, as in England, the formal government provides a point or points of power the possession of which enables the winning party to make effective whatever policies it wishes. If such a concentration of power can be achieved in the American constitutional system, he believed, bossism will disappear and responsible party government will follow shortly; for

party triumph would then be a matter of might in debate, not of supremacy in subterfuge. The two great national parties—and upon the existence of two great parties, with clashings and mutual jealousies and watchings, depends the health of free political institutions—are dying for want of unifying and vitalizing principles. Without leaders, they are also without policies, without arms. With leaders there must be followers, there must be parties. And with leaders whose leadership was earned in an open war of principle against principle, by the triumph of one opinion over all opposing opinions, parties must from the necessities of the case have definite policies. Platforms, then, must mean something. Broken promises will then end in broken power. . . . Eight words contain the sum of the present degradation of our political parties: *No leaders, no principles; no principles, no parties.*[48]

ESTABLISHING PARTY GOVERNMENT IN THE AMERICAN SYSTEM

Throughout his academic career Woodrow Wilson held to the central idea that in order to establish responsible party government in the United States it will be necessary first to provide for concentrated leadership and power inside the official governmental structure itself. Only thus, he believed, will parties be induced to operate openly and publicly within the government; for only thus can a situation exist in which, for their own survival, the parties will have to be concerned primarily with the creation and execution of programs of public policy.[49]

At various stages in his career, however, Wilson proposed two quite different programs for obtaining concentrated leadership within the constitutional system. During much of it he proposed the adoption of cabinet government and ministerial responsibility on the English model. The basis for this proposal was his conviction, noted above, that Congress had become by far the most powerful branch of the government, and that the President could never become an effective leader. Believing these things, he reasoned that if concentrated leadership is to be achieved at all in the American system, it will have to be leadership *by* Congress as well as *in* Congress. Since the great barrier against effective leader-

---

[48] "Cabinet Government in the United States," pp. 159-60. The emphasis is Wilson's. See also *ibid.*, pp. 146-50.

[49] Cf. *The New Freedom*, pp. 123-24.

ship *by* Congress is the separation of powers, the remedy indicated seemed to be ministerial responsibility; and since the barrier against concentration of leadership *in* Congress is the committee system, the solution was to place the real control of Congress's activities into one powerful committee, or "cabinet."

Wilson's notion of the practical measures needed in order to install cabinet government and ministerial responsibility in the American system varied from time to time. In "Cabinet Government in the United States" he said that the best method was to oblige the President to choose his cabinet members from among congressional leaders, and to give the cabinet the power of initiating legislation. This would automatically ensure ministerial responsibility, he said, for no proud man would continue to serve in the cabinet if Congress consistently voted down his proposals.[50] In "Committee or Cabinet Government?" the problem seemed somewhat more complicated to him. He realized that some constitutional amendment would probably be necessary, and so he proposed that Article I, section 6, clause 2 [51] be amended so as to exempt cabinet members.[52] In *Congressional Government* he made no specific suggestions, but confined his efforts to recommending, in general terms, the adoption of cabinet government. In both "Leaderless Government" and "Government Under the Constitution" he again proposed permitting cabinet members to sit in Congress and initiate legislation, but said nothing about constitutional alterations to permit the President to pick his cabinet from congressional leaders.[53]

Whatever constitutional changes might be required to achieve it, however, cabinet government seemed to Wilson in his early years as perhaps the only method by which responsible party government might be achieved in the United States:

Cabinet government has in it everything to recommend it. Especially to Americans it should commend itself. It is, first of all, the simplest and most straight-forward system of party government. It gives explicit authority to that party majority which in any event will exercise its implicit powers to the top of its bent; which will switch control if control be not given it. It is a simple legalization of fact; for, as every one knows, we are not free to choose between party government and no-party government. Our choice must be between a party that rules by authority and a party that, where it has not a grant of the right to rule, will make itself supreme by stratagem. It is not parties in open and legitimate organization that

[50] "Cabinet Government in the United States," pp. 150-52.

[51] This clause reads as follows: "No Senator or Representative shall, during the Time for which he was elected, be appointed to any Civil Office under the Authority of the United States which shall have been created, or the Emoluments whereof shall have been increased during such time; and no Person holding any Office under the United States, shall be a Member of either House during his continuance in office."

[52] "Committee or Cabinet Government?", pp. 112-14.

[53] "Leaderless Government," pp. 356-69; "Government Under the Constitution," pp. 176-78.

are to be feared, but those that are secretly banded together, begetters of hidden schemes and ugly stratagems.[54]

In *Constitutional Government in the United States,* however, Wilson took quite a different tack. He abandoned the notion that Congress was the only possible source of leadership in the American system, and at the same time gave up the corollary that cabinet government was the only hopeful substitute for "committee government" in Congress as a means of establishing concentrated leadership in the governmental structure. He declared instead that the greatest promise for such leadership lay in the development of presidential leadership—in the formal government and in the parties.

The potentialities for leadership in the Presidency now assumed huge proportions in Wilson's eyes. The President, he argued, was the only national officer elected by all the people and representing all the people. He was therefore the one national officer in whose activities the people were really interested, and who might therefore be legitimately and effectively held responsible by the people for how the whole government was carried on.[55]

The President also had the potentiality of becoming the great national leader of his party. After all, Wilson said, the stakes of power embodied in the Presidency were so great for American parties that the President could not help being leader of his party if he wished.[56]

In the President, concluded Wilson, the American system had precisely what it needed: a truly national leader of the formal government, elected by and responsible to no single section of interest but rather the representative of all of the people. Thus his power of leadership depended, not upon compromises and deals, but upon the power of public opinion. The President was also a potentially powerful party leader, whose office was the one great goal for both parties. And, most important of all, said Wilson, the Presidency united both government and party leaders *in the same person.* Thus the whole nature of the Presidency made for exactly the kind of identification of the party leader with the official governmental leader that would constitute the foundation of responsible party government. As he summed it up:

He cannot escape being the leader of his party except by incapacity and lack of personal force, because he is at once the choice of the party and of the nation. He is the party nominee, and the only party nominee for whom the whole nation votes. . . . He is not so much part of its organization as its vital link of connection with the thinking nation. He can dominate his party by being spokesman for the real sentiment and purpose of the country, by giving direction to opinion, by giving the country at once the information and the statements of policy which will enable it to form its judgments alike of parties and of men.[57]

[54] "Committee or Cabinet Government?" p. 114.
[55] *Constitutional Government in the United States,* pp. 126-27.
[56] *Ibid.,* pp. 63-66.
[57] *Ibid.,* pp. 67-68.

And again:

He may be both the leader of his party and the leader of the nation, or he may be one or the other. If he lead the nation, his party can hardly resist him. His office is anything he has the sagacity and force to make it.[58]

There is no direct evidence regarding the reasons for Wilson's complete change of mind about the Presidency and the leadership it might provide in the American system. Certainly the period from 1879 to 1900, during which he advanced his cabinet-government proposals, was the nadir of the Presidency's power and prestige, and the administrations of men like Grant, Hayes, Garfield, Arthur, Harrison, and even Cleveland afforded considerable evidence for his failure to be impressed by the office's possibilities. One may also surmise that eight years' observation of Theodore Roosevelt's presidency disclosed to Wilson possibilities in presidential leadership he had not seen before 1900. It is also possible that he lost his earlier confidence that the installation of cabinet government and ministerial responsibility would involve no serious revisions of the American constitutional system, although he made no explicit statement to that effect.

Whatever the reasons for it, however, Wilson's abandonment of cabinet government for presidential leadership did not affect his fundamental position that responsible party government is the best means for establishing genuine popular control of American government, that the existing American parties are not providing party government, and that such a system cannot be achieved in the United States until leadership is concentrated in the formal governmental structure.

APPRAISAL

Any theory of the proper function of political parties in the American system must take account of Woodrow Wilson's analysis of the problem. The comprehensiveness of that analysis is in itself a reason for giving careful attention to what he said about parties—the more since he did much of his writing at a time when few other American political scientists regarded the problem as deserving scholarly investigation.

Those who today are concerned with the viability of the doctrine of responsible party government might well pay special heed to Wilson's analysis; for he was the first American writer to advance the doctrine of responsible party government, and his exposition of it remains among the most thorough and thoughtful ever made.

Wilson's first contribution to the party-government position was his conception of how parties should be studied. His writings were based upon the assumption that all political parties have a twofold nature involving two sepa-

[58] *Ibid.*, p. 69.

rate but equally important functions: They are agencies for making nominations and conducting elections *and* they are agencies for carrying on government. Since Wilson's time, much of the American literature about parties, and particularly about party history, has been concerned solely with the first of these two functions.[59] This literature limits itself to the question of how parties make nominations and appeal for electoral support. Its specific concerns are the propaganda techniques used by parties, the various economic, social, racial and religious groups whose support they enlist, and the organizational patterns they set up for making nominations and conducting campaigns. When examination of the election or elections is completed, and it has been proved that this or that electoral technique has been most effective in producing victory for the winning party, the scholars of this persuasion feel their job of studying the nature of parties has been performed. What the winning party does while it is in power; what techniques (if any) it employs to put its program into law; what, in short, it does *as an agency of government*—these questions are ignored.

Now Wilson was certainly interested in parties as agencies for conducting elections and in no sense minimized this aspect of their activity. But he felt strongly that neglecting their other aspect—as agencies which do in fact carry on government, in however unsatisfactory a fashion—is methodologically unsound. In his opinion one cannot understand why parties act as they do in their electioneering activities—why, for example, their principles are meaningless and their propaganda is designed to 'becloud the real issues—unless one understands what, if anything, they are trying to do *after* elections in their capacity as agencies of government. So he determined to study party government as well as party propaganda techniques and nominating procedures.

Those modern scholars whose investigations have profited by the adoption of this double-edged approach to parties owe Wilson a great debt; [60] for it was he who first suggested it in America and demonstrated its usefulness in his own writings.

Wilson is also important for the party-government writers because he asked

---

[59] In Wilson's time the leading party histories using this approach were: Rufus Blanchard, *The Rise and Fall of Political Parties in the United States* (Chicago: The National School Furnishing Company, 1892); and W. M. Sloane, *Party Government in the United States of America* (New York: Harper and Brothers, 1914). The principal analytical works illustrating this approach were: Jesse Macy, *Party Organization and Machinery* (New York: The Century Company, 1904); and J. H. Patton, *Political Parties in the United States: Their History and Influence* (New York: New Amsterdam Book Company, 1896). At the present time W. E. Binkley, *American Political Parties: Their Natural History* (New York: Alfred A. Knopf, 1943) is the leading party history using this approach; and E. M. Sait, *American Parties and Elections* (3d ed.; New York: D. Appleton-Century Company, 1942), in an analysis of contemporary parties, also illustrates this approach.

[60] As indicated in the preceding chapter, the author believes that the works of such men as Schattschneider, Finer, Barker, and Herring—not all of whom take the party-government position—are the leading present-day writers who take this approach to the study of parties.

most of the questions and arrived at most of the answers which go to make up their point of view. In particular his analysis of the nature and conditions of responsibility has become an important foundation of their position. His conviction, as pointed out above, was that full responsibility depends upon the possession of full power—that no man (or group of men) can reasonably and effectively be held responsible for what the government does unless he (or they) possess the full power of the government. Nor, he argued, can their responsibility be made effective unless there is sufficient publicity concerning the real loci of power to assure that the people always know *who* really is running their government.

However axiomatic these propositions may seem to present-day political scientists, their very self-evidence is in large part a product of Wilson's exposition. Certainly his attack upon the Whig-Federalist theory of government, according to which government should be compounded of "rival antagonisms," was a devastating one, the more since he followed it up by demonstrating that the theory was inappropriate to a time when government must act swiftly, efficiently, and with direction.[61] This criticism has become a commonplace for most contemporary political scientists, but they are in large part indebted for it to the cogency and popularity of Wilson's writings.

In at least one instance Wilson, the founder of the party-government view, made a more thorough analysis of it than any of its present-day exponents. As pointed out in the preceding chapter, the latter do not discuss in any detail the question of why the existing American parties are boss-controlled, decentralized, and therefore irresponsible. They confine themselves largely to the suggestion that the Constitution—by setting up such institutions as separation of powers, staggered terms of office, and federalism—makes it impossible for a party to capture full power or to assume full responsibility. Wilson made the same points; but in addition he showed the consequences of the complete separation of the parties from the formal government, and the sharp distinction between party agencies and leaders and governmental agencies and leaders—a line of inquiry which might well be resumed by the party-government writers of the present.

There are, however, certain gaps in Wilson's analysis which make it impossible for the present-day political scientist to accept it *in toto*. He asked and tried to answer most of the important questions; but this is not to say that he asked all of them, or that all his answers were equally thoughtful. For one thing, he failed to explore thoroughly the fundamental question of the nature of democracy. As pointed out above, he realized the importance of clarity on this point, and stated clearly his belief that democracy means popular control of

---

[61] It should also be remembered that Wilson launched this attack at a time when the Whig doctrine in general, and the *Federalist* papers in particular, were widely considered to be repositories of the final truth about popular government.

(though not participation in) government; and he added that this, in turn, means the popular choice of alternative responsible ruling groups. Yet nowhere in Wilson's writings can one find a thorough discussion of *why* democracy should be defined in this manner. There are bits here and scraps there, but no systematic, comprehensive consideration of the several alternative conceptions of democracy. Some of the alternative conceptions were, moreover, much more widely held in Wilson's day than his own; and his failure to consider them is a more serious defect of his thought than his early flirting with antidemocratic notions.[62] He soon became an avowed democrat, but his frequent statements that party government is democratic because democracy means the choice of ruling groups involved considerable question-begging.

Again, Wilson never dealt seriously with the problem of the nature of party membership. In the eyes of one who expected so much unity, discipline, and organizational strength from parties, the question of who should be considered party members should have assumed great importance. But Wilson did not explicitly face the problem at any time; he merely took for granted whatever conception of party membership seemed most appropriate to the particular argument at hand. This is a source of much of the inconsistency and confusion in his writing about parties.

In *Congressional Government,* for example, he speaks of "real parties" and their "real leaders" in a way that indicates his scorn for the dilettante-reformer and his appreciation of the man who works hard in politics. One gets the idea from this that he believed the "real parties" were made up only of those who worked for the party. In *The New Freedom,* on the other hand, he strongly recommends direct primary legislation as the surest means of "restoring" party control to "the parties' members." Here he clearly assumes the ticket-voter conception of party membership; [63] and such a conception is incompatible with the kind of compact, disciplined parties his system of party government clearly called for.

His various proposals for achieving party government in the American system, however, led him into his greatest theoretical blunders. When he was expounding cabinet government and ministerial responsibility as well as when he was emphasizing presidential leadership, Wilson was capable of side-stepping important questions and of proceeding on his way with the most extravagant assumptions. For example, his earlier notion that cabinet government is the answer to all our party problems is open to criticism from both these points of view. Since so many of his ideas about party government were drawn from English experience, especially as interpreted by Bagehot, Wilson might with

---

[62] For the nature of some of these alternative conceptions, and for a discussion of some of the problems they create, see Austin Ranney and Willmoore Kendall, "Democracy: Confusion and Agreement," *Western Political Quarterly,* IV (September, 1951), 430-39.

[63] *The New Freedom,* pp. 112, 224-25.

great profit have asked himself such questions as these: How much of what Bagehot describes depends upon peculiar, non-transferable English circumstances, and how much is therefore inapplicable to the United States? What about the relative smallness of England, the homogeneity of its population, the absence of a written constitution and judicial review, the existence of a genuine ruling-class, and the tradition of the gentleman in politics? Do these things perhaps account for party government in England? It is quite possible that Wilson's answers to these questions would have been that the essential conditions producing party government in England are not uniquely and non-transferably English, and that English experience is therefore applicable to the United States. It is quite possible also that he could have made out a convincing case. The point is that he did not face up to the question at all.

Again, Wilson's proposals about cabinet government ignored a great many real difficulties. Would not, for example, the existence of a genuine bicameral legislature in the United States—as opposed to what is, for most purposes, really a unicameral legislature in England—make cabinet government and ministerial responsibility impossible here? Wilson, by remaining silent on this point, clearly begged the question whether insoluble problems would be created by the independence and strength of the United States Senate.

It can be argued that when Wilson abandoned cabinet government in favor of presidential leadership as the great remedy for our party ills he met many of those objections; but the later conception is open to the same criticisms. Carried away by his new enthusiasm for the potentialities for leadership in the Presidency, Wilson, in Constitutional Government in the United States, failed to distinguish between potential leadership and actual leadership. By his own statement, he was searching for an institutionalized, formalized leadership so integral to the American governmental structure as to operate effectively regardless of the variables involved. But the kind of presidential leadership he described could, clearly, be exercised only by a certain kind of President. It was therefore a personal rather than institutional leadership.[64] Wilson's conception of presidential leadership thus ignored most of the stumbling-blocks in the path of even a strong President: the inertia created by the separation of powers, the confusion induced by the staggering of congressional, presidential, and senatorial terms of office, and the anomaly of the defeated presidential candidate's pseudo-leadership.

Perhaps Wilson's difficulties with presidential leadership are a part of a greater difficulty one can readily observe in his writings, namely, his curious reluctance to realize and follow up some of the implications of his doctrine of party government. For example, Wilson not only believed in judicial review

---

[64] This sort of presidential leadership, as Herbert Croly pointed out, tends to destroy party strength and party leadership rather than to strengthen it. Progressive Democracy (New York: The Macmillan Company, 1914), pp. 337-46.

but also was confident that a system of responsible party government would "establish rather than shake those arrangements of our Constitution . . . to which our national pride properly attaches, namely, the distinct division of powers between the state and federal governments, the slow and solemn formalities of Constitutional change, and the interpretative functions of the federal courts." [65] On the other hand, one of his most fundamental doctrines was that responsibility is the concomitant of power, from which he drew the corollary that no party can be genuinely responsible unless it holds the full power of the government. Apparently he was blind to the fact that a party cannot hold full power while a court, selected for life, and largely beyond any direct party or popular control, can declare its leading measures null and void. Wilson believed in responsible party government and in judicial review; and he never officially noticed the possibility of conflict between the two institutions.

All these criticisms do not, however, lessen Wilson's importance as the first American exponent of the doctrine of responsible party government; nor do they detract from the value of his writings as constituting, for the reasons mentioned above, one of the most comprehensive and suggestive expositions of that doctrine made in his time or since.

---

[65] "Government Under the Constitution," pp. 179-80.

CHAPTER FOUR

A. Lawrence Lowell

Abbott Lawrence Lowell's ultimate position upon the function of political parties in the American system was a considerable departure from that of Woodrow Wilson. His preliminary analysis, nevertheless, was in many respects closely parallel to Wilson's.[1] Lowell was a distinguished scholar in the field of English government; and he greatly admired the English system, as did Wilson. Like Wilson, he believed political parties to be the most effective agency available to democracies for expressing the popular will and translating it into governmental action. And, like Wilson, he derived his concern with the problem of parties and their place upon the conviction that the most fruitful approach to the study of government is one which goes behind its legal façade and examines the forces which make it work.

It is necessary, Lowell conceded, to study the formal constitutional structure of government; for that, after all, is one of its most important parts. The real mistake is to isolate that (or any) part and attempt to understand it apart from its place in the whole governing process.

Any one who attempts to study a carpet loom, or even an ordinary steam engine, when at rest, will find its mechanism hard to understand. He may examine the several parts, note their size and shape, and the materials of which they are made; but unless he watches them in motion he will not easily appreciate their bearing upon one another, or their functions in the working of the machine. The same principle applies to the study of politics, for the real mechanism of a government can be understood only by examining it in action. It has, indeed, been far too common to study the constitutions of various countries statically, if I may use the term; and this has led to a habit of describing the nature, composition, and

---

[1] Lowell's ideas about the function of party are to be found primarily in these works: *Essays on Government* (Boston: Houghton Mifflin Company, 1889); *Governments and Parties in Continental Europe* (2 vols.; Boston: Houghton Mifflin Company, 1896); "Oscillations in Politics," *Annals of the American Academy of Political and Social Science*, XII (July, 1898), 69-97; *The Government of England* (2 vols.; New York: The Macmillan Company, 1908); "The Influence of Party upon Legislation in England and America," *Annual Report of the American Historical Association for the Year 1901* (Washington, D.C.: Government Printing Office, 1902), I, 321-542; and *Public Opinion and Popular Government* (New York: Longmans, Green and Company, 1913). He also published a later relevant volume: *Public Opinion in War and Peace* (Cambridge: Harvard University Press, 1923). This volume, however, contains nothing on the problem of party which Lowell had not stated in his previous works.

powers of the different factors in the government without seeking to know the actual scope of their several operations, or the extent of their control over one another.[2]

If this initial promise is correct, Lowell continued, it follows that the study of the nature and function of political parties is a task of great importance for political scientists everywhere. Parties are, he pointed out, a phenomenon characteristic of every contemporary popular government; and they should therefore be studied as thoroughly as formal constitutional law and legislative procedure.[3] But little value will be derived from such a study, he warned, unless scholars approach parties with some sympathetic understanding of their problems and some real attempt to place themselves imaginatively inside party activities. Otherwise, Lowell said, they will fall victim to the same sort of errors as Ostrogorski, who

appears to look on democracy, and on party machinery in particular, from the outside, as something artificial and weird, rather than the natural result of human conduct under the existing conditions. He does not seem to put himself quite in the shoes of . . . men who have come into contact with party organizations, and ask what he himself would, or might, have done in the same position. Hence his analysis has a slight air of unreality, and does not wholly approve itself as a study of ordinary political motives.[4]

Only by avoiding this "air of unreality," Lowell was convinced, can scholars hope to understand the nature and function of parties in a democratic system.

THE NATURE OF DEMOCRACY

The foundation of Lowell's theory of party government was his conception of popular government as "the control of political affairs by public opinion."[5] The fundamental assumption of popular government, he contended is "that public opinion should be carried into effect." There are two reasons why this should be done: "The first is based, not on any supposition that the opinion of the people is always right, but on the belief that it is on the whole more likely to be right than the opinion of any other person or body which can be obtained. The second reason is that contentment and order are more general, and the laws and public officers are better obeyed, when in accord with popular opinion, than otherwise."[6]

---

[2] *Essays on Government*, pp. 1-3.

[3] *Governments and Parties in Continental Europe*, I, v-vi.

[4] *The Government of England*, I, 467-68, note 1. The work Lowell referred to in this criticism was: M. I. Ostrogorski, *Democracy and the Organization of Political Parties*, translated from the French by Frederick Clarke (2 vols.; New, York: The Macmillan Company, 1902).

[5] *Public Opinion and Popular Government*, p. 4.

[6] *Ibid.*, p. 239.

Lowell repeatedly asserted, however, that popular government must be government by *genuine* public opinion; and he conducted an elaborate analysis of the nature of "genuine" public opinion. The result of the analysis was that such opinion exhibits two basic traits: In the first place, it is the lasting, considered, mature judgment of the people. It must not, he warned, be mistaken for temporary popular whims produced by the volatile passions of the moment. The more fundamental importance a society attaches to a given matter, Lowell further contended, the more it should impose constitutional limitations upon the ordinary processes of legislation in order to protect such a matter against easy revision as the result of passing and ephemeral popular whims.

Matters that ought to be beyond the reach of party politics had better be so hedged about that they can be dealt with only by something more authoritative than a party majority, or else time enough ought to be required for their consideration to permit a political oscillation to take place. In one form or the other this is effectually done by our constitutions in the case of a great many subjects. It has been said that a constitution limits the whim, not the will, of the people, and in view of the rapid alternations of party, the desire of a mere party majority cannot be said to express the lasting popular will. The tendency to political oscillations in a democracy teaches, therefore, the ever growing value of constitutional limitations.[7]

Still more important is the second trait: Genuine public opinion can emerge, said Lowell, only from an abiding consensus among the people about the ends of government, and about the nature of the framework within which governmental decisions should be made.

A body of men are politically capable of a public opinion only as far as they are agreed upon the ends and aims of government and upon the principles by which those ends shall be attained. They must be united, also, about the means whereby the action of the government is to be determined, in a conviction, for example, that the views of a majority—or it may be some other portion of their numbers—ought to prevail; and a political community as a whole is capable of public opinion only when this is true of the great bulk of the citizens. . . . The consent required is not a universal approval by all the people of every measure enacted, but a consensus in regard to the legitimate character of the ruling authority and its right to decide the questions that arise.[8]

Where fifty-one per cent of the community is committed to effecting a certain policy at all costs and where forty-nine per cent is irrevocably committed to resisting it, genuine public opinion cannot exist for the simple reason that no real community exists. The presence in any community of a significant number of such "irreconcilables," Lowell maintained, makes real popular government—govern-

---

[7] "Oscillations in Politics," p. 97.
[8] *Public Opinion and Popular Government,* p. 9.

ment by genuine public opinion—impossible.[9] Nor is it enough, he said, that the irreconcilable minority be frightened into acquiescence by the threat of the majority's superior force. The minority must feel that it *ought* to accept the majority's decision:

So far as the preponderating opinion is one which the minority does not share, but which it feels ought, as the opinion of the majority, to be carried out, the government is conducted by a true public opinion or by consent. So far as the preponderating opinion is one the execution of which the minority would resist by force if it could do so successfully, the government is based upon force. . . . Even when there is no resort to actual force it remains true that in any case where the minority does not concede the right of the majority to decide, submission is yielded only to obviously superior strength; and obedience is the result of compulsion, not of public opinion.[10]

Genuine popular opinion can thus exist only under certain conditions, Lowell believed. There must be sufficient homogeneity of population to encourage consensus.[11] And there must be freedom of dissent in order that the minority will realize that the majority really is the majority, and so that the minority will have a perpetual opportunity to become the majority.[12]

Lowell did not make the mistake, however, of assuming that wherever genuine public opinion exists it will automatically be translated into governmental action. There was, he observed, a widespread belief in America that popular government is a simple proposition and that converting the popular will into governmental action is a matter of no great difficulty. This belief, in his opinion, was at the bottom of much of the righteous and futile indignation of so many Americans about the state of their political institutions.[13] Much of this pointless furor could be avoided, he believed, by careful exploration of the question of what kind of institutional machinery is most conducive to popular government. His own analysis of this question led him to the conclusion that popular government can be organized only as the popular choice of and control over alternate ruling groups: "For more than a hundred years it has been the habit to talk of government by the people, and the expression is, perhaps, more freely

---

[9] *Governments and Parties in Continental Europe*, I, 102-03; *Public Opinion and Popular Government*, pp. 32-34.

[10] *Public Opinion and Popular Government*, p. 11. Lowell believed that this was substantially what Rousseau had meant by his doctrine of the "general will": that when people vote upon a public measure, their votes register not their personal wishes upon the matter but rather their opinions as to what the general will is. Thus the minority never has its *wishes* flouted; what happens is, rather, that its judgment is overruled. Everyone wants the general will carried out. And Lowell also believed that, in making this argument, Rousseau was pleading for the same kind of consensus he (Lowell) was arguing for. *Ibid.*, pp. 8-9.

[11] *Ibid.*, pp. 34-36.

[12] *Ibid.*, pp. 36-40.

[13] *Ibid.*, p. 100.

used today than ever before, yet a superficial glance at the history of democracy ought to be enough to convince us that in a great nation the people as a whole do not and cannot really govern. The fact is that we are ruled by parties, whose action is more or less modified but never completely directed by public opinion." [14]

He arrived at this conclusion through the following reasoning: If democracy means government by public opinion, the democrat must know the sort of questions about which the people are capable of having an opinion. It is quite clear, Lowell asserted, that most people are incapable of having real opinions upon intricate points of law, complex social and economic problems, technical matters of administrative management—all those matters, in fact, which are the day-to-day concern of government.[15] But it by no means follows, Lowell said, that "government by public opinion" is impossible, or that

because people have no true opinion on a question, they have no opinion on the method by which it ought to be decided. They may be incapable, and recognize that they are incapable, of forming an opinion about an intricate point of law, or about the guilt of a man accused of crime when the evidence is conflicting; and yet they may have a very definite opinion that the matter shall be decided by a court of law, and that its decision shall be enforced. The public may have no opinion about dealing with an epidemic, and yet it may have a very strong opinion that it ought to be combatted by physicians who have proved their competence. This suggests a point of practical importance, for it is obviously wise, so far as possible, to submit to the judgment of the people the questions on which they have, or may have, opinions, and not those on which they have none.[16]

Thus, Lowell concluded, a democratic government should submit to the people such questions, for example, as: Do they feel a particular problem is being settled to their satisfaction? In short, do they approve or disapprove of how the group which controls the government at the moment is running things? Government in which public opinion is for the most part called upon to answer only the question of *who* shall rule is none the less government based upon "the control of political affairs by public opinion." Indeed, Lowell avowed, in a modern highly populated and complex society, it is the only conceivable organization for such a government.[17]

It was from these assumptions concerning the nature of democracy that Lowell proceeded to develop his conception of the function of political parties in a democratic system.

THE FUNCTION OF POLITICAL PARTIES

Like Woodrow Wilson, Lowell believed that political parties are both in-

---

[14] *Governments and Parties in Continental Europe*, I, 69.
[15] *Public Opinion and Popular Government*, pp. 46-49.
[16] *Ibid.*, pp. 25-26.
[17] *Ibid.*, pp. 26-27.

evitable and desirable in any large-scale popular government. Unlike Wilson, however, he was willing to admit that there might be some democracies in which parties are neither inevitable nor particularly desirable. In such a society—Switzerland, for example—he felt that much could be said for eliminating political parties:

Party government has merits as well as defects. Under many circumstances, it is both unavoidable and beneficial, and lack of parties has its peculiar dangers. But in a community which has enough native honesty and intelligence to prevent personal corruption in its public men, and which does not require the friction of parties to stimulate progress, it is certainly a great advantage to get rid of the agitation, the partisanship, and the absence of a perfectly ingenuous expression of opinion, which are inseparable from party government.[18]

Such considerations are irrelevant for any consideration of the function of parties in the United States, however; for, said Lowell, American democracy is large-scale democracy and, as long as it remains so, political parties will continue to be the only possible agency for accomplishing a number of important functions. In the first place, he declared, political parties perform the function of "brokerage" and thereby enable public opinion to express itself.[19] Lowell was the first American political scientist to employ the term "brokerage" for this function of parties; and his exposition of it was one of his most original contributions to discussion of the problem.

The most striking characteristic of modern life, Lowell began, is its increased social mobility: people are moving from place to place, from job to job, and from class to class with much greater freedom than they have ever moved in the past. The psychological consequence of this characteristic is that people are much more ready than formerly to break with the past and to try new things. It is therefore an age of advertisers, Lowell said, of men who take advantage of this universal willingness to change. It is equally an age of brokers—of men who are not quite sellers and not yet buyers, but whose function it is to bring together buyers and sellers.[20]

The growth of population and extension of the suffrage, Lowell continued, has brought about the same result in politics. The very size of the population

---

[18] *Governments and Parties in Continental Europe*, II, 317. See also *Public Opinion and Popular Government*, pp. 101-02.

[19] In discussing the "function" of "parties" here and subsequently, Lowell was guilty of the same interchangeable use of two meanings for each of these terms that marred Wilson's analysis. Throughout his discussion of this point he was clearly using "parties" in sense (b) and "function" in sense (2); for in a later section he pointed out that the existing American parties were not performing these ideal functions. Clearly, in this part of his argument, Lowell had the English parties in mind as models of what parties *should* be and do; but the fact that, in this discussion, he also used American examples whenever they seemed to serve his purpose indicates that he never carefully and explicitly distinguished between what American "parties" *should* do and what, in fact, they *were* doing.

[20] *Public Opinion and Popular Government*, pp. 57-60.

means increased diversification of opinion; and the fact that most people have to be concerned more with bread-winning than with public affairs has made necessary a group of *political* brokers, or "politicians." Their function is to bring together the voters and the government; and their main instrument for accomplishing this purpose is the political party.[21]

Parties, Lowell argued, frame the issues for public discussion, and thus enable the voters to act in masses. If the nation depended upon the spontaneous emergence and concentration of opinion upon public measures and public officers, government would be unable either to know what public opinion is or to respond to it. Political parties, however, provide a sort of anode and cathode around which the "electrolysis" of public opinion takes place: "In short, any body of men, be it a board of directors, a legislative assembly, a mass meeting, or the electorate as a whole, can express itself intelligently only by answering 'Yes' or 'No' to a question submitted to it; or if, as in the case of most elections, the matter is to be determined by plurality, it can only select one from a list of candidates presented to it." [22]

If voters in the mass can answer only "Yes" or "No" to public questions, Lowell continued, then some agency must frame the questions which public opinion is called upon to answer. Political parties are the only feasible agency for doing the job: "They have become instruments for carrying on popular government by concentrating opinion. Their function is to make the candidates and the issues known to the public and to draw together people in large masses, so that they can speak with a united voice, instead of uttering an unintelligible babel of discordant cries. In short, their service in politics is largely advertisement and brokerage." [23]

Lowell was under no illusion that political parties, in performing their brokerage function, express all the shades of public opinion with perfect accuracy. He recognized that it is often difficult to determine the people's motives for deciding a given election, and that parties inevitably distort and falsify public opinion to that extent.[24] But this does not mean, he maintained, that it is therefore nonsense to talk of parties as the best available agency for expressing public opinion. Rather than considering this question in a vacuum, he argued, it is necessary to realize that parties *do* express public opinion accurately upon the greatest of all questions in any government: *Who* shall rule? It is also necessary to realize how much greater would be the distortion and falsification of public opinion in the absence of parties:

---

[21] *Ibid.*, pp. 61-67.

[22] *Ibid.*, pp. 67-69. Schattschneider makes this point in almost the same language: "The people are a sovereign whose vocabulary is limited to two words 'Yes' and 'No.' This sovereign, moreover, can speak only when spoken to." *Party Government*, p. 52.

[23] *Ibid.*, pp. 65-66.

[24] *Ibid.*, pp. 71-75, 86-92.

Suppose, for example, that no political parties existed in the United States, and that some candidates were nominated who stood for a more vigorous national control of corporations and a tariff for revenue only, others who stood for a similar control and a protective tariff, others for prohibition and restriction of immigration, and so on through all the possible combinations of political creeds. . . . It has already been pointed out that in such a case no single candidate would probably receive more than a small minority of the total vote, and if so what would the result of the election signify? What would it tell us about public opinion on any of these questions. . . . The confusion would certainly be far greater than it is today. In short, the function performed by the parties in framing the issues for popular judgment is not rendered useless by the fact that it is fulfilled very imperfectly.[25]

The second great function of political parties, Lowell contended, is to translate public opinion into governmental action—in other words, to establish popular control over government. For reasons to be discussed below, Lowell nowhere explained in any detail *how* parties accomplish this function. He seems rather to have assumed that if public opinion is accurately expressed upon the fundamental question of who shall rule, then popular control over government is, by definition, established. English parties perform this function particularly well, he pointed out, because in England the voters tend to vote for the *parties* and not for individual members of Parliament: "The fact is that . . . the intelligent voter votes not so much for Mr. X or Mr. Y as for the Ministry or the Opposition, and hence he rarely cares enough about the personal opinions or discretion of any candidate to jeopardize the success of his party by encouraging the nomination of a third person." [26] This is the situation, he pointed out, because each English party stands or falls *as a unit* behind its program and leaders:

In England the party that has a majority in the House of Commons must hold together and support the cabinet on all important measures, or it will fall and be replaced by a cabinet of the opposition. Conversely the cabinet must avoid a policy that divides its followers seriously. Hence a general election is far less a decision on the merits of individual candidates for Parliament than a judgment on the national party leaders who stand on a fairly definite policy. . . .[27]

Thus an indispensable prerequisite for party responsibility, Lowell believed, is the existence of parties that, as in England, are unified and disciplined on matters of public policy.

Lowell also drew the important corollary that a two-party system establishes popular control much more effectively than a multi-party system, even though the latter may more faithfully reflect the complex shadings of public opinion:

When there are only two parties . . . the electorate is offered a pair of alternatives and chooses between them. The issue is Republican or Democrat, Conserva-

---

[25] *Ibid.*, pp. 75-76. See also *Ibid.*, pp. 71-72.
[26] *The Government of England*, II, 54-55. See also *Ibid.*, II, 47.
[27] *Public Opinion and Popular Government*, pp. 76-77.

tive or Liberal; it is essentially a case of "Yes" or "No." But when a number of political groups exist no question is presented to which the people can answer "Yes" or "No." They cannot decide which of the groups shall be in power, because that will depend upon the combinations or coalitions formed in the representative body itself when it meets. . . . The existence of several groups may produce a legislative body that reflects the complex state of the public mind better than a division into two parties, and that may or may not result in wiser legislation, but it does not give to public opinion so direct a control over the government.[28]

Under Lowell's conception of ideal party government, therefore, the primary functions of parties are to express public opinion by framing issues for popular decision, and to establish popular control over government. In addition he believed that parties should accomplish at least two other tasks, both of which would also aid the production of genuine public opinion. For one thing, parties should operate as checks upon the popular whims and vagaries of the moment, and thus help to ensure that whatever public opinion finally emerges would be mature, considered, and permanent: "If political parties always distort public opinion in some degree, they also prevent still larger distortion caused by sudden waves of excitement. As great ecclesiastical bodies tend to frown upon religious excesses, so party organizations are inclined to check political vagaries. They are essentially conservative, setting their faces against new experiments." [29]

Party's greatest contribution to the production of genuine public opinion, however, should be the conciliation of antagonisms and the consequent encouragement of the basic consensus which Lowell believed to be an important precondition of popular government. It is beside the point, he said, to deplore the fact that political parties in America and England constantly tend toward the center of political gravity in order to garner the maximum number of votes. Ideological sharpness is admittedly lost thereby, but something much more important is gained in its stead: "The good side is found in the fact that political leaders strive to carry out so much of their policy as is attainable, instead of clinging obstinately to ideals which cannot possibly be realized. Such conditions tend to promote, on the essentials of democracy, a popular accord from which no leading statesman is far estranged; and they tend to eliminate irreconcilable and revolutionary elements in the state." [30]

In highly populated, relatively polyglot nations like England and the United States, Lowell concluded, any agency which tends to promote the democratic consensus performs an invaluable service; and there is, in his judgment, no agency which can provide that service so well as political parties.

---

[28] Ibid., pp. 82-83.
[29] Ibid., pp. 96-97.
[30] The Government of England, II, 97-98.

THE NATURE OF POLITICAL PARTIES

Unlike Woodrow Wilson, Lowell made careful inquiry into the nature of political parties.[31] As a result of this inquiry, he concluded, in the first place, that American and English parties are "not academic bodies for the expression of abstract ideas, but . . . essentially instruments of government; and it is only by regarding them in this light that they can be fruitfully studied as a phenomenon in modern democracy." [32] It was for that reason, he continued, that there is no point in criticizing them for accepting into their ranks men with differing points of view, or for abandoning ideas "merely because they are unpopular," or even because their primary concern is getting power rather than advancing great principles. Nor, he said, are English parties different from American on this score:

In truth the parties in England are not, as they are over much of the continent of Europe, collections of men bound together by their faith in a fixed political creed, but rather instruments of government, representing general political tendencies, and ready to govern the nation in accord with those tendencies so far as circumstances will permit. . . . The proximate aim of the two great parties is to get into power, and hence they no longer stand for abstract principles without regard to their popularity. They urge only measures for which there is at least a reasonable prospect of securing immediate support; and if a policy proves permanently unpopular it is abandoned.[33]

It is idle, Lowell argued, to rail at English and American parties for not living up to some vague ideal. The important thing is the fact that the kind of parties that exist are capable of performing valuable functions in their respective governments.

In the second place, Lowell pointed out, it is quite true, as many critics of parties in both nations were constantly charging, that they are controlled by very small percentages of their members.[34] But after all, he asked, what large

---

[31] The "parties" whose nature Lowell here discussed were clearly the *existing* parties— parties in sense (a). For purposes of this analysis he made no distinction between American and English parties, although, as will be pointed out below, when he came to evaluate the existing American parties he compared them unfavorably with English parties—which, in fact, were his model for what parties *should* be, although he never explicitly described them as such. Here again, therefore, his argument was confused by his inability to make clear in what sense he was using the term "parties."

[32] *Public Opinion and Popular Government*, pp. 84-85.

[33] *The Government of England*, II, 97. See also *ibid.*, II, 114-15; "Oscillations in Politics," pp. 93-94; and *Public Opinion and Popular Government*, pp. 84-85.

[34] In making this admission, Lowell obviously accepted without question the ticket-voter conception of party membership described in the second chapter of the present study. He further admitted the "oligarchy" charge arising from that conception. His reply, as the text indicates, was that oligarchical control was an inevitable attribute of large bodies of men, and that it was a price well worth paying for the many valuable services of parties. He seems never to have inquired whether the ticket-voter conception of party membership was a proper one.

body of men is not so controlled? "Government in every land and in every period of the world's history, whether of a nation, a church, a business enterprise or anything else, has been habitually conducted by a few guiding spirits whatever be the form of the organization; and that will continue to be the case so long as men differ in ability, in force of character, and in the amount of effort they are willing to put forth to prevail in their opinions and their desire to rule." [35] If oligarchy is thus inevitable in any large group of men, Lowell was convinced, any reform designed to "restore" party control to all the party members, such as the direct primary, cannot avoid failing of its purpose:

The party itself is so large a body that someone must present the candidates for nomination to its members. Even if all the Republican voters in a state could come together in a mass meeting, a name to be discussed and voted upon would have to be proposed by someone, and this is certainly not less true when the members of the party never meet together, but cast their ballots singly in polling booths. . . . To have any chance of success the candidate and his qualifications must be made known to the voters, and that involves an organization with branches throughout the community.[36]

Finally, as Lowell had pointed out in another connection, English and American parties are never very far apart on matters of public policy. But again he found this to be a strength rather than a weakness. He was aware that many critics of the existing parties in both nations were calling for a realignment so that the entire Left could enter one party and the entire Right could join the other. To such critics, he replied that where class parties are formed for mortal combat with other class parties there consensus disappears and genuine popular government becomes impossible: "So long . . . as party lines are vertical, popular government is on a sound basis. But if all the rich men, or all the educated men, are grouped together, the state is in peril; and if the party lines become really horizontal, democracy is on the high road to class tyranny, which leads, as history proves, to a dictatorship." [37]

The party alignment most conducive to democratic government, Lowell concluded, is

one where they are far enough apart to stand for real differences of policy, and yet sufficiently controlled by their moderate elements to be fairly close together. This is the best condition, because it is one that brings both of them near to the political centre of gravity of the whole people, neither of the alternatives offered to the voters being very repugnant to the average man. In such a case the parties

---

[35] *Public Opinion and Popular Government*, p. 99. See also *The Government of England*, I, 491.

[36] *Public Opinion and Popular Government*, pp. 149-50.

[37] *Governments and Parties in Continental Europe*, II, 65-66.

perform their function of framing issues for the people, and yet falsify public opinion to the smallest extent.[38]

The foregoing paragraphs should make it clear that, in his discussion of the nature of English and American parties, Lowell was never clear as to whether he' was talking about the existing parties or about some ideal to which, in his opinion, they should conform. When he came to consider the American party system in particular, however, this ambivalence disappeared, and he confined his observations strictly to the existing American parties.

EVALUATION OF AMERICAN PARTIES

Lowell had much the same conception as Woodrow Wilson had of an ideal responsible party government, drawn from the English model. He was, however, even more guilty than Wilson, as the preceding pages show, of expounding that ideal under the guise of a description of the existing party systems in both England and the United States. For that reason it is often difficult for the reader to separate the functions Lowell believed parties, in sense (a), *do* perform from the functions he believed parties, in sense (b), *should* perform. This confusion seems to have been worst when he was defending both English and American parties against the various charges leveled against them by their critics. When he came to evaluate the existing American parties in particular, however, Lowell clearly based his judgments upon a Wilsonian view of responsible party government as the most effective means for establishing popular control. He agreed with Wilson, moreover, that American parties are incapable of providing party government in that ideal sense, and that their fundamental deficiency is irresponsibility.

Lowell produced statistical evidence of the irresponsibility of American parties in his pioneer study for the American Historical Association of the strength of party lines in the House of Commons, Congress, and selected state legislatures. In explaining the purpose of his study, Lowell pointed out that it was common in America to denounce political parties for their "despotic" control of legislators and legislation. He was aware that in a system of effective party government parties would and should exercise such control; but he felt that the extent to which parties actually do control legislative action should be determined before praise or blame is awarded.[39] He therefore selected five "typical" Congresses and five "typical" state legislatures, and examined their

---

[38] *Public Opinion and Popular Government,* p. 96. See also *The Government of England,* I, 438. Here Lowell seems to be talking about parties in sense (b), for, as subsequent paragraphs will show, he did not believe that the existing American parties provide "real differences in policy." Again his (apparently unconscious) alternation between a defense of the existing English and American parties and the creation of a standard to which they should conform produced real confusion in his analysis.

[39] "The Influence of Party upon Legislation in England and America," p. 321.

voting records in order to determine how much voting along strict party lines exists in American legislative bodies, by contrast with the House of Commons.[40] His investigation revealed that in the House of Commons twenty-three per cent of the votes on major public issues were party votes, whereas in Congress only seven per cent were party votes, and in the state legislatures the proportion varied from one to fifteen per cent.[41] In the United States, Lowell concluded, parties take effective party stands on considerably fewer public issues than in England.

Lowell further concluded that this breakdown of party lines in American legislatures means that American parties are irresponsible. In the United States, he said, the voter cannot hold a party responsible for the course of governmental policy; but in England, since party lines are more closely drawn, the situation is quite different:

Where . . . as in the American state legislatures, party lines are not often strictly drawn, a member will vote according to his own opinions or those of his constituents, with little regard to the effect his vote may have upon the prospects of the party in other places. Under these circumstances, it is obviously very difficult to hold a party responsible for the fate of public measures. But in England responsibility is perfectly definite, for the cabinet can almost always control the party, and every voter knows that in casting his ballot at a general election he is voting for or against the policy of the ministry. They virtually appeal to the country on a legislative programme which they have power under ordinary circumstances to carry out, and if they fail to do so the nation will pass judgment on that failure at the next election. They receive all the credit and all the blame for what the House of Commons has done, and left undone, so far as public measures are concerned.[42]

Thus in England, where the people can readily understand what is going on in their government, there is no disposition to distrust the processes of representative government; but in the United States, Lowell said, the people generally have contempt for their legislatures simply because they are

unable to unravel the tangled threads of politics, to follow the innumerable measures through the criss-cross divisions in the legislature, or to appreciate the reasons for a vote on a particular bill. English politics are much more simple. One has

---

[40] The five Congresses selected were: the Twenty-ninth (elected in 1844), the Thirty-eighth (elected in 1854), the Fiftieth (elected in 1886), the Fifty-fifth (elected in 1896), and the Fifty-sixth (elected in 1898). Sessions of the legislatures of New York, Ohio, Illinois, Pennsylvania, and Massachusetts were considered.

[41] "The Influence of Party upon Legislation in England and America," pp. 338, 341. Lowell defined a "party vote" as one in which more than nine-tenths of the members present of one party vote one way, and more than nine-tenths of the members present of the other party vote the other way. *Ibid.*, pp. 323-24. This nine-tenths requirement may well seem excessive to the modern student; but Lowell apparently felt that a really "despotic" party should be able to dragoon that many of its members into line whenever its leaders so desired.

[42] *The Government of England*, II, 532.

only to keep his eyes on the battle between the two front benches, which is waged in the game. But here, where the voting is far less on party lines and hence the party cannot be held responsible, where most of the work is done in many committees of Congress and the state legislatures, when the field is complicated and the public are suspicious of everything they do not see, it is easy to give credit to rumors that are hard to disprove.[43]

The immediate explanation of *why* American parties cannot muster discipline or unity on matters of public policy was clear to Lowell: the parties are really controlled, not by their national public leaders, but by a number of obscure local bosses. And the boss

does not act mainly as an exponent of public opinion or frame the issues therefor. Unless they affect his power, or private interests from which he can derive a revenue, he leaves such matters alone if he can. He cares little for public policy or legislation relating to the general welfare so long as he is allowed to pursue his trade in peace; and he deals chiefly in things that public opinion cannot reach, the distribution of minor offices and the granting of privileges great and small which the public can hardly follow. He is, indeed, a political broker, but one whose business relates far less to the subjects of a genuine public opinion than to private benefits.[44]

As a result, Lowell concluded, "Parties in America are not, as a rule, despotic on public questions, because they have little cohesion; but their influence, or rather the influence of the machine, or of the individual politician, is freely exerted in things quite apart from those issues of public policy which form the only rational ground for party activity. In short, the boss is not a prime minister who directs policy, but an electioneering agent and a private bill and office broker." [45]

Thus Lowell agreed with Wilson that American parties are really controlled by bosses—men who care nothing for public policy and who work in irresponsible obscurity. As a result the parties are unable to achieve any discipline and unity on such matters, and are thus irresponsible and incapable of providing genuine party government. It remained for him only to answer the questions: *why* is this so, and what, if anything, should be done about it?

EXPLANATION OF AMERICAN PARTIES

Up to a point, Lowell's explanation of why American parties are irresponsible and boss-controlled was similar to Wilson's, though neither as fully developed nor as incisive. For one thing, Lowell suggested that the founding fathers constructed our formal governmental structure with the purpose of making genuine

---

[43] *Public Opinion and Popular Government,* pp. 139-40.

[44] *Ibid.,* p. 105.

[45] *The Government of England,* II, 94-95. See also "The Influence of Party upon Legislation in England and America," pp. 349-50.

party government impossible. They fragmented power, divided and obscured responsibility, and designed a government which could act only with the greatest difficulty:

The American system furnished no machinery whereby a party could formulate its policy, select the candidates for high office, and insure that they should be the real leaders of the party and able to control its action; but in England the party policy is determined by the cabinet, and its members are the men who in the constant battles in the Commons have made themselves the leaders of their fellows. Our fathers would probably have felt a strong aversion for these objects had they been suggested, and certainly no attempt was made to attain them; and yet they are absolutely essential to a thorough government by party.[46]

But at the same time, Lowell continued, the fathers, by constructing an almost unworkable system, made the rise of parties inevitable. The result is, he said, that the United States has a governmental system which requires the services of parties if it is to work at all, but which at the same time makes it extremely difficult for parties to act as agencies of government. In consequence, American parties have been forced to operate entirely outside the formal governmental structure:

The form of government in the United States has thus made parties inevitable; and yet they were furnished with no opportunity for the exercise of their functions by the regular organs of the state. There were no means provided whereby a party could formulate and carry through its policy, select its candidates for high office, or insure that they should be treated as the real leaders of the party, and able to control its action. The machinery of party, therefore, from the national convention to the legislative caucus, has perforce been created outside the framework of the government, and cannot be nicely adjusted thereto.[47]

Another great barrier against party government in the United States, Lowell believed, is the tendency of American politics to turn upon largely local, private matters. This tendency encourages—indeed, almost demands—decentralization of the parties and the scattering of their leadership among numerous obscure local bosses who care nothing for matters of national public policy. In England, on the other hand, national questions are the only important ones, Lowell pointed out, and this is a powerful force in producing the centralization of party leadership which is so indispensable to the English system of party government. Lowell cited five major causes for this difference between England and the United States: (1) the responsibility of the English cabinet, as opposed to the independence of the executive in the American system; (2) the fact that the English Permanent Civil Service leaves almost no area in which the spoils system can operate, whereas in the United States merit system reforms

---

[46] "The Influence of Party upon Legislation in England and America," pp. 343-44.

[47] *The Government of England*, I, 441. See also "The Influence of Party upon Legislation in England and America," pp. 346-47.

have left a great many offices available for political disposition; (3) the fact that England's traditional free-trade policy makes it impossible for the various sections and interests to battle each other for tariff favors—a battle which, he observed, dominates so much of American politics; (4) the strong tradition in England that the central government should spend no money on local improvements, making impossible the struggle for federal expenditures in local areas which dominates much congressional action in America; and (5) the English quasi-judicial procedure for private bills, which removes the opportunity for the kind of log-rolling which characterizes so much of Congress' legislative activity.[48]

It is at precisely this juncture that Lowell parts company with Wilson. Up to this point, Lowell goes along with Wilson's analysis of (a) the nature and function of genuine party government, as exemplified by the English party system, (b) the character of the American party system, (c) the consequent inability of American parties to provide real party government, and (d) some of the factors producing their peculiar nature.

Here, however, their agreement ends. It is here that Lowell introduces his own characteristic explanation of the reasons why American parties are the way they are, and his characteristic position upon the issue of what should be done to change their nature. What he says on both points sharply diverges from Wilson's views.

Wilson, as the preceding chapter demonstrates, believed that the American people really want to establish effective majority-control over their government. Since he believed that only genuine party government can effect such majority-control and that the existing American party system is incapable of providing it, he concluded that the United States must make whatever changes are necessary to convert American parties into cohesive, disciplined, and responsible agencies of real party government.

Lowell, on the other hand, was convinced that the ultimate reason why American parties do not establish majority-control over government is that the people really do not want such control established—that the existing party system, in short, is entirely appropriate to the kind of government they want. In America, he argued, the primary desideratum in government is not its unfettered control by the majority; it is rather the preservation of individual and minority rights against any kind of oppression, whether oppression from the majority or from any other source. As he put it:

In the United States the object of government is . . . to protect the individual, to prevent the majority from oppressing the minority, and, except within certain definite limits, to give effect to the wishes of the people only after such solemn formalities have been complied with as to make it clear that the popular feeling

---

[48] *The Government of England*, II, 514-18. See also *Public Opinion and Popular Government*, p. 118; and *Governments and Parties in Continental Europe*, I, 225-26.

is not caused by temporary excitement, but is the result of a mature and lasting opinion. This is done, in the words of the Constitution of Massachusetts, "to the end that it may be a government of laws, and not of men," or, as we should put it to-day, a government by principles, and not by popular impulse.[49]

Every popular government, Lowell continued, is faced with the choice between two alternatives: the establishment of effective majority-rule, or the protection of individual and minority rights. It is not possible to have both. Where government is totally at the command of the majority, he avowed, private rights are even more likely to be abridged than if a monarch had sole control; for a monarch must temper his policies from fear of effective resistance, and the majority need have no such fear nor display such temperance.[50] If majority-rule is what a nation wants, he said, then it should set up parliamentary government and responsible party government as they operate in England. But, he warned, such a nation should be fully aware that sooner or later the majority will limit or even destroy private rights on the ground of "public necessity."[51] If, on the other hand, a nation's primary goal is the protection of private rights, then the American system is best. It has, for example, Bills of Rights for making it clear what rights are to be protected. And, by such devices as separation of powers, checks and balances, federalism, and judicial review, it provides the elaborate and complicated governmental machinery necessary for restraining the "popular impulse of the moment" from abridging those rights.[52]

American parties, he contended, are entirely appropriate to and of great assistance in maintaining such a government in the United States. Such of their attributes as the concentration of their leaders upon the personnel and the spoils of government rather than upon public policy, and their deliberate blurring of public issues and distortion of public opinion operate as powerful restraints upon the majority.[53] This does not mean, of course, that parties are superfluous in the American system. They still accomplish a number of necessary functions, Lowell said: the framing of issues and concentration of public opinion upon them, the conciliation of class antagonisms which are such a threat to private rights, and the furnishing of personnel through nominations for public office. It only means that in the United States political parties are not intended to translate the majority-will into governmental action regardless of what that will demands. The American people, in short, do not want their parties to provide them with real party government. The popular veneration of the Constitution and the popular outrage and resistance which always greet

[49] *Essays on Government*, pp. 21-22.
[50] *Ibid.*, pp. 63-68.
[51] *Ibid.*, pp. 78-84.
[52] *Ibid.*, pp. 84-96.
[53] *Ibid.*, pp. 107-08.

proposals for radically altering it are, he declared, proof that Americans want a government whose primary aim is the protection of private rights. And they have the kind of parties which are most appropriate to such a government.

In contrast to Wilson, therefore, Lowell felt no urge to make suggestions for changing the existing American parties. He did suggest in passing that the short-ballot would remove the more grossly corrupt bosses; but for the most part he considered the question of reform only to criticize the changes proposed by others. In particular he attacked Wilson's proposals for establishing cabinet government in the United States. He took great pains, for instance, to demonstrate the fallaciousness of Wilson's belief that installing cabinet government here would involve no major institutional changes and is therefore quite feasible. On the contrary, Lowell pointed out, in order to establish cabinet government in the American system it would be necessary to reduce the Presidency to the status of an elective constitutional monarchy, to destroy the powers of the Senate so that a unicameral legislature would exist, to abolish fixed terms of office and institute the power of dissolution, to destroy federalism, and to abandon judicial review. Lowell believed in neither the possibility nor the desirability of such root-and-branch changes in our governmental system.[54] He believed instead that, for the government in which it operates—for the kind of government the American people really want—the existing parties are quite satisfactory and should in no major way be tampered with.

APPRAISAL

Whatever may be the final estimate of A. Lawrence Lowell's ideas about the function of political parties in the American system, it must be conceded that he made a number of valuable contributions to the general discussion of the problem, and, despite his ultimate disagreement with them, added some weapons to the armory of the party-government writers. Of particular value for their purposes is his discussion of the possibilities of parties as "brokerage" agencies: bodies, that is to say, for framing the issues for popular decision and for

---

[54] *Essays on Government*, pp. 25-45. While it is true that Lowell explicitly stated the position summarized here only in his earliest published work, there are several grounds for supposing that it remained his basic point of view in all his subsequent considerations of the American party system. For one thing, there is the recurrence in all his works of the theme (noted above) that it is desirable to check the popular "whims" of the moment by employing constitutional machinery to remove private rights from the power of an ordinary legislative majority—and that most Americans agree upon the desirability of such limitations. Again, the purpose of much of his discussion of the characteristics of the existing American parties was only to show that they differed from English parties— not, as with Wilson, to show their inadequacy. And finally, Lowell's almost complete ignoring of the problem of changing American parties, aside from his criticisms of the proposals of others, seems again to indicate that he believed that on the whole the existing parties are appropriate to the kind of government Americans want—a government that protects individual and minority rights above all else, and therefore a government made safe from complete domination by a mere popular majority.

enabling the meaningful expression of public opinion by simplification of the alternatives placed before it. This argument, as pointed out in the second chapter of the present study, has become a major contention of the present-day exponents of the doctrine of party government. But there has probably never been as thorough or as lucid an exposition of it as Lowell's.

Then, too, Lowell opened up an important question for the party-government position which Wilson barely touched upon: What are the conditions which produce the nature of English parties? He developed a fairly complete answer to this question, although he said little about the questions which logically follow: To what extent are those conditions uniquely, non-transferably English? And to what extent, therefore, is the English party system a model which American parties cannot, within the predictable future, emulate? Since, as the foregoing chapters indicate, the doctrine of party government depends heavily upon the English party system as its model, these are questions that exponents of that doctrine must (and in the author's judgment, all too often do not) face up to. Even though his answers were far from complete, it was to Lowell's credit that he at least raised the questions. And, among other things, his consideration of these questions enabled him to show the fallaciousness of Wilson's view that cabinet government could be installed in the United States without producing any fundamental changes in its governmental system.

Lowell's pioneer study on party voting in Congress and the state legislatures is also a valuable contribution to the discussion of the general problem. Not only does it provide convincing proof of the weakness and lack of discipline of American parties on matters of public policy, but it also demonstrates the viability of this particular method for determining the nature of parties. The results of his study, no doubt, are dated; but the possibilities of the *method* for discovering other characteristics of American parties than merely the strength or weakness of their party lines in legislatures remain considerable, and in recent years a number of political scientists have used it with real profit.[55]

Perhaps Lowell's greatest contribution to the discussion of responsible party government in America, however, was his explanation of why American parties are the way they are. Briefly restated, Lowell's position was this: American parties do not provide responsible party government because the people do not want them to. Why not? Because party government would establish effective majority-rule; and majority-rule means a constant threat to private and minority rights. Above all other things, the American people want their private, individual rights protected. They therefore cling to the kind of formal government most calculated to protect those rights, *and* the kind of party system most appropriate to such a government. The existing governmental structure and

---

[55] For only two examples, see Julius Turner, "Responsible Parties: A Dissent from the Floor"; and E. E. Roady, "Party Regularity in Congress, 1913-1921" (Unpublished doctoral dissertation, University of Illinois, 1951).

party system are exactly what they want; and for that reason, Lowell concluded, the people will resist any attempt to change the basic nature of either the government or the parties. Thus American parties, while continuing to perform their functions of organizing elections and expressing public opinions, can never and should never, in his opinion, perform the function of translating the majority-will into governmental action.

Lowell here posed a problem that the advocates of responsible party government, either in his time or our own,[56] have never even recognized, let alone solved. Their position has always been that the main barrier to the achievement of responsible parties in America is simply a failure in popular understanding: The People *want* effective majority-rule democracy, but they don't yet understand that responsible parties will give it to them. As soon as they are educated along these lines, responsible parties can be achieved without any formal amending of the Constitution. Lowell's denial of their major premise—that Americans want effective majority-rule democracy—is one of the most devastating and fundamental criticisms ever made of the party-government school, and one to which we shall return in the concluding chapter of this study.

This is not, of course, to say that we must totally accept Lowell's *factual* conclusion that Americans prefer inviolable minority rights to unlimited majority-rule, any more than we must accept the others' assumption that Americans believe the opposite. What evidence we have indicates no clear answer to this important question, and in any case the only thing that *is* clear is that we do not have enough evidence (or do not sufficiently understand the evidence we do have) to make flat assertions about how the people feel about majority-rule democracy. But it is eternally to Lowell's credit that he, unlike all the others, saw the basic importance of asking the question.

It must be recognized, however, that the clarity and incisiveness of this particular insight does not illuminate Lowell's entire analysis. Like the others, he too used the terms "parties" and their "functions" in differing senses, apparently without being aware that he was doing so. Or, to put the same criticism from another angle, he never explicitly stated his *ideal* of party government, as opposed to his description of the *existing* English and American party systems. Thus in one place he wrote of "parties" as performing the "function" of enabling the expression of public opinion by giving the people real alternatives to choose between; and here he cited this "function" as one of the items in his defense of the existing parties in both countries. But in another place he criticized the existing American parties for their failure to provide real alternatives. It is therefore difficult to say whether he conceived this "function" to be something the existing parties *should* perform or something that they *did* perform. For

---

[56] For a discussion of the present-day party-government school's failure to recognize this problem, see Austin Ranney, "Toward a More Responsible Two-party System: A Commentary," pp. 492-99.

purposes of exposition, the author has, in the preceding pages, attempted to separate Lowell's picture of an ideal party government from his description of the existing party systems. No such separation existed in Lowell's own writings, however; and the resulting confusions are the most serious deficiency in his total analysis.

These confusions seem to have led Lowell into perhaps his greatest error of all: his belief that American parties can do a good job of framing issues for public decision and thereby enable the emergence of concentrated majority-opinions on them—and at the same time not only fail to translate them into governmental action but even actively prevent their effectuation. In short, he seems to have believed that the election-conducting functions of parties are quite separate and distinct from their government-conducting functions, and that American parties could behave (and, for that matter, actually *were* behaving) like responsible parties in their former aspect while behaving like irresponsible parties in their latter aspect. And this despite the fact that his own description of the existing American parties showed, like the descriptions by the other writers, that they were behaving like irresponsible parties in *both* aspects.

If Lowell had analyzed the relationship between these two aspects of party functions as carefully as Wilson had done, he might have learned, as Wilson had, that these two functions are in fact *not* separable, and that a party system cannot perform one badly or not at all and still perform the other satisfactorily. Lowell's thorough knowledge of English experience should have disclosed to him (as it had to Wilson) that where parties really frame meaningful issues and produce a concentrated majority-opinion upon them, that majority is not satisfied until its opinion is translated into governmental action. Lowell may possibly have sensed this difficulty in his position when he argued that the issues parties frame are not issues of *what* the government should do but rather *who* should be its rulers; but that does not get him out of the difficulty. As Wilson pointed out, a party system cannot produce a clear and concentrated majority-opinion upon the question of who should rule—i.e., whether the party in power should continue to rule—unless the party in power has in fact been ruling, unless, in other words, it has had full possession of the power of the government.

Lowell's failure to grasp this point was the basic cause of his failure to apply satisfactorily his general analysis to the American party system. Wilson avoided this difficulty by proceeding from the assumption that it is possible to understand why a party system performs a certain function in a certain manner only by understanding how it performs *all* of its functions. If this premise is correct, said Wilson, it explains a great deal about the nature of American parties. Those parties in fact do *not* express public opinion well, he pointed out; on the contrary, they confuse the issues and blur the expression of public opinion.

Their failure as agencies of government grows out of their failure as agencies of opinion. And by the same token, Wilson concluded, American parties can never be made to express public opinion faithfully until they become responsible agencies of government. In short, the American party system cannot express the majority-will faithfully until and unless it is capable of translating that will into governmental action. But this was an insight which evaded Lowell; and his inability to see things in these terms prevents our accepting his total analysis as the final word on the proper function of political parties in the American system.

CHAPTER FIVE

Henry Jones Ford

Henry Jones Ford's professional life and point of view both reflected the influence of Woodrow Wilson, who in 1908 persuaded Ford to abandon a successful career as a newspaper editor and come to Princeton as a professor of politics, his first academic post.[1] The inspiration and methodological tools for Ford's analysis of the function of political parties in the American system clearly derive from Wilson's earlier works on politics.[2]

The first principle underlying Ford's approach to political science, for example, is that which forbids the scholar ever to confuse politics with ethics, with the corollary that nothing is to be gained by explaining political phenomena in terms of the struggle between "good men" and "bad men." What should be studied, said Ford, is the *system* and not the moral righteousness of the men involved in the system. He believed that Wilson's "remarkable and significant" undergraduate article on "Cabinet Government in the United States" had made this point unanswerable, and he accepted Wilson's position, which he articulated as his own:

At that period politics and ethics were confused in the accepted manuals, as indeed they still are in schoolbooks on civics. The regular way of treating constitutional arrangements was to impute to them the merit of their intentions and to account for their failure in practice by the machinations of politicians or by the ignorance and perversity of the electorate. Hence the people are always to blame when things go wrong, and it follows that political improvement is to be sought through moral improvement. . . . [Young Wilson grasped] the principle that the quality of power is determined by the conditions under which it is exercised, and that good

---

[1] E. S. Corwin, "Henry Jones Ford," in *The Dictionary of American Biography*, edited by Allen Johnson and Dumas Malone (New York: Charles Scribner's Sons, 1931), VI, 515.

[2] By far the most comprehensive statement of Ford's views on party was contained in his earliest published work, *The Rise and Growth of American Politics* (New York: The Macmillan Company, 1898). Also important, however, are his review of Frank J. Goodnow's *Politics and Administration,* in *Annals of the American Academy of Political and Social Science,* XVI (September, 1900), 177-88; "Municipal Corruption," *Political Science Quarterly,* XIX (December, 1904), 673-86; "The Direct Primary," *North American Review,* CXC (July, 1909), 1-14; *The Cost of Our National Government* (New York: Columbia University Press, 1910); and "American and Canadian Political Methods," *North American Review,* CXCIV (November, 1911), 685-96. His last work, *Representative Government* (New York: Henry Holt and Company, 1924), is a useful summary of his matured views, but it contains nothing new on the subject of parties.

management of the public business is as much a matter of sound organization as good management of private business.[3]

Ford thus entered upon his investigation of party and its place with this Wilsonian axiom: "The quality of power is determined by the conditions under which it is exercised."

Again like Wilson, Ford maintained that the student of politics must look behind formal constitutional arrangements at the realities they sometimes conceal. In order to understand the true nature of a given governmental system, Ford wrote, the scholar must see the whole complex of customs, usages, and ideas which interact with formal constitutions to produce the actual governing system. Thus, in explaining why Montesquieu had drawn his principle of separation of powers from observation of English government at a time when no such separation in fact existed, Ford observed:

Montesquieu erred, just as innumerable students of politics have erred since, by taking constitutional documents at their face value, which is never a safe thing to do. They are operative only so far as they affect the actual distribution of political force, and the working constitution of a country can never be accurately inferred from its written documents alone. Usage and not the legal form determines the actual character of a constitution, and usage takes its shape from the conditions that arise, quite irrespective of the ideas and intentions with which the conditions are brought about.[4]

In Ford's opinion political science was in his own time undergoing a fundamental change, a change which he welcomed and with which he wished to align his own work. He conceived of his method as breaking with the deductive method characteristic of earlier writers, whom he accused of proceeding upon "traditional assumptions as to the nature of constitutional government, which were treated as axioms" and of drawing conclusions about particular governments "not according to the circumstances in which they act, but according to ideals deduced from the plan and purpose of the organic law."[5] The future of political science, he believed, lay with the "new method" which he described thus:

Political phenomena are observed and classified, and generalizations are made from data thus collected. . . . Instead of considering first what ought to be, the aim is to consider first what is. As a result treatises on government are appearing that are not doctrinal in character, like our older manuals on civics and politics, but are descriptive and expository, taking simply and plainly how the public authority under consideration is organized, how it works and with what results. They are

[3] *Woodrow Wilson: The Man and His Work* (New York: D. Appleton and Company, 1916), pp. 13-14. See also *The Cost of Our National Government*, pp. 35-37; and "Principles of Municipal Organization," *Annals of the American Academy of Political and Social Science*, XXIII (March, 1904), 195-209.

[4] "The Cause of Political Corruption," *Scribner's Magazine*, XLIX (January, 1911), 55.

[5] *Ibid.*, pp. 54-55.

studies of political structure and functions, conceived in the same scientific spirit as that of a zoologist examining the fauna of a particular region.[6]

It was thus in the firm belief that he was employing the new empirical, inductive, objective, and scientific approach to politics that Ford attacked the problem of the function of political parties in the American system. That problem always seemed to him to be one of the most important areas for scholars of politics to explore, and he deplored the fact that, as he believed, they had hitherto so largely neglected it.[7] He felt confident that the new political science would fill this gap, and set himself the task of helping the job along.

THE NATURE OF DEMOCRACY

Ford's ideas about the function of political parties in the American system were grounded in a conception of the nature of democracy and democratic organization that closely paralleled those of Wilson and Lowell. Democracy, Ford said, cannot profitably be thought of as meaning either direct popular participation in or supervision of governmental activities:

If direct popular supervision of the conduct of government had the importance which the dominant school of reformers attach to it, municipal government should be best administered, since it comes closer to the people than state or national government, and the consequences of maladministration are more direct and immediate in their effect. By like inference, state government should be superior to the national government in quality of administration; but, as a matter of fact, the gradation of satisfactoriness is just the other way. . . .[8]

It is meaningless, Ford argued, to talk of taking government away from the politicians and giving it to the people. Politics will always be carried on by politicians—by men who have the special aptitude, training, and interest required, and who will devote to it the immense amount of energy it requires:

One continually hears the declaration that the direct primary will take power away from the politicians and give it to the people. This is pure nonsense. Politics has been, is and always will be carried on by politicians, just as art is carried on by artists, engineering by engineers, business by business men. All that the direct

[6] *Ibid.* Ford's conscious adoption of this "objective" and "scientific" approach to the study of politics had several important effects upon his analysis of the function of parties—effects which will be noted below.

[7] "Political Evolution and Civil Service Reform," *Annals of the American Academy of Political and Social Science*, XV (March, 1900), 147.

[8] Review of *Politics and Administration*, pp. 182-83. It should be pointed out that in this passage Ford was being quite as "deductive" as any of his predecessors: he proceeded, that is, from the assumption that administrative "satisfactoriness" is the standard of good government, and concluded that, since this quality was least in evidence at the governmental level where direct popular supervision was most common, such supervision was not important to good government. This is only one of a number of instances where Ford failed to be "inductive" and "scientific" within his own definition of those terms.

primary, or any other political reform, can do is to affect the character of the politicians by altering the conditions that govern political activity, thus determining its extent and quality. The direct primary may take advantage and opportunity from one set of politicians and confer them upon another set, but politicians there will always be so long as there is politics. The only thing that is open to control is the sort of politicians we shall have.[9]

Does this mean that the people are helpless in the grip of a small band of politicians and that popular government is therefore impossible? Not at all, said Ford. Democracy should be thought of as popular *control* over government, not as popular participation in its activities: "The people are called upon to control the government, not to administer it; and they can do the one because they do not have to do the other." [10] In short, so long as the politicians are held strictly accountable to the people for how they exercise their power the requirements of democracy are satisfied; and Ford believed that any misguided attempt to make the people do more than this will result only in depriving them of the power they possess:

It is obviously impossible for the people to select officers for innumerable places except by some means of agreement and cooperation, which means is ordinarily supplied by the activity of the political class. *It may be laid down as a political maxim, that whatever assigns to the people a power which they are naturally incapable of wielding takes it away from them.* It may be argued that this principle carried to its logical conclusion implies that the people are unable to select their own rulers in any case. This is perfectly true. The actual selection will always be made by the few, no matter how many seem to participate. The only value of popular elections is to establish accountability to the people, but this rightly used is quite enough to constitute a free government.[11]

But, he warned, no group of politicians can be expected to be truly responsible for what the government does unless they have genuine power over it. Responsibility, he believed, can grow only out of power: "While the suffrage is incapable of serving as an organ of administration, it is capable of serving as an agency of control; but to be an efficient instrument of control, it must act upon some organ of government possessing administrative authority so complete that it may be held to full accountability for the results. . . ." [12]

It was because he believed that giving the people more power than they can exercise results in the destruction of effective popular control that Ford distrusted any proposal for creating "direct democracy." It was because he conceived of democracy as the popular control of government through the choice

---

[9] "The Direct Primary," p. 2.

[10] Review of *Politics and Administration*, p. 187.

[11] *The Rise and Growth of American Politics*, p. 299. The emphasis is added. See also Ford's "The Initiative and Referendum," *Harper's Weekly*, LVII (July 4, 1913), 8, 26.

[12] "Municipal Corruption," p. 681.

of accountable rulers that he believed responsible party government to be the best possible organization of democracy.

THE FUNCTION OF POLITICAL PARTIES IN THE AMERICAN SYSTEM

Ford's treatment of political parties can best be set forth in terms of a distinction between the functions parties should perform in any democracy, and the functions American parties are, in his opinion, called upon to perform because of the peculiar nature of our governmental system.[13] Insofar as he dealt with functions of the first of these two types, Ford's ideas in large measure followed those of Woodrow Wilson. He took it for granted, for instance, that parties should express public opinion. Though he nowhere elaborated the point, again like Wilson (but unlike Lowell), Ford perceived that political parties are agencies for carrying on government quite as much as agencies for conducting elections and expressing public opinion. The two functions are, to his mind as to Wilson's, inseparable; and he argued that it is impossible for parties to express public opinion faithfully unless they are prepared to translate that opinion into governmental action. "Non-partisanship is still preached as a civic duty, but it has never been reduced to practice and it never will be. The reason is very simple. No law of human nature is better known than that action is the correlative of desire. The very existence of public opinion implies the seeking of means for giving effect to it in the conduct of public affairs, and in a free country this produces party action." [14]

The major function of political parties in any democracy, Ford seems to have assumed, is to establish the responsibility of the government to the people by offering them alternative sets of rulers who can be held accountable for how they exercise public power.[15] In addition to this function, said Ford, parties should also encourage popular participation in government in the way such participation can be carried on: by popular interest in and discussion of public issues and officers. If parties stir up popular excitement through their campaigning activities, he argued, that is all to the good:

The true office of the elaborate apparatus used to work up popular excitement over party issues is to energize the mass of citizenship into political activity. . . . [Party] spirit . . . draws . . . together [the various classes] by ardent sympathies which elicit a copious and constant supply of political force. Their operation extends

---

[13] In Ford's own writings no distinction was made between these two types of functions. In fact, he never made explicit his position upon what functions parties should perform, as distinct from the functions they do perform. There was, however, a position upon the former question implicit in his judgments of the existing parties, and the author has, for purposes of exposition, attempted to infer the nature of that position from the character of Ford's judgments. The probable reasons for his failure to make explicit his ideal of party government will be discussed below.

[14] *The Rise and Growth of American Politics*, p. 94.

[15] Cf. *ibid.*, pp. 299-300.

far beyond the sphere of the intelligence, for they thrill and penetrate the bottom strata of character—the inheritance of ancestral habit moulded by tribal discipline, the deposits of race experience throughout the ages, bringing into play those deep instincts of which we are unconscious, but which constitute the wisest part of us.[16]

A still more important party function, in Ford's view, is that which parties perform with respect to class, religious, racial, and other antagonisms. Though he made no such elaborate exposition of the point as Lowell, Ford was just as certain that genuine popular government cannot exist within a fundamental consensus among the people on how political decisions should be made. He had a strong sense of the danger to that consensus contained in the clash of interest groups. And, like Lowell, Ford believed that political parties are a primary factor operating to moderate this clash, to compromise the differences, and to preserve the consensus. This he labeled the "conservative function" of party:

Party . . . contains a principle of conservatism, inasmuch as it must always seek to keep faction within such bounds as will prevent it from jeopardizing party interests. . . . [This] conservative function of party is not duly appreciated. . . . [Even] in times of the most contagious excitement there must be some modification of purpose among large bodies of citizens. It is reasonable to infer that the habitual calculation of consequences, essential to the training of every political leader, must affect his deference to the behests of his supporters. It may be stated as a fact, which acquaintance with the interior working of politics will verify, that the influence of party leaders is chiefly exerted in soothing the prejudices and moderating the demands of their followers. If party action were an accurate reflection of the passions, animosities, and beliefs of the mass of individuals composing the party membership, politics would be as tremendous in their instability as ocean waves. . . .[17]

And again: "The violence of politicians does not usually go higher than their lips. . . . [A] curious circumspection . . . attends the periodical national mood of party frenzy. . . . Burke's expressive metaphor fits the case exactly. 'The parties are the gamesters; but government keeps the table.' No matter how passionately they contend, they will take care that they do not kick over the table and lose the stakes."[18]

Thus in any democratic government, according to Ford, political parties have a challenging task. They should express public opinion, translate it into governmental action, provide the agency for establishing effective popular control over government, encourage popular discussion of public affairs, and promote the basic consensus necessary to democracy. But in addition to these, he argued, American parties in particular are forced by the peculiar nature of our formal governmental structure to perform still other functions. The most important of these is that of breaking down separation of powers.

---

[16] *Ibid.*, pp. 305-06.

[17] *Ibid.*, pp. 127-29.

[18] *Ibid.*, pp. 304-05. See also *ibid.*, pp. 306-07; and "Municipal Corruption," pp. 685-86.

Throughout Ford's writings there ran this leading theme: The formal separation and independence of the executive agencies from the legislative violate all the tenets of sound governmental organization; and this is the fundamental cause of our political ills, whether national, state, or local.

The breakdown of representative government in the United States and the substitution of methods which give the custody of political power to particular interests, are the direct and natural consequence of the application of the doctrine of the separation of the powers. Viewing the situation from the standpoint of political pathology, it may be concisely described as a case of constitutional disease from specific infection. The case is a perfectly typical one, for which many parallels are to be found in history, the only marked difference being the remarkable vitality and endurance of the patient. In all other national constitutions which have experienced that infection, the breakdown was so rapid that all semblance of constitutional government rapidly disappeared. . . . History affords no instance of economical and efficient government constituted on the principle of the separation of powers. On the other hand, it appears that where the rule of the people is most vigorous there the connection is closest.[19]

Since, however, the independence of one from the other cannot be maintained if government is to act at all, the American people must, on Ford's showing, however much lip-service they may pay to Montesquieu's old error, seek a way of *uniting* the executive with the legislature. And political parties are the only agency, Ford believed, capable of doing this indispensable job: "[Party] organization continues to be the sole efficient means of administrative union between the executive and legislative branches of the government. . . . Whatever tends to maintain and perfect that union makes for orderly politics and constitutional progress; while whatever tends to impair that union, disturbs the constitutional poise of the government, obstructs its functions, and introduces an anarchic condition of affairs full of danger to all social interests."[20] He saw evidence at all levels of American government that whatever cooperation is achieved between the executive and the legislative branches is due to the parties:

The boss system is enormously expensive, but so great is the value of concentrated authority in business management that one may hear it said among practical men of affairs that a city needs a political boss in order to be progressive. . . . The state boss is the natural complement of the situation produced by the dissolution of executive authority in state government. The office restores outside of the formal constitution what is lost inside of it—efficient control. In the national government no such dissolution having taken place, the case is different. There is no national boss but the President, and that is what the people put him there to be. If he does not boss the situation, he is a political failure, no matter what else he may be.[21]

[19] *The Cost of Our National Government*, pp. 73-74.

[20] *The Rise and Growth of American Politics*, p. 356. See also "Principles of Municipal Organization," pp. 211-13.

[21] *The Rise and Growth of American Politics*, pp. 301-02.

American parties have, according to Ford, still another special function to perform, namely, that of fighting the powerful centrifugal force of localism so characteristic of American politics, especially as manifested in Congress. Congress, he argued, is not in and of itself a legislative body at all:

The House of Representatives takes its character from the fact that it represents, not the nation, but the districts into which the nation is divided. It is powerfully acted upon by the external agencies of party rule, but there is in its constitution no embodiment of national control to which particular demands and impulses must be subordinated. Hence it lacks the faculty of self-government which, whether in the state or in the individual, implies the supremacy of reason over desire. The consequence is that, when the House is not acting under a party mandate, it is a scuffle of local interests in which every member must take his part under penalty of losing his seat. "What has he done for his district?" is a question which applies the test by which ordinarily the value of a representative is gauged. While eminent party service will add to his reputation, it does not lessen his dependence upon his local constituency. The dominant idea is that it is the proper business of a member to represent his district, and most people would be surprised to hear that any other idea could be entertained.[22]

In respect of its procedure, its results, and its members' attitudes, Ford continued, Congress is rather like a diplomatic convention, in which representatives of autonomous local areas meet to negotiate for special favors:

Business is shaped and arranged for consideration, as in a diplomatic gathering, by action of Congress itself. It supplies itself with the necessary organs by subdivision into as many committees as it sees fit. . . . It breaks itself up into numerous segments, each a little congress in its way, with both the dominant party and the opposition represented in its membership. The formative stage of legislation is carried on in diplomatic privacy, while the public feeds on gossip about what is going on behind the closed doors. Hidden influences are at work determining results. The conduct of business is a negotiation between diverse interests, and it is only after the conclusions reached are reported that Congress gets a chance to act. And yet the committees assume no responsibility, for the theory is that they are simply agents of Congress, appointed for its convenience.[23]

The result is, argued Ford, that the United States has no overall government engaged in promoting the public interest: "Where, in this struggle of interests, this jostle of legislation, does the government [that is, a responsible management, defining national policy and shaping legislative proposals] come in? For such a government, our present constitutional system makes no provision. . . . It may seem like a sarcasm to say that Congress represents every interest except the public interest, but just that is implied by the attitude which Congress takes with regard to public demands." [24] This, in Ford's view, is the breach into which the political parties are called upon to step. In order to win the huge

22 *Ibid.*, pp. 239-40.
23 *Ibid.*, p. 224.
24 *Ibid.*, pp. 232-33.

stakes of power embodied in the Presidency they must strive for national support; and in order to win that support they must elaborate national programs.
Ever since Jackson's administration, he contended, the parties have provided
presidential leadership of Congress through the majority-party's agencies in
both Houses.[25] For Ford, then, political parties are the only possible source
of unity, coherence, and direction in the American system; and providing these
elements is one of their major functions.

THE NATURE OF POLITICAL PARTIES

As A. Lawrence Lowell had done, Ford sought to explore the nature of
political parties, and his findings were in many respects similar to Lowell's. He
agreed with Lowell, for instance, that parties are inevitably run by a small
group of managers and can therefore lay hardly any claim to representing party
members:

The theory of party organization is that its power emanates directly from the
people, by means of a system according to which the party membership, at primary
elections, chooses delegates who meet to state the party principles and name the
party candidates. In practice, few people besides the politicians have any share in
the transaction. As a rule, the vote at primary elections is very small, and even
when exceptional circumstances bring out a large vote, it is still small as compared
with that polled at a regular election. In many cases there is hardly the pretense
of an election by the party membership, but the politicians frankly bargain among
themselves who shall attend the conventions and figure as party representatives.[26]

As this passage makes clear, Ford accepted (as Lowell had) the prevailing
ticket-voter conception of party membership and agreed with other writers of
his day that party management is unrepresentative of the party members. This
was, however, as far as he was prepared to go with them; and on the question
of whether the unrepresentative character of the parties was injurious to democratic government he took sharp issue with them: "[There] appears to be no
connection between the extent to which a constituent quality has been imparted
to a convention, and the force with which its decisions appeal to public confidence and support." [27]

The task of party management, he contended, is to provide disciplined and
cohesive party organizations capable of bridging separation of powers, cen-
tralizing administration, and establishing popular control over government.
Beside this, representation was a minor issue. He, therefore, made no sense of
Frank J. Goodnow's insistence that, although parties need strong organizations,
party control should be wrested from the managers and "restored" to the party
members. Goodnow, he felt, was trying to have it both ways:

---

[25] *Ibid.*, pp. 193-94, 250-51, 281-84. Ford's conviction that in the United States party
leadership must be presidential leadership will be discussed below.

[26] *Ibid.*, pp. 295-96. See also *ibid.*, pp. 71, 133-34.

[27] *Ibid.*, pp. 296-97.

It seems . . . to be a strange *non sequitur* when later on one finds Professor Goodnow advocating a wholesale scheme of party disintegration. The very statement of the proposition involves a contradiction in terms which should suggest its fallacy. The inorganic condition which it is supposed to create by diffusing the exercise of party function through the whole mass of party membership excludes the idea of party organization. *Structure and function are correlative, and the notion that administrative capacity and corporate responsibility would somehow survive in party after the extirpation of the organic structure with which they are associated, finds no parallel except in the case of the Cheshire cat, whose grin remained after the cat had disappeared.*[28]

Ford was as little disturbed as Lowell by the preoccupation of American parties with winning elections and getting power instead of stubbornly clinging to consistent sets of great principles. He viewed party policies as the product of the political necessities of the moment, rather than abstract, selfless, and logical analyses applied to public affairs: "Politicians employ their logic to defend the positions they feel impelled to take; their action is the result of circumstances operating upon their endowment of character and habits of thought. Their personal relation to the events of their times has much more to do with shaping their policy than any abstract theory of government which they may profess. . . . Political structure grows like coral rock, the product of multitudinous activities incited by individual needs." [29] Ford was also able to make his peace with the fact that diligent service to the organization, rather than eloquent exposition of party principles, sends a man to the top in the party hierarchy: "Ability in the public championship of party principles has declined in importance, as compared with assiduity in service to party organization. Claims of distinction resting upon capacity in party service, either by craft of management or by ability to finance party organization, receive increasing recognition." [30]

In short, Ford never tired of reminding his readers that parties have important functions to perform and must therefore have powerful and disciplined organizations, and that the critic who wishes them to become debating societies or collections of like-minded philosophers merely misses the point.

EVALUATION OF AMERICAN PARTIES

Henry Jones Ford more vigorously defended American political parties than any other writer considered in this study. The unfavorable criticism of the parties with which he was familiar consisted, in his view, largely of unwarranted conclusions drawn from erroneous premises; and he devoted much of his writing to an exposure and refutation of such criticism. This does not mean that he supposed American parties to have no shortcomings, but only that, in

[28] Review of *Politics and Administration*, pp. 185-86. The emphasis is added.
[29] *The Rise and Growth of American Politics*, pp. 106-07.
[30] *Ibid.*, p. 269.

view of the difficult circumstances in which they are forced to operate, they, on balance, deserve our gratitude:

Not even the great industrial development of the nation affords so striking an exhibition of American inventive genius and faculty for organization as that huge, complicated mechanism which, in default of any provision for direct party control of legislative procedure, has been extended to every part of the government—national, state and municipal—so as to reach and subject to some degree of public responsibility the political activities finding expression in the various state legislatures and Congress. Nowhere else in the world, at any period, has party organization had to cope with such enormous tasks as in this country, and its efficiency in dealing with them is the true glory of our political system. . . . The conclusions may be distasteful, since it is the habit of the times to pursue public men with calumny and detraction; but it follows that when history comes to reckon the achievements of our age, great party managers will receive an appreciation very different from what is now accorded them.[31]

Ford was, on the other hand, fully aware that American parties do not perform their functions as well as might be desired. Here he followed the main outline of Woodrow Wilson's diagnosis, according to which the parties' basic deficiency is to be sought neither in their control by bosses nor in their love of power rather than principle but in their irresponsibility. And, like Wilson, Ford demonstrated the nature of that irresponsibility by contrasting American with English parties. He directed attention, for instance, to the procedures for voting legislators salary increases in the two countries:

[In England] the allowance cannot be made unless recommended by the administration, which thus must assume the responsibility for it before the electorate, and if members should attempt to force the government they could not do so without being regarded by their constituencies as bolters, and hence would forfeit their party standing. But in the case of the American Congress, no such responsibility exists. Members of all parties can work together to help themselves, and at the same time manage to avoid responsibility. The thing may be wrapped up in some essential bill and members in ticklish districts may be provided with specious pleas to the effect that they had to submit in order to save important legislation. It is a thing which is admitted by congressional politicians to require nice handling, since if any location of responsibility can be made by the voters, there may be an upsetting upheaval.[32]

The voters, however, cannot locate responsibility by comparing party performances with party platforms, for: "Conventions have no power to contract binding engagements. Their declarations are merely expressions of sentiment made for electioneering use, and those raised to office may decide for themselves to what extent and in what way they will recognize party obligations. Indeed explicit party pledges may be flatly repudiated."[33]

[31] Ibid., pp. 309-10.
[32] The Cost of Our National Government, pp. 90-91.
[33] Ibid., p. 70. See also ibid., pp. 72-73.

While Ford's analysis of the irresponsibility of American parties thus paralleled Wilson's, the implications and consequences of that irresponsibility appear to have disturbed him much less than they had disturbed Wilson. Wilson's analysis was designed to demonstrate the superiority of responsible parties over the existing parties. Ford, on the other hand, wished his readers to be aware primarily of the blessings of the existing parties, and called on them to consider where they would be with no parties at all. This emphasis colors his explanation of why American parties are as they are and of what, if anything, should be done about them.

EXPLANATION OF AMERICAN PARTIES

In his search for reasons for the irresponsibility of American parties, for their control by men who have no interest in public policy, and for the corruption that so often results from their activities, Ford again followed Wilson's lead. The quest led him, as it had led Wilson, back to the Constitution of the United States.

Responsible party government, Ford was aware, is a way of organizing democracy, of establishing popular control over government. It presupposes a governmental system amenable to majority-control. But certain aspects of the American constitutional structure, especially the separation of powers, make impossible real popular control. This is *not,* he said, because there are "bad men" operating our democratic institutions in an undemocratic way, but rather because the institutions themselves are not democratic and never were:

No one now disputes popular sovereignty, but the people are in the position of the Grand Turk, who can cut off the head of an offender, but whose affairs are so out of control that he is robbed left and right by his servants. What makes the situation more exasperating is that it is becoming a matter of common knowledge that democratic control is more complete and effective in some other countries than in our own; but the usual inference that we have somehow lost what our institutions were intended to secure is a fallacy. Our institutions have not lapsed from democracy into plutocracy; they never were democratic, and their present plutocratic character arises from the substitution of money power for the original aristocratic control.[34]

And again:

Means do not exist for action in the sole interest of the general welfare, for the essential characteristic of the scheme is that all action shall be subject to the consent of privileged interests distinctly represented in the government. The scheme was not made for democratic use and is not susceptible of conversion to democratic use. This is the secret of the disharmony between American society and American politics. The rule of the people cannot be made effective for lack of appropriate institutions. Their sovereignty cannot become concrete and practical without an organ in which it can reside. Wherever the rule of the people is effective, it will

[34] "Municipal Corruption," p. 685.

be found that there is such an organ, formed by the connection of the executive and legislative branches.[35]

Ford made it his task to point out the way in which the peculiar nature of our governmental structure affects the character of our political parties. The Constitution, he felt, forces them to operate entirely outside the formal government, and thus obliges them to become something essentially different from parties which operate in a more favorable environment: "Party is as old as politics, and the operation of party in working the machinery of government is seen in all countries having free institutions; but of party as an external authority, expressing its determinations through its own peculiar organs, the United States as yet offers to the world the only distinct example, although tendencies in that direction are showing themselves in England." [36] Parties forced entirely outside the formal government must, in Ford's view, be irresponsible as a matter of course:

What is peculiar to American politics is that party organization is so situated that it cannot negotiate as a principle, but as a go-between. Unlike an English party, it cannot itself formulate measures, direct the course of legislation, and assume the direct responsibility of administration. All that it can do is to certify the political complexion of candidates, leaving it to be inferred that their common purpose will effect such unity of action as will control legislation and direct administration in accordance with party professions. The peculiarities of American party government are all due to this separation of party management from direct and immediate responsibility for the administration of government. Party organization is compelled to act through executive and legislative deputies, who, while always far from disavowing their party obligations, are quite free to use their own discretion as to the way in which they shall interpret and fulfill the party pledges. Meanwhile they are shielded, by the constitutional partitions of privilege and distributions of authority, from any direct and specific responsibility for delay or failure in coming to an agreement for the accomplishment of party purposes. Authority being divided, responsibility is uncertain and confused, and the accountability of the government to the people is not at all definite or precise. When a party meets with disaster at the polls, every one may form his own opinion as to the cause. It is purely a matter of speculation.[37]

Ford also found in the separation of powers a satisfactory explanation (for him) of the lack of popular interest in and understanding of public affairs:

As a natural consequence of the detached and subordinate position of party organization in the conduct of the government, public opinion is not concentrated upon

---

[35] "The Cause of Political Corruption," p. 60.

[36] *The Rise and Growth of American Politics*, p. 294. Though Ford never specifically referred to the "tendencies" in England he had in mind here, it seems probable that he was thinking of such developments as the Birmingham Caucus, the national party conferences, and the national party unions—all of which were important party bodies outside Parliament.

[37] *Ibid.*, pp. 326-27.

its acts with steady scrutiny and vigilant supervision. The activity of party is largely concerned with details of its own business management, not possessing much interest for the mass of the people who have their own affairs to attend to. Its contentions are largely personal squabbles, whose political results may be very important, but which do not themselves present political issues. They are like the intrigues which used to go on among the English gentry, over court honors and official emoluments, in the Georgian era of English politics, the mass of the electorate but dimly comprehending what was going on and regarding the strife with disgust and aversion, although quickly roused to activity by issues appealing to their political instincts. The true public opinion of the nation is ordinarily in a state of suspense. The minds of people are preoccupied by too many interests to attend closely to the transactions of politicians, and not until the issue is thrust upon the public in a definite form by some pressing emergency is the genuine expression of public opinion evoked.[38]

Similarly, the separation of party agencies from governmental agencies seemed to him to account for the fact that American parties rarely take a firm stand on public issues:

Party organization not being directly burdened by the difficulties and necessities of government feels at liberty to court public opinion in all its vagaries. Great art is employed in framing platforms so as to be susceptible to various interpretations. Concerning issues which are settled, party speaks in a clear, sonorous voice. But on new issues it mumbles and quibbles. Subdivisions of the party organization make such professions as will pay the best in their respective fields of activity. If the issue cannot be dodged, straddling may be resorted to. Declarations really incongruous in their nature are coupled, and their inconsistency is cloaked by rhetorical artifice. . . . Such practices are results of the ordinary instincts of party in all countries, and obtain such monstrous growth in America because of extraordinarily favorable conditions.[39]

If the Constitution drives the parties outside the formal government, Ford continued, it nevertheless leaves it up to them to make the system work. Bridging the separation of powers, counteracting localism, making nominations for the myriad elective offices created by our federal system—all these tasks are, so to speak, forced on American parties by our constitutional system. And in order to perform them, the parties acquire a complex structure—as well as quite a special relation to the government itself:

The magnitude and extent of the functions assumed have been sustained by an appropriate elaboration of structure, giving to party organization in America a massiveness and a complexity unknown in governments whose constitution leaves to party only its ordinary office of propagating opinion and inciting the political activity of citizenship. In England party elicits the expression of the will of the nation; in this country it must also provide for its execution, so that it is virtually a party of the apparatus of government itself, connecting with the executive and

[38] *Ibid.*, pp. 328-29.
[39] *Ibid.*, pp. 330-31.

legislative departments, and occupying the place which in the parliamentary type of government is fulfilled by the ministry.[40]

Along with huge and elaborate organizations comes domination by the party managers, and the need for large-scale financial backing; and since no method exists for obtaining the necessary funds officially, parties must support themselves by graft and patronage.[41] In such a situation, Ford asked, how can the party managers be expected to concern themselves with public affairs instead of money-making? "An extensive field for the formation and sale of political power as a business pursuit has long existed. . . . In such conditions party organization exists rather as a means of controlling nomination patronage than as an agency of opinion; and hence, although party organization cannot detach itself from opinion, it tends to confine opinion to traditional forms, and seeks to repress the development of new issues." [42]

Ford continually reminded his readers, then, that the real villain is the weird, complicated, and undemocratic constitutional system which produces the "bad" bosses, and not the bosses themselves. "The remarkable thing," he observed at one point, "is not that the system breeds corruption, but that it should work at all." [43]

To associate corruption with partisanship, or to assume that the two must necessarily go together, was to Ford's mind quite unwarranted. On the contrary, he wrote, "They are really antagonistic principles. Partisanship tends to establish a connection based upon an avowed public obligation, while corruption consults private and individual interests which secrete themselves from view and avoid accountability of any kind." [44] In fact, he argued, the only hope for removing corruption from the American system is to *strengthen* party organization and party control over government: "The weakness of party organization is the opportunity of corruption. Party organization undertakes to supervise the conduct of legislative bodies only so far as party interests distinctly require, and it has no warrant to go further. This permits a latitude of action in regard to general legislation which abounds in pernicious reactions throughout the business world. In proportion as party control is strengthened, a counteracting force is brought to bear." [45]

Ford insisted that American parties are as they are, in the last analysis, because their nature and their potentialities as agencies of popular government are generally misunderstood. Wherever he looked he found strong prejudices

---

[40] *Ibid.*, p. 220.

[41] *Ibid.*, pp. 311-20.

[42] *The Cost of Our National Government*, p. 87.

[43] *Ibid.*, p. 60. See also "Political Evolution and Civil Service Reform," pp. 154-55; and "The Direct Primary," pp. 7-8.

[44] *The Rise and Growth of American Politics*, pp. 322-23.

[45] *Ibid.*

against political parties and politicians, and he came to recognize that these prejudices are characteristic of traditional American thinking about politics. He saw the primary cause of this antiparty bias in the persistence of the Whig check-and-balance theory of government:

The doctrine of a distribution of authority, so that the various branches of the government shall check and balance one another to protect the public welfare, still possesses the public mind. Although the working of the constitution has undergone profound change, the theory has remained almost intact. That the constitution does not work well in practice is freely admitted; but of course that is not its fault. The constitutional idea is noble; but the politicians are vile. If only the checks could be established beyond the strength of the politicians to disarrange,—or, above all, if some barriers could be erected, so tight and strong as to shut the politicians out altogether,—the constitution would work perfectly. Therefore, more checks upon the abuse of power; more contrivances to baffle the politicians, whose machinations pervert the constitution and corrupt the government! [46]

Thus Ford's general position was that, considering the extremely unfriendly circumstances in which they are forced to operate, American political parties perform a number of valuable functions for which the nation might well show itself more grateful than, in his view, it was yet prepared to do. And he was not willing to countenance any indictment of the parties that ran in terms of alleged inherent deficiencies of parties as such, without regard to the fact that they are forced to operate in a governmental system which necessitates huge organizations, drives those organizations entirely outside the formal government, provides them with no legitimate means of support, and generally makes their operation as difficult as possible. Any project for reforming American parties, he was convinced, must fail if it strikes at the parties themselves rather than at the context that makes them what they are.

THE REFORM OF AMERICAN PARTIES

Henry Jones Ford believed that it is neither possible nor desirable to "reform" American parties—at least in the sense in which the word was customarily used in his time. The sort of "reform" envisioned by the advocates of direct primary legislation, for example, seemed to him not only futile but also dangerous. Parties will always be run by small groups of managers, he argued; and, in any case, the direct primary proposal rests upon an incorrect analysis of bossism:

[The direct primary] scrambles power among faction chiefs and their bands, while the people are despoiled and oppressed. The fact that the thing is done in the name of the people, and with the pretence that it is done for the people, ought not to obscure the patent facts of the situation. . . . We are always pulling down bosses, because transient combinations of would-be bosses and reformers may develop strength enough to overthrow a particular boss or a particular machine. But while bosses and machines come and go, the boss and the machine are always with us.

[46] *Ibid.*, pp. 334-35. See also *ibid.*, pp. 93-94.

From the standpoint of the public welfare, it is the system that is important and not the individuals who act in it.[47]

The direct primary, indeed, insofar as it affects things at all, tends to make them worse:

The direct primary does not remove any of the conditions that have produced the system, but it intensifies their pressure by making politics still more confused, irresponsible and costly. In its full application it is the most noxious of the reforms by which spoilsmen are generated, for it parallels the long series of elections with a corresponding series of elections in every regular party organization. The more elections there are, the larger becomes the class of professional politicians to be supported by the community.[48]

In the absence of the direct primary, the parties assume at least some responsibility; but with the direct primary, the American system tends toward complete irresponsibility:

As the late Speaker Reed frankly declared: "We have at present irresponsible government, so divided that nobody can tell who is to blame." In this situation party organization performs a great service, because it roughly locates power somewhere, thus assuming a vague but real responsibility for the behavior of government. The direct primary impairs this responsibility by making power the football of faction. Power will rest somewhere just the same, but few will know where, so that it will be released from any responsibility for results.[49]

Party reform, Ford argued, should look not to the elimination of bosses and to the end of graft per se, but rather to the development of real party responsibility. And for this purpose, he believed, the experience of England in the eighteenth century was full of lessons for nineteenth-century America—the more since politics in eighteenth-century England were markedly similar in some ways to American politics in the 1890's. England's eighteenth-century governmental system, Ford pointed out, was founded on distributed authority and confused responsibility, and the Whig and Tory parties were notoriously corrupt, boss-controlled, and devoid of real programs. This led to a profound popular distrust of all public men as stupid and venal. Some of the better people (like Addison in the *Spectator*) preached non-partisanship as the indicated remedy. Others (like Bolingbroke) hoped for a "patriot King" who would "rise above party" and rule for the good of all. Nevertheless, the actual political situation continued to deteriorate until, in 1770, Edmund Burke pointed out a new solution: frankly accept the rule of party, he said, by giving the parties full and open power over the government, thus forcing them to assume full responsibility—which they could do only if they first reformed themselves.[50] Burke's

---

[47] "The Direct Primary," pp. 3-4.

[48] *Ibid.*

[49] *Ibid.*, pp. 11-12.

[50] *Thoughts on the Cause of the Present Discontents* (2d. ed.; London: printed for J. Dodsley in Pall Mall, 1770).

analysis, according to Ford, was at first received with scorn; but it was precisely the kind of partisanship Burke recommended that, beginning with the first ministry of the younger Pitt, accomplished the desired result.[51]

Ford drew the moral from this story as follows: Our task in the United States, he said, is to lodge in the majority-party full power over government, and then hold it accountable for how it exercises that power: "It is not by limitations of power, but by pressure of responsibility that good government is secured." [52] Under the pressure of such responsibility, Ford believed, American parties will clean house just as the parties had cleaned house in eighteenth-century England. Perhaps they will not "reform" themselves; but if only parties could be made genuinely responsible, Ford was willing to leave them "unreformed."

There remained for Ford the crucial problem of *how* power might be centralized and responsibility fixed in the formal governmental structure of the United States. He saw in the existing structure no place where power can be centralized except in the Presidency, and he insisted therefore that the only kind of party leadership possible in the United States is presidential leadership. As to whether or not presidential leadership will prove adequate he was inclined to be optimistic: "While all that a President can certainly accomplish is to force a submission of an issue to the people, yet such is the strength of the office that, if he makes a sincere and resolute use of its resources, at the same time cherishing his party connection, he can as a rule carry his party with him, because of the powerful interests which impel it to occupy ground taken for it by the administration." [53] And again: "It is the rule of our politics that no vexed question is settled except by executive policy. Whatever may be the feeling of Congress toward the President, it cannot avoid an issue which he insists upon making. And this holds good of presidents who lose their party leadership as with those who retain it. Tyler, Johnson, and Cleveland, although repudiated by the parties which elected them, furnished the issues upon which party action turned." [54]

On the other hand, Ford was aware of the existing institutional barriers to presidential leadership: "The function of general representation that has settled upon the presidential office as the only available basis for it, lacks appropriate institutions for its discharge. The people look to the president to do what he is denied means of doing." [55]

Ford nevertheless brought forth no proposals to centralize power in a fashion that would remove the barriers and thus open the way for real party responsibility. Indeed, the curious concluding chapter to *The Rise and Growth of*

[51] *The Rise and Growth of American Politics*, pp. 335-49.

[52] "American and Canadian Political Methods," pp. 692-93.

[53] *The Rise and Growth of American Politics*, p. 281.

[54] *Ibid.*, pp. 283-84.

[55] *The Cost of Our National Government*, pp. 111-12.

American Politics, where he looked ahead to what he called the "Ultimate Type" ("the new type of government which American democracy is perfecting"),[56] seems quite inconsistent with this emphasis in his thought. The Ultimate Type, according to Ford, will be a sort of parliamentary government, in which the President will become a largely honorary and ceremonial figure.[57] The government will consist of Representatives, and will represent the popular will as expressed in presidential elections. It alone will have the formal power to propose, defend, and "direct" legislative programs. Congress will retain its power of opposing the government's program, and when such opposition occurs the people will know whether the government or Congress is to blame. The purely administrative agencies will remain formally independent of Congress and under the President's control.[58] In such a system huge party organizations will no longer be necessary, and the parties will concentrate upon cultivating public opinion.[59] The bosses will disappear.[60] Thus, concluded Ford, genuine democratic government will, by natural evolution, at last establish itself in the United States.

One great advantage that Ford claimed for his Ultimate Type was that it will require no formal amendment of the Constitution. That our normal political evolution is producing it was his position; and when public opinion and the parties are ready to embrace it, the Constitution can be "interpreted" to allow for any necessary changes. He reminded his readers, in this connection, of the metamorphosis of the Electoral College; and he saw no reason why similar developments should not occur in the future.[61] He was, indeed, highly critical of any proposals for changing our governmental structure by formal amendment. Such amendment, he held, is difficult to obtain, uncertain in effect, and unnecessary. In a discussion of J. Allen Smith's thesis that only formal amendment of the Constitution will enable genuine democracy to arise in the United States,[62] Ford wrote:

It would be worth while for Mr. Smith to observe that where democratic government has been actually established it has been secured not by framing democratic constitutions but by instituting democratic procedure. Mr. Smith notes that "Our

---

[56] *The Rise and Growth of American Politics,* p. 365. That Ford believed he was making predictions in this chapter rather than constructing a Utopia is difficult of proof; but in view of his pride in being "objective" and "scientific" this seems to the author a likely hypothesis. Certainly in his later works he made no proposals for bringing about the kind of government described in this chapter.

[57] *Ibid.,* pp. 368-69.

[58] *Ibid.,* pp. 366-67.

[59] *Ibid.,* p. 370.

[60] *Ibid.,* p. 371.

[61] *Ibid.,* p. 161.

[62] This thesis was developed by Smith in his book, *The Spirit of American Government* (New York: The Macmillan Company, 1907).

Constitution was modeled in a general way after the English government of the eighteenth century." That is true. But the English have the same old eighteenth century form of government still intact and yet they have erected democratic government within that form. There is no *a priori* reason why the American people cannot do the same with their eighteenth century form. The way is as open to them as it was for the English, but they find it not, chiefly because they have been persuaded to dally with nostrums which English democracy ignores.[63]

Thus, while Ford believed that any reform of American parties must come as a consequence of the centralization of power and responsibility, presumably in the President, he had no real suggestions to make about how to obtain that centralization; and in describing the new kind of government which he believed to be evolving he found himself thinking in terms of a Presidency even less powerful than that obtaining in his day.

APPRAISAL

In his works on politics, Henry Jones Ford's avowed purpose was to describe the political system of his day as it actually was, and not (as he felt others were doing) as it should be. This approach was, of course, consistent with his conception of "the new political science" as a science divorced from ethics, objective in view, empirical in method, and concerned only with "is's," never with "ought's." Placed against this background, many otherwise puzzling aspects of his ideas become more understandable, and the weakness and strength of those ideas are more sharply outlined.

For example, his constant striving for objectivity enabled Ford to approach political parties with real feeling for the problems of politicians and real sympathy for their point of view. This led him to a number of insights that were denied to the majority of his contemporaries. He was aware, for example, of the importance of the functions devolving upon American parties; and he saw clearly that these functions can be performed only by elaborate and costly organizations. He was also prepared to face the fact that such organizations need large amounts of money and will obtain them any way they can. Such insights place him in a considerably different world of discourse from that of most writers of his time, who contemplated "machines" and "graft" with righteous indignation alone.

Perhaps it was his ability to see things as the party managers saw them that produced Ford's analysis of "intraparty democracy." Whatever the cause, he alone of all the writers in this period (and, with the exception of Professor Schattschneider, of our own time) asked the question: What relationship has democracy *within* the parties to democracy *between* the parties? And his well-reasoned conclusion that any serious attempt to achieve the former will inevitably

---

[63] Review of J. Allen Smith's *The Spirit of American Government*, in *American Political Science Review*, III (February, 1909), 138.

prevent the latter remains a point which most party-government advocates today might well ponder.

Ford, in fact, was at his best when defending American parties against the kind of criticism that was current in his time. Nothing spurred him on so much as the pronouncements of some critics that America would be better off with no parties at all than with the kind of parties it has. And even more fully than Wilson or Lowell, Ford described the nature and importance of the functions our parties perform—functions which the American system badly needs to have performed and for which there is, in his view, no other agency available.

Ford's attempt to be "objective" about American parties, on the other hand, was also the source of several weaknesses that the reader may readily observe in his analysis—among others, his uncritical acceptance of the ticket-voter conception of party membership. This is particularly surprising in view of his unwillingness, so unusual in his time and our own, to condemn American parties for their oligarchical and boss-controlled organization. Ford had no patience with this line of criticism, but his reply to its authors ran in terms of an insistence that the unrepresentativeness of the parties was made necessary by the functions the parties were called upon to perform, and did not lessen their value as agencies for establishing popular control over government. He seems never to have asked himself whether the conception of party membership on which the criticism was based might be fallacious, although the objective method he believed himself to be using should have lent itself to analysis of this kind of question.

A far more serious consequence of his attempt to consider only what actually exists is his failure to make explicit and complete his picture of how responsible party government should work. Nowhere can the reader find Ford's point of view on this question. He must piece it together for himself, by inference from a few fragmentary remarks, some of which deal primarily with other matters. Now Ford would probably have insisted that it was not his function as a political scientist to discuss how parties *ought* to behave—that his only job was to show how they *do* behave. Nevertheless, Ford often did in fact take positions involving "ought's." His statements on the alleged irresponsibility of American parties, for example, are meaningless unless predicated upon a conception of how parties *ought* to behave. His disavowal of value judgments did not prevent him from making them; and insofar as he makes them he is accountable to the reader for a statement of their bases.

Perhaps the most serious deficiency in Ford's analysis, however, was the part that dealt with the question of what should be done to make American parties more responsible. Of course Ford would have claimed that he dealt with no such question—that his chapter on the Ultimate Type was merely the recording of an observed trend. Yet, even if we take him at his own word, this answer is demonstrably not good enough. He cited no evidence showing that such a trend was in fact discernible; he made no attempt to show why the Ultimate Type was taking the particular form he described rather than another form; and he did not try to demonstrate that that particular type would produce responsible party government.

Ford's Ultimate Type was in fact a Utopia, and a Utopia at least as far removed from the political realities of his time as Wilson's early proposals for cabinet government had been. Though Ford labeled it "the new type of government which American democracy is perfecting," he could not successfully disguise its character. He shied away from discussing the values he wanted to see realized and from making proposals for achieving those values. Instead he left the former unstated, and attempted to disguise the latter as a "trend."

Thus the very conception of an objective political science that had enabled him to make so many shrewd and valuable observations about the nature and functions of the existing political parties in a sense prevented him from dealing profitably with the question of what should be done to improve them. Thus his analysis, which for the most part may be read with great profit even today, breaks down at just the point at which he might have used it to affect the course of events.

CHAPTER SIX

Frank J. Goodnow[1]

Frank J. Goodnow's works, unlike those of the other writers considered in this study, were for the most part written in the fields of public administration and municipal government. They displayed a concern with the details of public law which the others did not have, and all but one touched upon the subject of political parties only in passing.

Goodnow did not, however, see himself belonging to the considerable number of American political scientists of his time who believed that public law is the basic discipline of their science and that parties are not a subject fit for scholarly investigation. In one of his earliest published works, *Politics and Administration,* he not only developed a theory of the nature and function of party, but also stated a conception of the proper approach to the study of politics that was in essential agreement with the view of Wilson, Lowell, and Ford:

The tendency of most writers on governmental subjects has been to confine their study to the more striking facts which become apparent as a result of considering alone the formal governmental organization. Thus, most writers on American government begin and end their work with the Constitution. Some, it is true, endeavor to treat of the history of the Constitution as well as its present form, but few have attempted to get back of the formal governmental organization and examine the real political life of the people. The cause of this method of treating our political institutions is unquestionably to be found in the fact that most of the writers who have their impress on American political science have been lawyers, and are therefore not accustomed to look beyond the provisions of positive law. No method of treatment, however, is more likely to mislead the student in the formation of his judgment of a nation's real political life; for the character of a governmental system is determined just as much by extra-legal as by legal institutions. Indeed, it is not infrequently the case that extra-legal institutions have more influence than the mere legal system in which it may be framed.[2]

---

[1] A substantial portion of this chapter has appeared under the title, "Goodnow's Theory of Politics," *Southwestern Social Science Quarterly,* XXX (March, 1950), 268-76.

[2] *Politics and Administration* (New York: The Macmillan Company, 1900), 1-2. The other works of Goodnow in which some aspect of the problem of party is considered are: "The Tweed Ring in New York City," Chapter LXXXVIII in James Bryce, *The American Commonwealth* (1889); "Political Parties and City Government," *The International Monthly,* I (June, 1900), 618-31; *Municipal Problems* (New York: Published for the Columbia University Press by the Macmillan Company, 1907); *Municipal Government* (New York: The Century Company, 1909); and *City Government in the United States* (New York: The Century Company, 1910).

Thus Goodnow set out upon his exploration of the problem and the place of parties in the firm belief that he was studying something quite as important as public law.

THE NATURE OF DEMOCRACY

One of Goodnow's fundamental principles, which has since become an axiom in most public administration manuals, was that the traditional American division of public functions into executive, legislative, and judicial is false and misleading. There are really only two kinds of governmental activity, he said: policy-making and policy-executing, to which he gave the labels "politics" and "administration."

Political functions group themselves naturally under two heads, which are equally applicable to the mental operations and actions of self-conscious personalities. That is, the action of the state as a political entity consists either in operations necessary to the expression of its will, or in operations necessary to the execution of that will. The will of the state or sovereign must be made up and formulated before political action can be had. The will of the state or sovereign must be executed after it has been formulated, if that will is to result in governmental action. All the actions of the state or its organs, further, are undertaken with the object, either of facilitating the expression of this will, or of aiding in its execution. This would seem to be the case whatever may be the formal character of the governmental system.[3]

In any individual person, he went on, the two functions are carried on almost simultaneously and by largely the same organs. The greater complexity of political society, however, makes it necessary to develop differentiated governmental agencies for each function.[4] While complete separation of the two functions into two entirely different sets of organs is impossible, Goodnow said, it is nevertheless highly desirable to keep them as distinct as possible.[5]

Keeping them distinct, however, does not mean making them autonomous. Unlike some subsequent students of public administration, Goodnow was deeply convinced that in any government which calls itself democratic politics must control administration. It may be said, in fact, that most of his writings were devoted to the search for a means of establishing effective political control of administration. He therefore made a careful inquiry into the nature of democracy and democratic control, the result of which, as suggested above, closely resembled the ideas of Wilson, Lowell, and Ford.

Goodnow's first contention was that, whatever else it might be, democracy certainly is not direct popular participation in the day-to-day activities of governmental agencies on the town meeting model. In particular he attacked the reform polemics of Albert Stickney, S. E. Moffett, and Charles C. P. Clark.

[3] *Politics and Administration,* p. 9.
[4] *Ibid.,* pp. 10-12.
[5] *Ibid.,* pp. 14-20.

Their argument proceeded from the assumption that democracy cannot be said to exist unless the people do in fact participate in governmental activities in that sense. They argued, therefore, that all organizations—such as political parties—interposed between the sovereign citizen and his government will have to be destroyed or by-passed if genuine democratic government is to be obtained in the United States.[6] Democracy of that sort may well exist in rural New England towns, Goodnow said.[7] But it cannot exist in highly populated urban areas:

The only country . . . having an important urban development in which the referendum or initiative has any great importance is the United States. The reasons for its adoption would seem to be two in number. The first is the democratic idea that everything possible should be decided by direct appeal to the people which underlay the town meeting of New England. But the success which it unquestionably had in the towns of New England is not an argument of great value in favor of its adoption in the much more complex conditions of the modern American city. Like the elective principle which is also characteristic of the New England town, it was adopted in the place of its origin for districts whose population was most homogeneous and whose needs were quite simple. Because it worked successfully in those conditions, we may not predict that it will work successfully in the totally different conditions which characterize urban populations.[8]

In any complex, highly populated area, whether urban areas or the nation as a whole, Goodnow argued, "the attainable in democratic government is not as much the deliberate choice of officers and the positive determination of policies by the people, as the power of veto and the power to change party leaders . . ." [9] In other words, Goodnow believed that party government—the popular choice of alternate ruling groups—is as close as we are likely to get to democratic government in the United States: "Where conditions of life are at all complex, *i.e.*, where the population is numerous and not thoroughly homogeneous, where the territory to be governed is extended and the distribution of wealth and intelligence is not comparatively equal, the necessities of the case have developed alongside of the formal governmental system more or less voluntary extra-

---

[6] Albert Stickney, *The Political Problem* (New York: Harper and Brothers, 1890); S. E. Moffett, *Suggestions on Government* (New York: Rand, McNally and Company, 1894); and Charles C. P. Clark, *The "Machine" Abolished and the People Restored to Power* (New York: G. P. Putnam's Sons, 1900). The argument of these writers will be more fully discussed and criticized in the chapter on Herbert Croly. It should be noted here, however, that they assumed that political parties will always be exactly like the existing parties. One of Goodnow's major objections to their position was that they underestimated the possibilities for improving parties (through such reforms as the direct primary).

[7] *Municipal Problems*, pp. 174-80.

[8] *Municipal Government*, p. 154. See also *Municipal Problems*, pp. 180-86.

[9] *Politics and Administration*, p. 248. See also *ibid.*, p. 149.

governmental organizations, which exercise a controlling influence on the formal government." [10] And again:

Now, in order that government under parties shall be popular, conditions must be such, both that the party, in whom the people as a whole do not have confidence, shall retire from the active control of the government, and that party leaders who in like manner have forfeited the confidence of the party shall retire from active control of the party. If these conditions do not exist, the system of government cannot be said to be popular. If they do exist, the government is probably as nearly popular as government ever has been or ever can be expected to be in any except the most primitive and simple social conditions.[11]

Goodnow, then, conceived of democracy as government *responsible* to the people, and not as government carried on by them. In order to make this responsibility effective, he pointed out, the power of the government must be concentrated so that one man or set of men can easily and identifiably possess it at any given time. Full responsibility, he was convinced, can arise only from full power. What is true of municipal government in this respect is true at all levels: "The desire to concentrate all executive power in the mayor in order to secure that responsibility for the municipal government without which popular control cannot exist, and also to secure greater administrative efficiency, has resulted in the very general adoption of what are called single-headed departments." [12] And again:

Whatever plan of representation is adopted, the supreme powers of the city should be concentrated in some one authority. Only in this way is it possible for the city population, which finds it so difficult under the most favorable conditions to cooperate, to exercise a control over the city government. When governmental powers are distributed among many officers and authorities each one of whom is within the limits of the statutes a law unto himself, official responsibility for acts of government is so difficult of attainment as to be practically impossible except in a most homogeneous population and in political conditions of the greatest simplicity. The only way to ensure a popular control over city government in the conditions which obtain in modern cities is to focus the attention of the voters upon a single person whose character and views are well known.[13]

For Goodnow, then, as for Wilson, Lowell, and Ford, democracy is popular control of government through the choice of alternate responsible sets of rulers —responsible because one of them is clearly in full possession of the government's power at any given time. Such a view became, at least, the foundation of his conception of the place of parties in the American system.

---

[10] *Ibid.*, pp. 149-50.

[11] *Ibid.*, pp. 151-52. By the "party" whose confidence the party leaders may forfeit, Goodnow meant all those voters who vote for its particular ticket. The influence of this conception of party membership upon his general position will be commented upon below.

[12] *Municipal Government*, p. 225.

[13] *Ibid.*, p. 383.

THE FUNCTION OF POLITICAL PARTIES

The first function political parties should perform in a democracy, Goodnow believed, is to assure responsibility of the government to the people.[14] His model for how this should be done was party government as he conceived it to operate in England:

That such a political system is, in the case of the English people, an admirable one, can hardly be doubted. It permits the development of government along the lines of least resistance, and therefore along the most natural lines. It permits, further, political development within the governmental organization, or at any rate in close connection with it, and has the great advantage of insuring responsibility, since persons whom the law can reach, that is, persons holding official position, are the persons actually exercising political powers. The fact that political responsibility is, comparatively speaking, easily fixed, that the people may force out of power political leaders who do not possess their confidence, makes the whole system one in which popular government is easily secured. For the party is made responsible and the leaders of the party who are the leaders of the government makes the whole political system a responsible one.[15]

The basis of popular control through party government, Goodnow pointed out, is the substitution of *party* responsibility for individual responsibility: "It is important, if harmony in government is desirable, that all the candidates of one or the other of the great parties in a given administrative district should be elected. The individual candidate must be sunk to a large extent in the party. Individual responsibility must give place to party responsibility." [16]

Once it establishes the responsibility of the political side of the government to the people, Goodnow continued, the next function of party is to enable politics to control administration—a control which he believed to be essential to democratic government:

Either the executing authority must be subordinated to the expressing authority, or the expressing authority must be subjected to the control of the executing authority. Only in this way can the expression of the real state will become an actual rule of conduct generally observed. . . . Popular government requires that it is the executing authority which shall be subordinated to the expressing authority, since the latter in the nature of things can be made much more representative of the people than can the executing authority.[17]

There is always the danger, he admitted, that parties will extend their control

---

[14] It should be emphasized that Goodnow was, in this context, talking about the functions parties *should* perform—that, in short, he was here setting up his ideal of responsible party government. He was perhaps less guilty than any other writer considered in the present study of confusing the functions parties *should* perform with those they *do* perform.

[15] *Politics and Administration*, p. 157.

[16] *Ibid.*, p. 34.

[17] *Ibid.*, p. 24.

beyond that necessary to control administration, and thereby make the "formal" will of the state differ from its "actual" will. The remedy, however, is not to abolish parties but merely to watch them closely and to make sure that their power remains within its proper limits.[18]

In the United States in particular, continued Goodnow, the nature of the formal governmental structure is such that political parties are called upon to perform certain functions which do not fall to them, for example, in England. He agreed with Ford's analysis of the fallacious principle and harmful effects of the separation of powers, and joined with Ford in arguing that parties are the only agency available in America for inducing some kind of coordination and harmony between the legislative and executive branches:

There was [in America from the start] a great need of strong government. The system as originally established was not strong because so many authorities had to pull together in order to accomplish anything. But as the system of government adopted was incorporated in documents which were difficult if not impossible of amendment, the formal system of government could not well be changed. Since that system provided in no way for that co-ordination of governmental departments without which harmonious and effective action could not be ensured, means to secure the desired end had to be sought for outside the system. This means was found in the organization of well organized and disciplined political parties, which strove by every means within their power to get control of all governmental departments in the belief that in this way and in this way only could they force these departments to act in harmony and thus secure a solution of the problems before the country.[19]

Thus in England the formal government itself makes for concentration of power and the establishment of responsibility; but in the United States those necessary conditions of democracy can be established, Goodnow argued, only through the agency of party:

Responsibility, if it is to be found at all, must be found outside of the government and in the party which largely reflects the conditions existing in the government. The governmental system of checks and balances, whatever its advantages may be from other points of view, makes it difficult for the electors to hold public officers to account. For it is almost impossible under it to fix the blame or award the credit for any concrete thing that is done or left undone by the officers of the government. The electors must, therefore, look to the party . . . [which] is, under our present system, almost the only protection against anarchy, the only means of progress.[20]

Then, too, continued Goodnow, if politics is to control administration in the American system, parties must be the agency whereby that control is established; for

---

[18] *Ibid.*, pp. 128-31.
[19] *Municipal Government*, p. 104.
[20] *Politics and Administration*, pp. 174-75.

it has been impossible for the necessary control of politics over administration to develop within the formal governmental system on account of the independent position assigned by the constitutional law to executive and administrative officers. The control has therefore developed in the party system. The American political party busies itself as much with the election of administrative and executive officers as it does with the election of bodies recognized as distinctly political in character, as having to do with the expression of the state will. The party system thus secures that harmony between the functions of politics and administration which must exist if government is to be carried on successfully.[21]

The goal of good government, Goodnow affirmed, should be to keep politics and administration as separate as possible while retaining control of the latter by the former. But this is not possible, in his opinion, unless the administration is first centralized. Here again American parties have performed an important function, he believed. The formal government has been unable to centralize the administration, but the parties have accomplished it—largely for spoils purposes, to be sure. Now that they have finished this job, he concluded, they should be entirely removed—with thanks—from the purely administrative sphere through merit-system reform.[22]

Goodnow therefore believed that political parties have a big job to do in any democratic system; but the special nature of the formal governmental structure in the United States either makes their job more difficult or, failing that, adds entirely new tasks to their burden. Thus, like Ford, he had a strong sense of the enormity of the job imposed on American parties by the Constitution—and of the importance of the services they are called upon to perform.

THE NATURE OF POLITICAL PARTIES

Goodnow's conception of the nature of political parties, in general, closely resembled that of Ford. In the first place, he saw that parties are not only agencies for debating public policy and conducting elections but also agencies for carrying on government: "A political party is formed for the accomplishment of certain ends. These ends are not accomplished unless, in the first place, a law is put upon the statute books which, in the second place, is actually enforced and becomes a rule of conduct observed by the citizens of the state." [23] He studied parties in both aspects—indeed his attention was so centered upon their governmental aspect as, sometimes, to obscure their opinion-expressing side.

Then, too, Goodnow went more deeply into the problem of the nature and conditions of party leadership than any of his contemporaries. He agreed with

---

[21] *Ibid.*, pp. 25-26. Here Goodnow is still talking about the functions American parties *should* perform. For reasons to be discussed below, he believed that the existing parties *do* in fact bridge separation of powers, fix responsibility, and establish political control of administration.

[22] *Ibid.*, pp. 128-31.

[23] "Political Parties and City Government," p. 622.

Lowell and Ford that, because parties have so much to do, they must, particularly in the United States, be closely controlled by the party managers, and that the party members cannot possibly participate directly in the day-to-day processes of decision-making:

The maintaining in all its integrity and power of the party organization and the preservation of successful party leadership are so necessary to the attainment of the ultimate ends of the party that the role of the members of the party ceases to be the positive determination of party policy, and is reduced to the amendment or negativing of propositions made by the party leaders. A body in which all shades of opinion exist and find expression is apt to be a debating society merely, incapable of positive action. They must therefore follow rather than lead, and in order that they may follow they must have leaders capable of originating a policy which will approve itself to the party membership.[24]

But, he warned, the party leadership must use its strength despotically if party is to serve as an agency of democratic government: "A popular, representative form of government with an autocratic party organization controlled by an oligarchy or a party despot may not result in as really a popular political system, *i.e.*, may not permit of as ready an expression of the popular or state will, as a less popular form of government combined with a less autocratic form of party organization."[25]

It is therefore necessary, argued Goodnow, for the party leaders to be held responsible by the party members. But who are the party "members" who should exercise this control? Clearly, said Goodnow, they are those voters who signify their wish to vote in the party's primary. He would not even restrict party membership to those who can prove past party loyalty. In reply to those who criticized the "open primaries" on the ground that they permit persons other than bona fide members of a party to exert control over its nominees, Goodnow wrote:

Such an objection is, it must be admitted, not devoid of force. It is still to be remembered, however, that it is based largely on the theory that party membership is to be determined by past action rather than by present intention. This theory, if adopted, seriously limits the rights of the citizen, inasmuch as it presupposes that no one as a result of his citizenship has the right to do more than exercise a choice at the polls between candidates, all of whom are objectionable, and in the selection of none of whom he has had anything to say. The voter's choice is not in reality free if he is precluded in any way from participation in the selection of candidates.[26]

Thus Goodnow believed that the kind of parties needed to perform the many functions that fall to parties in the American system are those with strong leadership capable of providing unity and discipline within their ranks. He

[24] *Politics and Administration*, pp. 150-51.
[25] *Ibid.*, pp. 27-28.
[26] *Ibid.*, p. 234.

went a step further, however, and argued that the party leaders must be responsible to the party members in precisely the same sense that the parties themselves should be responsible to the voters at large—that within his meaning of the terms, there must be democracy *within* the parties as well as *between* the parties. This notion of responsible party leadership did a great deal to shape his subsequent analysis of the existing American parties as well as his proposals for improving them.

EVALUATION OF AMERICAN PARTIES

Up to this point in the argument, there is no discernible conflict between Goodnow's point of view and that of Wilson, Lowell, or Ford. In describing and evaluating the existing American parties and in analyzing what is wrong with them, however, he broke with their analysis in several important respects.

Goodnow's description of American parties, for one thing, is often so different from that offered by these other writers that the reader finds it difficult to believe that he was talking about the same party system. They saw American parties as weak, leaderless, and therefore incapable of unified, responsible action on matters of public policy. Goodnow's picture, by contrast, ran in terms of rigid control by powerful bosses who whip their legislative puppets into line and grind out public policy in a despotic but highly efficient manner. Here is a typical passage in this vein:

When it is remembered that it is the party which controls both the legislature and the administration, and it is the party leader or "boss," as we have accustomed ourselves to call him, who controls the party, it will at once be seen what a commanding position is accorded by the American political system to the bosses. . . . They control the making of laws and their execution after they are made. As Mr. Horace E. Deming has said: "The deliberative functions of the legislature as conceived by the 'fathers' have absolutely ceased to exist for many purposes." It registers as automatically the will of a third party and as little the results of its own deliberation as the Electoral College. The form of a legislature survives, but the substance and spirit have vanished. . . . The legislative power . . . is exercised by one man or a small self-constituted group through dummies who are still in name representatives of the people.[27]

Goodnow even went so far as to assert that unless a man is "right" in his views on public policy the party bosses will deny him even the most minor public office:

In order to build up the parties, administrative efficiency in both the national and state governments was sacrificed through the introduction of the partisan political maxim that "to the victors belong the spoils." Public office was given as a reward for partisan political service, and little attempt was made to secure official incumbents because of their fitness for the discharge of the administrative duties attached to the offices which they secured. The questions asked were: does the

---

[27] *Ibid.*, pp. 169-70.

applicant hold the proper opinions on the extension of the suffrage, on states rights and slavery; and will he, if given the office, further the policies of the party which has selected him? [28]

So deep, indeed, was Goodnow's disagreement with Wilson, Lowell, and Ford on this kind of question, that he was capable of drawing a contrast between the "weak" political parties in France and the "strong" political parties in the United States, and of drawing it in such a way that any of the other three writers would willingly have accepted his description of French parties as a description of American parties:

There are no strongly organized national parties such as are to be found in either the United States [sic] or England. There are, instead, groups of persons who are accustomed to act together, either based largely on local considerations or owing personal allegiance to some prominent public man. Party allegiance sits lightly on the shoulders of both people and politicians; and, such as it is, it is owed to a local clique or a man of national reputation. Parties, such as they are, have practically no national organizations, draw up no national platforms, and have no really national leaders. The national party leader is practically unknown, and the parties are merely more or less local cliques, which may or may not act together.[29]

Goodnow's point in making these observations, it should be remembered, was that such "weak" parties are incapable of providing responsible party government; but it seems never to have occurred to him that American parties were open to exactly the same charge:

The deputies controlled by these party leaders finally owe their election not to any appeal to party allegiance of their constituents. They owe their election to their personal popularity. This popularity has been obtained very largely because of past favors granted or future favors promised. One of the most common complaints in France is "that the deputies represent local and personal interests rather than national." . . . Such a condition of things is not conceivable in that part of American political life in which the influence of national parties is predominant.[30]

The readiest explanation of this blind spot is that Goodnow approached party politics on the national level on the basis of an uncriticized assumption that they differ in no important respect from party politics on the local level. Because of his lifelong concern with the problems of municipal government, he was well aware of the strength of local machines and the power of local bosses; and he seems to have thought of a man like Mark Hanna as a "national boss" in the same sense in which Richard Croker and Tom Platt were "local bosses." In a word, he expected to find the national parties being run with a discipline and effectiveness comparable to that which he had observed in Tammany Hall.

Goodnow did recognize some differences between the local machines and the

---

[28] *Municipal Government*, p. 104.

[29] *Politics and Administration*, p. 139.

[30] *Ibid.*, p. 143.

national parties, primarily in the motives which seemed to him to animate their respective leaders: "In the case of strong national parties there is after all some motive other than self-interest which leads to political action. In theory, at least, party allegiance is due to motives more or less ideal, however much practice may depart from the theory. In the case of local parties, which we are sometimes urged to put in the place of national parties, the basis of party cohesion is quite the reverse of the ideal. It is, on the contrary, grossly material." [31] In the last analysis, however, Goodnow recognized many more important similarities than differences between local and national machines: both, in his view, were despotically controlled by bosses irresponsible to the party members.

Naturally, therefore, Goodnow was less charitable to the existing American parties than Henry Jones Ford or even Wilson and Lowell had been. He did not go so far as to deny that parties are necessary in the American system and that we are better off with the ones we have than we would be with no parties at all. But he did not hesitate to insist that

the American political system as at present existing does not thus satisfy the demands of popular government, as they have been defined, in as full a measure as is desirable. It does not, in the first place, permit the easy retirement, from the control of public affairs, of a party which has lost the confidence of the people. It does not, in the second place, give the party members, in case they disapprove of policies proposed by party leaders, the power to bring about as easily as is desirable a change in party leadership.[32]

Believing this, Goodnow naturally sought to diagnose the malady, and he decided that the basic deficiency of American parties—basic in the sense that all other deficiencies flow from it—lies in the fact that the bosses are not responsible to the party members:

The mere fact that the boss is a political leader of great influence and power is a matter which to the student of politics is of very little importance. It is merely indicative of the trend which is noticeable in the development of almost all political systems. But that the boss is irresponsible is a much more serious matter. For power without reponsibility is a thing against which the human race has been fighting since its first attempts at political organizations. The frank recognition of the necessity of political leadership is one thing. The actual existence of irresponsible political leadership is quite another.[33]

Goodnow proceeded to spell out the consequences of this alleged irresponsibility of American party leaders. As a student of local government and an advocate of home rule he was especially preoccupied with the constant interference of national and state parties in local politics. He was, indeed, willing to

[31] *Ibid.*, pp. 144-46.
[32] *Ibid.*, pp. 165-66.
[33] *Ibid.*, p. 174.

place upon the boss-ruled state and national parties a considerable part of the responsibility for the undemocratic character of local government institutions:

[A] reason why constitutional provisions attempting to secure to local governments the expression and execution of the local will have not had the success which was anticipated from them is to be found in the partisan political system obtaining in the United States. . . . This party system has been formed primarily to attend to national and state politics, that is to facilitate the expression and execution of the will of the nation and of the state as a whole. This was so because the great political questions which we as a people have been called upon to solve have been national and state questions. The state and national parties, having thus important national and state questions to solve, have not scrupled to sacrifice the interests of the local communities to what they considered to be the interests of the state and nation. They not only have made use of the powers of the legislature over the localities in the interest of the state and nation, but also, by emphasizing the importance of national and state questions on the occasion of local elections, have drowned by their clamor the voices of those individuals who have attempted to call attention to the rights and interests of the local communities.[34]

It should be clear from the above passages that when Goodnow referred to "party irresponsibility" what he meant was that the party members are unable to hold the party leadership to account, or to depose unpopular party leaders. When, on the other hand, Wilson, Lowell, and Ford used the term, they assigned to it an entirely different meaning; i.e., what they had in mind was the failure of American parties to stand together as parties on matters of public policy so that they might as parties be held responsible by the people at large. Goodnow would, of course, wish the parties not to be irresponsible in this sense also; but he apparently took it for granted that the parties themselves will become responsible only when their leaders become responsible to the party members—in short, that democracy *between* the parties can come only as a result of democracy *within* the parties.[35] For the rest, he was so sure that the national parties are closely controlled and disciplined by national bosses, and so sure that this is the nub of the question, that their alleged weakness on matters of public policy seemed to him unimportant. Find out why the parties are boss-controlled, he insisted, go on from there to discover a means of preventing boss-control through democratization of the parties, and other problems will take care of themselves.

EXPLANATION OF AMERICAN PARTIES

Although he took issue with them on the question of *what* is wrong with American parties, Goodnow agreed with Wilson, Ford, and Lowell upon the

---

[34] *Ibid.*, pp. 62-63. See also *Municipal Home Rule* (New York: The Macmillan Company, 1895), pp. 26-27; "Political Parties and City Government," pp. 619-30; *Municipal Problems*, pp. 200-01; and *City Government in the United States*, pp. 81-82.

[35] Cf. *Politics and Administration*, pp. 197-98.

basic reason *why* they are as they are. For all of them that reason lay in the peculiar nature of the American constitutional system—primarily in separation of powers and the proliferation of governmental units and elective offices produced by federalism.

The Constitution, in Goodnow's opinion, encourages the subjection of American parties to the control of irresponsible bosses in two ways. In the first place, it imposes such heavy responsibilities upon them, by default at least, that they have to have elaborate and well-disciplined organizations in order to do their job:

The first cause of the irresponsibility of parties in the United States is to be found in the work demanded of the party. The party in the American political system has to do what in other political systems is devolved upon the formal governmental organization. . . . That is, the party does this work because the governmental system is so formed that it cannot do it, and if the party did not do it we would have anarchy instead of government. Further, the party organization is as strong as it is because the party has to do this work, its organization will probably continue much the same as it is at present.[36]

The necessity of strong organization, in turn, has done much to prevent the party members from insisting upon the responsibility of their leaders:

The individual members of the party have not only not been able to make the party leaders as responsive as might be wished, they have not desired to insist upon as full a measure of responsibility from party leaders as is desirable from their fear of weakening the party. This unwillingness on their part is in large measure due to their appreciation of the enormous task which our governmental system devolves upon the party, and to the feeling that the accomplishment of this task makes necessary that they evince willingness to forego a part of their political privileges if through such action the party to which they have attached themselves can be successful in obtaining control of the government.[37]

In the second place, the Constitution, by driving the parties completely outside the formal government, forces them to operate entirely under their own rules, which for the most part are worked out, secretly and irresponsibly, by the bosses themselves:

The irresponsibility of the parties is due, in the second place, to the position which we have assigned to the party. The enormous work which has been devolved upon the American political party, and which it would seem that the party must perform for many years to come, has really made the party a most important political organ. And yet the party is largely a voluntary organization governed by rules of its own making, which are enforced or not, according as their enforcement is or is not to the advantage of the few who have succeeded in getting control of the

---

[36] *Ibid.*, pp. 199-200.

[37] *Ibid.*, pp. 164-65. See also *ibid.*, pp. 105-08, 135-36; and *Municipal Government*, pp. 381-82.

party machinery. The courts as a general thing refuse to exercise any control over parties.[38]

The position of American parties entirely outside the formal government is, in Goodnow's view, an invitation to the seizure and retention of power by the irresponsible bosses; for, with no aid from the courts or any other official agency, the ordinary party members can unseat their bosses only by a "prolonged, continuous, and bitter struggle." And as a result "the almost invariable rule is that success will crown the efforts of those alone who are willing to devote practically their entire time to the struggle. Such persons do not scruple to make use of unfair means in their pursuit of power, largely because such a method of procedure is not effectively prevented by the law." [39]

He pressed the point still further: even the prevalence of spoils and graft as the characteristic method of party finance can be explained in terms of the extra-constitutional position of the parties: "[The party bosses] must be paid in some way. Indeed the work is so arduous as to take all of their time. They cannot live, therefore, if they are not endowed with this world's goods, unless pecuniary rewards are attached to the pursuit of party politics. If such rewards are not attached by law to this work, ways will and must be found outside of the law by which they will be provided." [40]

Goodnow was, in a word, talking about a quite different set of evils in American parties from that which Wilson, Lowell, and Ford presented. But his explanation of the basic situation in which, on either showing, evils arise, runs in terms strikingly similar to theirs. The similarity does not, however, extend to his proposals for reforming American parties.

THE REFORM OF AMERICAN PARTIES

Goodnow's major prescription for the ills of the American party system, as the reader will already have guessed, runs in terms of making party leaders responsible to the party members. He did not wish to destroy or even to weaken party leadership, for he believed that, given the functions American parties are called upon to perform, such leadership is both inevitable and desirable: "Political changes are naturally made more quickly nowadays, but still it may be years before our bosses become responsible and cease to be corrupt. But, in order that they shall be responsible, and shall cease to be corrupt, it is necessary for all who want good government to fight on, now for this reform, now for that one, always bearing in mind that the ultimate purpose should be not to

---

[38] *Politics and Administration*, p. 206.

[39] *Ibid.*, pp. 220-21.

[40] *Ibid.*, pp. 108-09. See also *ibid.*, pp. 110-13; and "Political Parties and City Government," pp. 628-29.

destroy the boss as an institution, but to make him amenable to the public will." [41]

Goodnow, then, sought an effective method for making the boss responsible to the party members. He was, however, deeply convinced that proportional representation, for all the claims being made for it by other writers, will not solve the problem, in part because it frequently eventuates in minority rule, and in part because it tends to strengthen rather than weaken the power of the boss.[42] He chose, rather, to place his bets on the direct primary; for he felt sure that it

will do much to make the party, and through it the boss, responsible. For it will put into the hands of the people the same control over nominations as they now have over elections. The people will not be confined in their political action to choosing between two undesirable candidates. They will also have the power to prevent the running, as candidates of their party, of persons in whom they do not have confidence. The same is true also of the general policy of the party. At present formulated in its outward expressions by conventions over whose deliberations the average party member has little, if anything, to say, if this method of primary elections is adopted such policy will be determined by bodies much more than at present representations of party membership.[43]

In other words, the direct primary, Goodnow believed, will make the bosses responsible; and he was prepared to make other claims for it as well. By drawing the parties into the orbit of the formal government, and giving them the status of official instrumentalities, the direct primary will subject the parties' internal processes to state control; and he was ready even to welcome the fact that this control will be enforced by the judges in the courts of law: "If some such system as the one outlined above is adopted, the party will have received full and frank recognition as a political organ of government of great importance. This recognition will have been accompanied by its subjection to public regulation, and by the guarantee to the individual citizen of the right, in virtue of his citizenship, to participate in the actions of party." [44] Furthermore, party finance will be purified: instead of depending upon spoils and graft for their support, the parties will, under the watchful eye of the courts, depend upon voluntary contributions by the party members.[45]

Better still, Goodnow claimed, there will no longer be any question of interference in local politics by state and national parties:

A national party by adopting specific municipal issues may attract to it as party members many persons who, while in sympathy with its municipal policy, would

---

[41] *Politics and Administration*, pp. 195-96. See also *ibid.*, pp. 197-98.

[42] *Municipal Problems*, pp. 167-68.

[43] *Politics and Administration*, pp. 248-49. See also *ibid.*, pp. 166-67, 232-33.

[44] *Ibid.*, p. 242.

[45] *Ibid.*, pp. 110-13.

not act with it if not permitted to share in the work of nomination. By permitting them to determine their party membership themselves in a local campaign, they will give the party with whose municipal policy they are in sympathy, their aid, regardless of their or its attitude on national or state questions. Municipal parties, which, whatever advantages are claimed for them, certainly tend to break up the national parties, considered apart from their municipal policies, would be unnecessary.[46]

All these last-named benefits of the direct primary, however, appeared minor and derivative to Goodnow; for he was convinced that they will flow as a matter of course from the breaking of the bosses' power and the lodging of party control in the party members.

APPRAISAL

Woodrow Wilson, A. Lawrence Lowell, Henry Jones Ford, and Frank J. Goodnow were the most prominent writers in the period covered by this study who advanced the notion that "representative government is party government." The present writer has therefore referred to them as the "party-government school." It should be remembered, however, that there were many dissimilarities as well as similarities among these four writers. And one way of measuring Goodnow's stature and determining the nature of his particular contribution to this school is to compare him with some of its other members.

First, then, let us consider Goodnow and Henry Jones Ford. Ford's great weakness as a writer on parties, as pointed out in the preceding chapter, lay in his unwillingness or inability to deal at any length with the theoretical aspects of the problem of political parties in a democratic system. Goodnow, by contrast, was at his best when considering those aspects; and his greatest contributions to the general discussion of the problem were undoubtedly made in that area. There was, for one thing, his attack upon the traditional tri-partite classification of governmental powers and his revised division of those powers into politics and administration. Goodnow's position on this point has, of course, become one of the commonplaces of political science,[47] and serves as a basis, as he showed, for such widely accepted doctrines as (a) that which asserts the desirability of assigning the two functions to differentiated governmental organs while recognizing the impossibility of separating them completely; and (b) that which asserts that in a popular government politics must control administration. All subsequent thought about parties has been noticeably affected by the clear implications of Goodnow's position regarding the interrelation of the various agencies of government; for once these implications are grasped, the

[46] *Ibid.*, pp. 236-37. See also *Municipal Government*, pp. 160-64.

[47] It is, however, under considerable attack from a number of present-day students of public administration. For the nature of much of this criticism, see Dwight Waldo, *The Administrative State* (New York: The Ronald Press, 1948), pp. 106-11, 114-23.

problem of parties must be restated in such fashion as to take account of them. Then, too, Goodnow opened up the whole question of the nature and conditions of party leadership in a way that Wilson, Lowell, and Ford never got around to doing. One need not accept his answers in order to recognize the importance of the questions he raised, and their value as possible lines of inquiry for subsequent students of party.

Ford, on the other hand, was at his best when describing and explaining the nature of the existing American parties; and the most obvious and probably the most serious deficiency in Goodnow's entire analysis was his rather complete misreading of their nature. Here also the contrast between Goodnow and Lowell becomes sharpest: for Goodnow never learned what Lowell might have taught him about the nature of the existing national parties. He must have been acquainted with Lowell's report on party voting in American legislatures, and yet he seems never to have felt it necessary to revise any of his ideas in the light of that report. Lowell's figures, however, constituted an unanswerable refutation of most of Goodnow's generalizations about the nature of American parties. There is, for example, no excuse for Goodnow's lumping together the local machines and the national parties, and merely assuming that what is true of one must also be true of the other. There is, if anything, even less excuse— in view of his own observations that the local bosses care nothing for public policy and everything for the spoils—for his argument that those bosses will not award even minor administrative jobs except to people who are "right" on the tariff, states' rights, etc. And, because no man's thought about parties is likely to rise far above his factual knowledge about parties, this weakness makes itself felt in every page and paragraph Goodnow wrote on the subject.

However, it is not possible for Goodnow's admirers to plead that his "party-government" colleagues did not attempt to go to his assistance in this regard. Ford, who reviewed *Politics and Administration* in the *Annals,* taxed Goodnow severely for his failure to understand the nature of the existing American parties and for his uncritical acceptance of the direct primary as the cure for all their ills. Ford's bill of particulars included these points: (a) recognizing, as he does, the need of disciplined and strongly led parties in the American system if they are to provide the popular control over the government which the Constitution makes impossible, Goodnow fails utterly to realize how weak, decentralized, and leaderless American parties really are; (b) not only does he ignore the crucial problem of how to strengthen party leadership, but his major proposed reform, the direct primary, is calculated to have the effect of disintegrating the parties still further; (c) under Goodnow's proposed reforms not only would the local bosses persist but the prospects of achieving genuine responsible party government would receive a serious setback; and (d) the result is that Goodnow worries about bossism as the major evil either where it does not exist at all (on the national level) or where it is the product of other factors (as on the state and local levels).[48] Goodnow not only did not reply to Ford, but his subsequent writings showed that he paid no attention to this criticism.

Why did this scholar, whose ability and industry have won for him the admiration of all subsequent generations of political scientists, refuse to face up to the real nature of American parties? A partial answer can be found in his uncritical acceptance of the ticket-voter misconception of party membership. In this he was no different from the other party-government writers of his time; but he accepted it in its most extreme form. Party membership in Goodnow's view, should not be restricted to voters who have supported the party in a given number of past elections, or who can pass any of the rudimentary tests of party "loyalty" embodied in some of the direct primary laws now extant. A party member should be, rather, anyone who signifies his desire to vote in a particular party's primary—which is to demand the most "open" kind of primary conceivable. This is the party member who, Goodnow continually asserted, has a *right* to vote in the primary and determine the party's policies. This right, he said, attaches to citizenship; and he seems to have thought of it as being of exactly the same nature as the right to free speech or the writ of habeas corpus. He was quite unaware of the difficulties involved in the notion of an association which, though voluntary, is yet of such a character that any person, merely in virtue of his citizenship, has a right to determine the association's policies without assuming any obligation other than that of expressing his opinion upon those policies. In view of his own conception of the parties' great responsibilities and their attendant need for strong leadership and effective discipline, Goodnow should have seen that his "right of membership" involved both a naive conception of rights and a naive conception of membership. He nevertheless based his entire analysis of what should be done about American parties upon this fundamental error.

Ultimately, as perusal of Wilson's and Ford's writings should make clear, Goodnow's error flowed from an unwillingness to put first things first. If the analysis of the nature of democracy and the function that political parties must play in it—upon which all four "party-government" writers based their argument—is correct, then the great need is to guide American parties toward that unity of action on matters of public policy without which they cannot be responsible to the people. Once this is accomplished, as Ford pointed out, the parties' internal processes will probably become more democratic and their leadership more responsive—as they had in fact become in England *after* the parties themselves had developed sufficient unity to become responsible agents of government. But even if the parties do not "reform" internally, Ford and

---

[48] Review, of *Politics and Administration*, pp. 185-86.

Wilson believed, it will not particularly matter so long as their responsibility to the people at large remains effective.

It therefore seems fair to conclude that the more Goodnow dealt with the nature of the existing American parties and with proposals for their reform, the less he was able to escape the consequences of certain of his misconceptions and the less valuable were his conclusions for the modern student of parties. What he had to say about the nature of democratic government, however, about the relation of politics and administration in such a government, and about the functions political parties should perform in ordering those relations, represented a great step forward.

Part Three

Party as the Enemy of Democracy

CHAPTER SEVEN

M. I. Ostrogorski

Moisei Iakovlevitch Ostrogorski, who was born in Russia and educated in France, is the only non-American considered in this study.[1] He is included for several reasons; the broad scope of his analysis; the distinctive point of view from which he wrote; and the frequent citation of his works by modern American textbooks, which indicates that he has exercised a considerable influence upon American teaching about parties.[2]

Ostrogorski devoted over twenty years to the study of the English and American party systems. He was convinced that the political scientist, if he is to understand the true nature of the political process, must "study political *forces* instead of political forms." [3] The natural point of departure for such a study, he believed, is an examination of the organization and operation of political parties:

It was necessary in the first place to find in political life a field where the modes of action are in a way concentrated and systematized, a field offering a clearly defined sphere for observation and a firm vantage-ground for the observer. . . . The material organization of parties appeared to me to offer the required post of observation, and its historical growth the landmarks for tracing the development of the political tendencies and forces themselves, which would enable me to ascend from the present to the past, from the effects to the causes, and to consider the working of democratic government as a whole, not in the inanimate fabric of political forms, but in the midst of living society.[4]

Although his works are packed with a still-unsurpassed wealth of detail about

---

[1] Biographical information about Ostrogorski is inadequate. There is a helpful though brief sketch of his career by A. W. Macmahon in *Encyclopaedia of the Social Sciences* (New York: The Macmillan Company, 1937), VI, 503-04. A few useful facts are also included in reviews of his works by J. H. Finley in the *Atlantic Monthly*, XCI (March, 1903), pp. 422-25; and by Jesse Macy in the *American Political Science Review*, V (August, 1911), 472-74.

[2] To mention only two examples, Ostrogorski is cited eighteen times in P. H. Odegard and E. A. Helms, *American Politics* (2d ed.; New York: Harper and Brothers, 1947), and these authors seem to accept his values and judgments on a number of matters. He is cited seventeen times in E. M. Sait, *American Parties and Elections*, although Sait is somewhat more critical than Odegard and Helms of Ostrogorski's position. V. O. Key's *Politics, Parties and Pressure Groups* is the only modern textbook in which he is not cited at all.

[3] *Democracy and the Organization of Political Parties*, (1902), I, li-lii.

[4] *Ibid.*, I, lii-liii.

the organization of English and American parties, Ostrogorski never sought details for merely descriptive purposes, but only as they seemed to him to cast light upon the nature and problems of democratic government.

THE NATURE OF DEMOCRACY

Ostrogorski had his own views as to the nature of democracy, and these views are the ultimate source of his sweeping denunciation of political parties. Democracy, he insisted, is more than just "popular control of government" or "rule by the majority." [5] He was, moreover, unwilling to equate democracy with "government by public opinion." Every government, he reminded his readers, relies on opinion; and the crucial question is whether that opinion is determined by "prejudice and sentiment, crystallized in tradition" [6] or by "reason asserting itself in discussion." [7] Thus, while he was convinced that "the first postulates of democracy is the active participation of the great mass of the citizens" such participation was, for Ostrogorski, merely a means to the end of rational, judicious, and unimpassioned popular discussion of public affairs.[8] In a healthy democracy, he wrote, "public spirit"—which he equated with a plenitude of popular concern for the common weal and a universal willingness to work for it actively—is indispensable. But this does not, he warned his readers, make it any easier for a democracy to achieve. "The advent of democracy," he wrote, "coincided with, and, to some extent, was caused by, a social evolution, which has made life more and more complex, has multiplied and intensified private interests—cares as well as pleasures—both of a moral and of a material kind. Thus it came about that, from the time the public weal has demanded the greatest attention from each citizen, the great majority have found themselves less than ever in a position to respond. . . ." [9] In Ostrogorski's opinion, therefore, one of the first tests which should be applied to any supposedly democratic institution is: Does it tend to generate or to destroy public spirit?

Democracy nevertheless meant to Ostrogorski responsibility to the people on

[5] *Ibid.*, I, 215. Ostrogorski, in fact, was by no means convinced that really important public questions (e.g., Irish Home Rule) *should* be settled by a bare majority. *Ibid.*, I, 309. Cf. n. 12 below.

[6] *Ibid.*, II, 637. Ostrogorski seems to have believed, however, that democracy in this sense is possible only where the people are all well educated. Although he nowhere elaborated this point, he did make one passing reference to the deficiencies of the sort of average, uneducated people who attended ward caucuses in England. Such people, he said, "are only capable of showing approval or disapproval and can never elaborate ideas." *Ibid.*, I, 351.

[7] *Ibid.*, II, 623. He goes yet further, in an *obiter dictum* in the same paragraph, and asserts that "government pure and simple of opinion is only a despotism pure and simple."

[8] *Ibid.*

[9] *Ibid.*, II, 624.

the part of those in public office, and his conception of the nature of responsibility deeply affected his ideas about party. He believed, in sharp contrast to the writers taking the Wilsonian position, that responsibility, if it is to have any real meaning and effectiveness, must be purely *individual* responsibility. The "collective responsibility" associated in the minds of some scholars with party government in the English Parliament seemed to Ostrogorski to entail "general irresponsibility."

> It is the party that comes up for judgment before the electors, and whether it is convicted or acquitted, all its members are censured or commended without distinction, the good as well as the bad; it is not so much they and their merit or demerit that are involved, as the government which they support or oppose. The ministers, in their turn, easily hide behind the collective title; however incompetent or culpable they may be, it is impossible to punish one of them without punishing all. . . .[10]

That is to say that, in his opinion, neither the individual member nor the individual minister nor the ministry as a whole is really responsible to the people.

Clearly, as the above citation shows, Ostrogorski's conception of democracy was essentially atomistic. He thought of a democratic society as one in which isolated individuals engage in the rational discussion of public affairs, freely combining with other individuals on the basis of identity of views on particular issues. His picture of a really democratic political process as the constant formation and dissolution of these idea-groups, as will be pointed out below, underlay his recommendation in favor of "single issue parties" as the cure for the ills of popular government.

Ostrogorski was fully aware of the difficulty of finding the institutional machinery necessary for achieving democracy. Democratic thinkers had largely neglected this crucial question, he observed; in their easy assumption that democracy will function automatically he saw the major reason for their shock and disappointment at how democracy works out in practice.[11] If genuine popular government is to exist and prosper, he declared, some agency must be found to solve such of its problems as

> how to counteract the want of public spirit peculiar to democracies; how to check the general cowardice which characterizes them; how to transform fear into a sense of the moral responsibility which would bring the power of social intimidation to its maximum of elevation and, consequently, of efficiency; how to temper the despotism of public opinion, to protect minorities against majorities, and, in general, to strengthen the individual as against the sovereign multitude; how to promote the rise in democracy of an elite to guide it; how to prevent the ideal, which is its life-blood, from wasting away; how, in a word, to maintain and develop its living forces and not to allow the democratic regime to sink into an

---

[10] *Ibid.*, II, 716. See also *ibid.*, II, 523-24, 716-20.

[11] *Ibid.*, II, 607-13.

automatic contrivance without a soul and without a conscience, which would only fall an easier prey to selfish ambitions and appetites.[12]

Ostrogorski was, however, profoundly dissatisfied with the agency modern democracy had, in his view, called into existence to deal with these problems. The democracies, he insisted, had acted hastily in this regard, and had, without sufficient thought and study, pinned their hopes upon "a methodical organization of the electoral masses, by extra-constitutional means and in the form of disciplined and permanent parties." [13] On the other hand, he was by no means attracted to the current theory that something called "responsible party government" will provide the best available answer to these problems: "This theory appeared alluring enough to be adopted by some writers of prominence, and expanded, in certain cases, with brilliancy of literary style. It has, however, one defect: it is not borne out by the facts." [14]

Ostrogorski therefore set about his study of the English and American party systems with the avowed purpose of analyzing the actual performance of political parties as democratic agencies, and of testing the theory that they alone can provide the institutional machinery necessary for democracy.

ANALYSIS OF POLITICAL PARTIES

Unlike such writers as Woodrow Wilson and A. Lawrence Lowell, Ostrogorski recognized no important differences between English and American parties, and thus could make no sense of the notion that English parties should be taken as "models" that American parties might emulate. He did not, of course, regard American parties as identical with English parties, but he was able to point to four basic traits (permanence, domination by small cliques of "wire-pullers," the near-religious devotion and loyalty demanded of party followers, and the tendency to develop their real centers of power *outside* the formal government) that they shared with British parties; and he was convinced that, in the background of these common characteristics, any differences could be dismissed as relatively unimportant.

Among these four common characteristics, Ostrogorski laid his major emphasis upon the first—that is, on the fact that the parties were, on the record, *permanent* organizations designed for the exclusive purpose of capturing and retaining power, rather than (what he would have wished them to be) temporary organizations called into existence only to promote particular public policies. He cited as an example the Republican party in the United States which, despite the fact

---

[12] *Ibid.*, II, 646-47. See the concluding pages of the present chapter for the writer's comments upon Ostrogorski's concern, here and elsewhere, for minority and individual rights against the "unbridled majority." See n. 5 above.

[13] *Ibid.*, I, 3.

[14] *Democracy and the Party System in the United States* (New York: The Macmillan Company, 1910), p. 380.

that its apparent original objective was to combat the spread of slavery and to resist secession, had continued to exist and grow strong long after both of these issues were settled, and thus long after its avowed *raison d'etre* had disappeared. In England, similarly, the historic issues that had given rise to the Liberals and Conservatives had, in his opinion, been settled long ago; yet the parties persisted. Why? Because in both nations the party leaders and members were really interested only in getting and keeping power, and because particular issues and policies were important to them only insofar as they contributed to the winning of power. Ostrogorski believed, moreover, that all the other common characteristics of the English and American party systems could be traced to this one fundamental feature.[15] His language, indeed, often suggests that all four of the indictments he rests upon the four common characteristics are merely different ways of saying the same things.

Thus, with regard to the second of the four traits, Ostrogorski declared that in both countries political parties are always controlled by small groups of leaders rather than by the totality of their members, and that such party arrangements as the Birmingham Caucus, are mere shows of "representative control."[16] He was not willing to concede that these leaders are the parties' ablest statesmen, picked on the basis of receiving the widest public acclaim. They are, rather, the parties' most successful wire-pullers, and achieve party leadership because of their superior skill in the art of intraparty manipulation—the natural leaders, that is to say, for permanent organizations bent upon getting and keeping power for its own sake.[17]

The third of the four common characteristics is, recognizably, merely the obverse of the second: both English and American parties demand and receive from their members, in Ostrogorski's view, a blind adherence to dogma and a passionate organizational loyalty resembling nothing so closely as that exacted by a church. Without these things, indeed, the kind of leaders he described could not maintain themselves in power; and Ostrogorski did not hesitate to seize upon what seemed to him to be the obvious analogy:

Party came down to us as an inheritance of the theological and ecclesiastical age. Its organization resembled that of the adherents of a Church; its principles or programme constituted a creed invested, like the creed of a Church, with the sanction of orthodoxy and heterodoxy. The adherence had to be undivided; one could not differ from the party or any article of its faith any more than one could choose between the dogmas of a religion. Like the Church which takes charge of all the spiritual needs of man, Party demanded the whole citizen. Conformity with

[15] *Democracy and the Organization of Political Parties*, II, 656-58, 671-74.

[16] For Ostrogorski's comments and illustrations of this point with respect to English parties, see *ibid.*, I, 329-30, 332-34, 345-46. For the parallel discussion regarding American parties, see *ibid.*, II, 58, 128-29, 203-04, 208-09.

[17] For English parties as illustrations, see *ibid.*, I, 352, 529. For American parties, see *ibid.*, II, 216, 285.

the party creed was the sole rule of political conduct; like a religious faith it conferred saving grace on all its members, present and to come, without further effort on their part.[18]

From these three common characteristics the fourth flows as a matter of course: in both countries the parties tend to establish their real centers of power entirely outside the formal government and thus beyond the reach of the publicity and legal sanctions that might hinder the machinations of the party leaders and so reduce their power to exact unquestioning obedience from party members. Ostrogorski was aware that, traditionally, this tendency was more marked in the United States than in England; but he was confident that such party organizations as the Birmingham Caucus, the Liberal and Conservative Central Associations, and the annual party conferences would finally bring the English parliamentary parties under complete domination by non-parliamentary and extra-constitutional organizations. The trend, he believed, is for the English parties to become more like the American, rather than the reverse.[19]

Despite his insistence upon these four alleged basic similarities, Ostrogorski was willing to call up for examination certain differences between English and American parties; but given his assumptions it was inevitable that his sympathies should lie with the former. American parties, he argued, differ from English ones in that they are dominated by a particular type of party leader known as "the boss," whom he distinguished from the "wire-puller" who controlled English parties in two respects. In the first place, while English party leaders apparently desire power for a wide variety of ·reasons, the American party bosses enter politics for just one reason: the spoils. The bosses, that is to say, do not love power for its own sake, or because they want the thrill of being President-makers. Less still do the bosses wish to advance particular public policies. They are in politics to make money—as much as possible in any way possible.[20] In the second place, while English party leaders are concerned with national politics and are obliged to work through national organizations, the American bosses are strictly local figures working exclusively in local politics. He was fully aware that the national parties are made up of coalitions among various local bosses, but he was convinced that no individual boss ever attempts to extend his personal dominion beyond the limits of his particular state, and that few try to boss even so wide an area as a state. It is this fact, in Ostrogorski's opinion, that enables the American bosses to carry on their manipula-

---

[18] *Democracy and the Party System in the United States,* p. 436. See also *ibid.,* pp. 437-39; and *Democracy and the Organization of Political Parties,* II, 587-88, 621-22.

[19] Chapters 1 and 2, volume I, part two, of *Democracy and the Organization of Political Parties* are devoted largely to an elaboration of this point.

[20] *Ibid.,* II, 190-91, 197, 199-200, 300-01, 405. See also *Democracy and the Party System in the United States,* p. 413.

tions in a secrecy and silence that the wire-pullers of the English parties might well envy but cannot emulate.[21]

Ostrogorski was, however, indifferent to any claims to superiority that the English parties might rest upon the fact that their leaders are "wire-pullers" rather than "bosses"; and he vigorously dissented from the view that English parties should be taken as *the* standard in the light of which American parties should be reformed. As regards the effect of each of the two party systems upon its government, he felt (as Dr. Johnson felt about Rousseau and Voltaire) that they surpass each other in iniquity.

EVALUATION OF AMERICAN PARTIES

The English party system, in which men like Wilson and Lowell found so much to admire, in Ostrogorski's view serves merely to obscure the responsibility of the individual Members of Parliament, to discourage the country's able men from entering public life, to crush dissent and promote a slavish orthodoxy and truckling to the majority, and to ruin local government by introducing irrelevant national questions and national animosities.[22] But his verdict upon the American party system was no less severe. It has, he charged, (1) weakened and crippled American government in all its aspects, and (2) eliminated from the American political scene precisely those conditions under which it is possible for democracy to be born. The bill of particulars which he brought forward in connection with each of these two charges demonstrates, as the reader will see in the following paragraphs, the bitterness of Ostrogorski's condemnation of parties and the depth of his conviction that most of the ills of the American system can be explained in terms of the influence of parties.

Ostrogorski's first major charge, then, is that no single part of the formal constitutional government of the United States has escaped the crippling touch of party, and he invited his readers to consider, first of all, the Chief Magistracy. Intended by the founding father to be the symbol of the nation's unity and the apex of its power, he contended, the President, under the corrupting influence of party, has "ceased to be head of the nation," and has become the "head of a party." Even as the head of a party, however, he exercises powers that are merely nominal, and his position is devoid of dignity: "He was not at liberty to assert his initiative, to give the party a policy, to form comprehensive designs and far-reaching plans on its behalf, for all the interests of the party were reduced to the immediate preoccupations of its Organization, to its appetites,

---

[21] *Democracy and the Organization of Political Parties*, II, 195, 224, 406.

[22] The whole of the first volume of *Democracy and the Organization of Political Parties* is devoted to a documentation of these charges. For more specific references to them, however, the reader is referred to the following places, where the emphases listed above are, in that order, discussed: 300-06, 493-95, 605-12; 348-49, 490-91; 350-51, 587-95; and 492-94.

which sought satisfaction in the patronage entrusted to the President by the constitution. The President was left with the role of grand cup-bearer of the party." [23] With the Presidency subordinated to the party it is, moreover, impossible for the civil service to remain undefiled; and on Ostrogorski's reading of the record party had early "deteriorated the public service by destroying all stability in it, by setting up intrigue and favour in place of merit, competence, and professional zeal, and leaving the door wide open to adventurers and hungry mercenaries." [24]

Even more tragic from the democratic point of view, said Ostrogorski, is the degeneration of American legislatures—those bodies to which democratic government assigns the great task of debating and formulating public policy. The Congress of the United States, which should have been the greatest of all legislatures, has come in the course of time to be composed entirely of men who have "succeeded in 'getting the delegates,' or in ingratiating themselves with the Machine or the boss." Such men, said Ostrogorski,

enter Congress as slaves of the Machine and the boss, or sordid parochial considerations, or of powerful private interests, industrial or financial, which are so often in league with the Machine. One or another of these servitudes of mind and conscience, or even all combined, is what they have to pay for their seat. The House therefore is simply a diet of representatives of private or local interests, and it has been aptly remarked that every interest is represented in it but the public interest.[25]

Once in office, moreover, these minions of the machine naturally act as lackeys of the omnipotent caucus, and the legislature, itself dominated by a mere minority of its members, becomes an instrument for defeating the purposes of popular government:

Majority rule, which is the pretence and vindication of the caucus, is reduced to minority rule; not only is the minority of the party crushed out, but the majority of the legislative body is deprived of its will and its power. A corrupt minority may dictate laws. Freedom of speech is as much annihilated as freedom of vote, and legislation by discussion under the eye of the public is replaced by secret conclaves. Irresponsible bodies themselves, they free and shelter from all responsibility the representatives of the people; the most scandalous vote finds a ready excuse: "it was a caucus measure," they could not help it. Cowardly and servile to the behests of the party chieftains, these legislators may defy public opinion, which has itself conferred on them the power to do so by acquiescing in the false assumption of the sacredness of the caucus decision.[26]

[23] Ibid., II, 540-41. See also ibid., II, 34, 86-87, 129, 130-31; and Democracy and the Party System in the United States, pp. 365-67.

[24] Democracy and the Organization of Political Parties, II, 52.

[25] Ibid., II, 544-45.

[26] Democracy and the Party System in the United States, p. 292. See also ibid., pp. 284-90; and Democracy and the Organization of Political Parties, II, 394-96, 542-46.

Ostrogorski turned a deaf ear to the argument, advanced by Henry Jones Ford and Frank J. Goodnow, that American parties have performed a great service by counteracting the effects of separation of powers. Far from coordinating the legislative and executive agencies, he replied, parties have in fact widened the gap between them. After all, he pointed out, from Jackson's retirement to McKinley's administration, excepting only the unusual situation of the Civil War, the Presidency and both Houses of Congress had never been controlled throughout an entire four-year term by the same party. And whenever party control has been split, the legislative-executive animosity had intensified rather than diminished. He conceded that one party had controlled all branches of the government throughout the McKinley and Roosevelt administrations, but he denied, pointing to the continuous bickering between them through that period, that this weakened his point.[27] Parties have also, by putting weak tools of the caucus into both Congress and the White House, made it impossible for either (whether they were of the same party or of different parties) to check the other. In short, he concluded, "The Caucus, without preventing, as we have seen, the mischievous effects of the separation of powers, has nullified all its advantages." [28]

Finally, Ostrogorski charged that American parties have weakened the real training-ground of democracy: "Local self-government, which in Anglo-Saxon communities had, from time immemorial so to speak, set in motion the whole political machinery, has subsided under the action of the caucus. In its anxiety for the spoils of presidential patronage, it has subordinated all the elections, from those of the township up to the presidential election." [29] The inevitable and grievous result, he said, has been the bringing about of "a harmful centralization, which by stifling self-regulated local life and by enfeebling men's initiative and volition, dries up the sap of a political community and preys upon the very roots of its existence." [30] If local government, the fountainhead of a healthy democratic spirit, is corrupted and enfeebled, he warned, democracy cannot flourish in any part of the national life. In short, at all levels of the American system, from local government to the President and Congress, party has, in Ostrogorski's judgment, crippled the formal constitutional government, perhaps beyond repair.

In setting forth the second of his two grand indictments of parties, Ostrogorski moved from the recognition that the metamorphosis they have wrought in the formal government might have been well worthwhile *if* it had resulted in genuine democracy in the American system. His point was that this is precisely what the metamorphosis has *not* entailed, and that the very conditions

[27] *Ibid.*, II, 554.

[28] *Ibid.*, II, 546.

[29] *Democracy and the Party System in the United States*, p. 379.

[30] *Democracy and the Organization of Political Parties*, II, 553. See also *ibid.*, II, 384-85.

upon which democracy, in his judgment, depends have in large part ceased to obtain in the United States because of the impact of the parties upon American society. For one thing, the people have lost any meaningful power of choice they might have had vis-a-vis their public officials, so that the government is removed from any effective popular control. Under the convention system the parties created for making nominations,

[The people] were helpless. Imprisoned in the convention system and the dogma of "regularity," they could only ratify unconditionally the selections made for them, and Benton was not far from the truth when he said: "The people have no more control over who is to be the President than the subjects of kings have over the birth of the child who is to be their ruler." "And," added this old associate of Jackson and Van Buren, "until this system (the convention system) is abolished, and the people resume their rights, the elective principle of our government is suppressed." [31]

Ostrogorski, however, went much further than Benton: the parties, he said, have also made impossible the emergence of the able, courageous, and spirited leadership which democracy requires by liquidating the contextual presuppositions of such leadership:

Real leadership can be obtained in a political community only on four essential conditions: the men capable of exercising the leadership must have easy access to public life; these men who are allowed political influence must assume the responsibility attaching to it; for this responsibility to be a reality it must be enforced by proper control; to be efficacious the action of the leaders must be sure of continuity. Now, under the Caucus regime, ideas, convictions, character, disqualify a man for public life; they make him, to use the regular expression, "unavailable," whether it is a case of filling the Presidency of the Republic or the office of mayor of a city. The party Organization always gives the preference to colourless, weak, easily managed men.[32]

But the indictment is still incomplete: Ostrogorski called upon his readers to recognize that, in the situation American parties had created, the formation and expression of a genuine public opinion had come to be quite out of the question. Nothing resembling real public discussion of issues could take place, and therefore no legitimate public opinion could emerge, because the party regime "discouraged independence of thought, initiative, and self-confidence; it put a premium on the selfishness of the citizen who wanted to shirk concern for the public welfare and devote all his energies to money-making. Why, indeed, should he concern himself? Did not the party Machine provide the elector with his convictions, did it not prescribe to him his conduct, his political sympathies

---

[31] *Ibid.*, II, 91. See also *ibid.*, II, 389-90, 540; and *Democracy and the Party System in the United States*, pp. 364-65.

[32] *Democracy and the Organization of Political Parties*, II, 560. See also *ibid.*, II, 237-313, 562-66.

and antipathies, the choice of men—all cut and dried and ready for use?" [33]
And if, by some miracle, the people nevertheless had remained capable of
arriving at considered opinions about public matters, the parties had nevertheless deprived them of all facilities for giving them effective expression. There
was no longer anything to vote for except one or the other of the two great
parties, each with its "omnibus" platform laden with platitudes on every conceivable issue. Ostrogorski's is perhaps the classic statement of this recurrent
point of view regarding the party process in the United States:

Consequently, what was pompously called the national verdict was, as a rule,
tainted with ambiguity and uncertainty; a group of electors gave or refused its
approval to the party or to its champions in consideration of this or that point of
the composite programme which they put forward, another group did the same
on the ground of some other point. And after "the voice of the country had spoken,"
people did not know exactly what it had said, and very often were entitled to
wrangle over the meaning of the vote; for, however paramount a particular question may have been in the public mind, considerations foreign to it constantly
entered into the "popular verdict." [34]

Ostrogorski did not hesitate to drive the point home by restating it in terms
of his assumptions regarding the strategic role of public spirit in democratic
society. In effect, he was saying, the United States, by acquiescing in the development of the political parties he described, had invited its citizens to
develop an attitude of indifference towards the public welfare:

The first problem . . . which arises in democratic practice is the following: how
to so organize political action as to develop spontaneous and regular impulse, to
stimulate individual energies and not let them fall asleep. The party system offered
its solution: Let the citizens choose a party, let them enlist in it for good and all,
let them give it full powers, and it will undertake to supply the required impetus.
Put forward with every semblance of political piety, this solution found favour
with the citizens, and enabled them to sink, with an untroubled conscience, into
their habitual apathy. . . . They raised political indifferentism to the level of a
virtue, and this aloofness has combined with the ignorance of the masses to repress
public spirit.[35]

Indifference to public welfare does not, however, mean indifference to party;
and Ostrogorski's thesis was that a full understanding of the American party
system involves the recognition that the "regularity" it demands and receives
is merely another word for slavish subordination, for pusillanimity, and at the
margin, for an adulation incompatible with freedom:

The ritual cult with which it surrounds the "majority," the "party," gives a quasi-

---

[33] *Ibid.*, II, 566-67.

[34] *Ibid.*, II, 618-19. See also *ibid.*, II, 231, 261-63, 278-79; and *Democracy and the
Party System in the United States*, pp. 391-92.

[35] *Democracy and the Organization of Political Parties*, II, 625-26. See also *ibid.*, II,
569-71.

concrete form to the undefined authority of numbers which strikes the imagination of the individual and casts a spell over his will; it makes this authority still more urgent, more irresistible. Party "regularity" sets up an external standard for political conduct, which thrusts back the unseen guide, conscience, which puts a sort of barrier between it and the citizen; he cannot cross this barrier without the risk of being caught in the very act of "irregularity" by the first passer-by; all eyes are upon him to see if he follows the route indicated by the visible sign; how can he help falling into line? The life of the party is, consequently, only one long school of servile submission. All the lessons the citizen receives in it are lessons in cowardice. . . .[36]

This state of affairs has led as a matter of course to the people's abdication of their democratic rights and duties, concluded Ostrogorski, and to the seizure of power by the plutocracy. American government has become merely the handmaid of the great business interests, and "democracy" a term with little relevance to the facts of American politics.[37] Ostrogorski held, indeed, that if the people's liberties have not yet entirely disappeared it is merely because "the American Constitution has made the fundamental rights of the man and of the citizen safe from oppression by placing them under the sovereign protection of the courts, which can annul as unconstitutional not only administrative acts, but laws themselves; and the judiciary, taken as a whole, is not yet under the thumb of the bosses." [38] In a word, the people have retained only such scraps of freedom as the Constitution has placed beyond the debasing influence of the parties.

It remains to examine Ostrogorski's account of why all this has happened, and his views as to what can conceivably be done to improve the situation.

EXPLANATION OF AMERICAN PARTIES

Ostrogorski was familiar with the argument that men like Wilson, Lowell, and Ford were advancing to the effect that political parties were prevented from producing better results in the United States because they were forced to operate in a hostile environment.[39] He flatly rejected the whole line of argument, however, and insisted always that the real trouble lay in the deficiencies of the parties themselves rather than in their environment.[40] Concretely, Ostrogorski held that the real issue turns on one of the fundamental characteristics of American parties (and of English parties also), namely the fact that they are permanent organizations, primarily concerned not with public policy or with popular discussion of issues or with promoting public spirit, but with

---

[36] *Ibid.*, II, 635-36.

[37] *Ibid.*, II, 572-74.

[38] *Ibid.*, II, 413-14.

[39] *Ibid.*, II, 560-61. The argument, he caustically observed, was advanced by "some with ability and vigour, others with more zeal than discretion." *Ibid.*

[40] *Democracy and the Party System in the United States,* pp. 380-87.

getting and keeping power. The question whether organizations of this basic character can serve the purposes of, or play a helpful role in, democratic government he did not regard as open. One of his axioms was: you have democratic government only where parties dissolve as soon as the particular issues they are interested in are settled. On Ostrogorski's showing, furthermore, this deficiency is the source of all the other traits that make American parties unfit for participation in truly democratic government: they can win power only if they maintain armies of professionals, only if they finance those armies with corruption and the spoils of office, only if they crush any deviation from party "regularity" among either the voters or public officials, and only if they do all the other things that corrupt the formal government and destroy the conditions necessary for democracy.[41] The axiom, more concisely stated, affirms that permanent parties cannot, in the very nature of the case, fail to act undemocratically, and that this would be true in any environment whatever. He attached great importance to the fact that the English parties, putatively operating in a "favorable environment," and American parties, operating in what was alleged to be an "unfavorable environment," amount to largely the same thing.

Ostrogorski proceeded to pose the question: why had Americans not seen all this for themselves, and repudiated their party system? He sought the answer, in a fashion typical of his age, in an assumed "national character." Americans had been too busy making money to bother much about civic affairs, or about the good health of their democracy.[42] Their concentration upon material success, he pointed out, had even had the incredible result of making many of them see in the successful boss "a master spirit. He excites admiration like those *conquistadores* who conquered and plundered empires. Even cultivated men of high integrity cannot always resist this feeling of admiration for the favourites of fortune, honest folk or rascals, which pervades the air of the New World. One would almost think that they are proud of the bosses." [43] Again, Ostrogorski observed, the inherent optimism of most Americans, their common belief that "things are bound to turn out for the best, if left alone," operates in favor of the machine,[44] as does their intense national pride. Because of their optimism they can, in Micawberish fashion, tolerate the machine's worst abuses without real fears regarding their ultimate consequences; and because of their pride they can turn a deaf ear to the complaints of "agitators" and "reformers" who might make them aware of what is amiss.[45] Finally, we find Ostrogorski observing that the individual American is an isolated and lonely

---

[41] *Democracy and the Organization of Political Parties,* II, 656-58; *Democracy and the Party System in the United States,* pp. 671-74.

[42] *Ibid.,* pp. 398-400.

[43] *Democracy and the Organization of Political Parties,* II, 407.

[44] *Democracy and the Party System in the United States,* pp. 400-01.

[45] *Ibid.,* pp. 401-08.

person who needs political parties which, while depriving him of responsibility, yet give him a sense of "belonging." [46]

In the final analysis, however, the key to Ostrogorski's analysis is his assertion that the machine feeds and thrives upon the very want of public spirit which it produces. This means, at the margin, that the "better people" in the community, who alone might provide the leadership necessary for breaking the grip of the machine, avoid politics—not because they deem politics reprehensible, but because it does not pay.[47] Democracy can exist, he was deeply convinced, only where the people desire it deeply enough to make its achievement and retention the central purpose of their lives. But this central purpose, he believed, is no longer to be found even among the potential leaders of the American community.

ACHIEVING DEMOCRACY IN THE AMERICAN SYSTEM

Ostrogorski was so convinced that the existence of permanent political parties is the major obstacle to the achievement of democracy in the United States as to believe that no proposal for reform that starts from any other premise deserves serious attention. He had no hope, for example, that the citizens can defeat a "bad" party by supporting its rival. All permanent parties are bad parties; and in any electoral contest between such parties the sure loser is democracy itself.[48]

Similarly, Ostrogorski denied that the direct primary proposals then current could effect any real reform of American parties. Everyone recognized, he said, that the direct primary, where it had been adopted, had been singularly ineffective in breaking the bosses' power; and he was certain it would continue to be ineffective.[49] Nor had there ever, in his opinion, been any good reason to expect it to change matters, since it had clearly been an attempt to make the state regulate something that lay beyond its reach: "The State is as powerless against the despotism wielded over the members by the party or its represen-

---

[46] *Ibid.*, pp. 409-12. Ostrogorski also suggested that Americans had not become worried by the bosses' seizure of power because government itself had traditionally occupied only a very small portion of their lives, and because, in the one area where government might have become very important, their individual liberties had been protected by the Constitution and the courts. Thus the machine's theft of the government had not entailed the consequences for the United States that it would in such areas as Europe or Latin America, where government had assumed great importance in the lives of all. *Ibid.*, pp. 412-15.

[47] *Democracy and the Organization of Political Parties*, II, 433, 438-39. Cf. Bryce's chapter on "Why the Best Men Do Not Go into Politics" in volume II of *The American Commonwealth*, pp. 37-43, in which he concludes that "in America, while politics are relatively less interesting than in Europe and lead to less, other careers are relatively more interesting and lead to more."

[48] *Ibid.*, II, 439-40, 457-58.

[49] *Ibid.*, II, 516-20, 532; *Democracy and the Party System in the United States*, pp. 345-48.

tatives, legitimate or not, as it is against the despotism wielded by the Church over its followers, each despotism being founded on the willing or passive assent of the very persons on whom it presses. The victims of this despotic power can only liberate themselves from it by liberating their conscience. If they are unable to do this, the arm of the State cannot help them." [50]

All attempts to incorporate parties into the state, he believed, were similarly doomed to fail of their purpose.[51]

The general line of attack for achieving democracy in the American system, on the other hand, seemed quite clear to Ostrogorski. It consists—naturally enough in view of the ideas summarized in the foregoing paragraphs—in striking at the *permanence* of the political parties, in "discarding the use of permanent parties with power as their end, and in restoring and reserving to party its essential character of a combination of citizens formed specially for a particular political issue. . . ." [52] Instead of the old permanent organizations, the country should build "special organizations, limited to particular objects." The parties will then cease to hold their members in a "vise-like grip," and public opinion will express itself in what Ostrogorski believed to be the ideal manner, that is, through "combinations forming and re-forming spontaneously, according to the changing problems of life and the play of opinion brought about thereby. Citizens who part company on one question would join forces on another." [53]

Ostrogorski labeled the new kind of political organization he envisaged "single issue parties"; and he was convinced that they could produce the desired results. The armies of professional politicians would disappear, and with them the root-cause of corruption. "Party regularity" would cease to have meaning. The citizens would concentrate their attention on the issues, discuss them rationally, and freely make up their own minds.[54] The will of the people would clearly express itself on each individual issue, because the voters "instead of being jumbled together in an ill-assorted compound and kept mechanically in the fixed grooves of permanent parties . . . [would] be able to combine and recombine at will, according to their natural affinities, in homogeneous categories." [55] Politics would once more be pure and meaningful; the able men of the community would come forward to enter public life; and, as a result of all these things, democracy would come into its own.[56]

The means Ostrogorski recommended for substituting single issue parties

---

[50] *Democracy and the Organization of the Political Parties*, II, 518.
[51] *Democracy and the Party System in the United States*, pp. 427-28.
[52] *Democracy and the Organization of Political Parties*, II, 658.
[53] *Ibid.*
[54] *Ibid.*, II, 658-63.
[55] *Ibid.*, II, 664-65.
[56] *Ibid.*, II, 669-70, 681-91, 712-16.

for permanent ones was a system of nonpartisan nominations and elections, the essential characteristics of which he conceived in the following terms: There would be a "preliminary" election, for which any aspirant to office would be eligible by petition. The three aspirants who poll the highest number of votes would be placed upon the ballot for the "final" election. In both elections the voters would be allowed to indicate their first, second, and third preferences, with a system of transferable votes to determine the victors; and in neither election would any candidate be permitted to have any kind of party label attached to his name.[57]

Although deeply committed to this proposal, Ostrogorski was not so blinded as to suppose that merely getting the relevant legal provisions on the statute book would turn the trick. He reminded his readers, as often and as unambiguously as anyone who has ever written on politics, that the effectiveness of any reform depends ultimately upon what happens in the minds of the people:

> Of course this victory over political formalism, if it is to be genuine, must be won first of all in the minds of the electors. . . . There is no legal authority which can issue and enforce the following decree: (1) Permanent parties are and shall be dissolved; (2) the pursuit of power is expressly forbidden to parties; (3) the electors shall henceforth display public spirit. To make such an enactment enforceable, it is necessary to change the mental attitude of the electors, to eradicate those conventional notions, those prejudices which have taken possession of their minds, and which make them believe that the citizen who follows his party blindly is a "patriot," and that the prostitution of power to a party is a pious action. These *idols*, as Bacon would say, must be destroyed.[58]

It was Ostrogorski's fondest hope that his works would in some significant measure contribute to the destruction of those idols.

APPRAISAL

Ostrogorski did his thinking about these problems on the basis of a still-unsurpassed mass of facts concerning party organization and history in the United States and England; and no reader who follows the inquiry from beginning to end will be disposed to question the earnestness of his attempt to explore all the facets of the problem or his willingness to pursue his line of

---

[57] *Democracy and the Party System in the United States*, pp. 432-33. See also *Democracy and the Organization of Political Parties*, II, 692-95, 702-12, 726-27. In his later work, despite his disavowal of legal "tinkering," Ostrogorski argued that a number of additional reforms would be necessary to produce single issue parties. Among these were: the drastic reduction of the number of elective offices at all levels of government, the recall of all public officials, the substitution of the general ticket system for representation by districts, proportional representation along the lines of the Hare system; and, at the national level in particular, abolition of the Senate's power over appointment, providing seats in Congress for cabinet members, and the creation of a number of "Associate Senators" who would directly represent the great economic interests and thereby eliminate the necessity of pressure politics. See *Democracy and the Party System in the United States*, pp. 446-54.

[58] *Democracy and the Organization of Political Parties*, II, 728.

argument wherever it might lead him. Even those subsequent writers who have been least willing to accept his conclusions have relied heavily upon his factual descriptions of the workings of party organizations.[59] Here, certainly, is a carefully documented attack upon the Wilson-Lowell-Ford-Goodnow position that any defender of that position must come to grips with.

For purposes of criticism, however, it is necessary to distinguish between (a) Ostrogorski the compiler of facts about party organization and (b) Ostrogorski the proponent of reforms calculated to cure the ills of modern democracy. Ostrogorski the descriptive analyst had torn to shreds the arguments of those who supposed that democracy could be called into existence by legal "tinkering"; but Ostrogorski the reformer had nothing to offer beyond new ventures in tinkering plus a vague plea for popular education against the "idols" of permanent political parties. Since, that is to say, Ostrogorski had himself proved, at least to his own satisfaction, that "permanent" parties had a way of turning such legal reforms as the direct primary, the nonpartisan ballot, and the recall to their own advantage, he is, on his own showing, estopped from appealing to such reforms as a means of producing his "single issue parties." [60]

This was not the only respect in which Ostrogorski revealed an incapacity to subject himself and his ideas to the kind of searching criticism he sometimes turned upon others. Leaving aside the question of whether his "single issue parties" could have been created in the way he proposed to create them, and assuming, for the sake of argument, that they could have been, we are entitled to demand of him an answer to a number of patently unavoidable queries about what would happen next. For example, the public officials, he tells us, are to be elected in the first instance because of their stand on a single issue. Will they not then have to be recalled as soon as a new issue arises on which they hold unpopular views? If so, what is to prevent the constant replacement of elective officials from leading to sheer chaos, or, failing that, to a situation in which the real power of the government will come to vest in permanent, irresponsible administrative officials, who alone can promise the continuity and cohesiveness necessary for the conduct of the affairs of a great nation? Ostrogorski had, in short, no answer to Wellington's question, "How is the King's government to be carried on?" Apparently he never attempted to find

---

[59] Cf. Schattschneider, *Party Government*, p. 213; and Merriam and Gosnell, *The American Party System*, p. 133.

[60] Cf. Frank J. Goodnow's judgment that "any one who has had the opportunity which [Ostrogorski] has had to study parties, can believe that such devices will have any permanent value, is almost incredible. That he should seriously propose them as remedies of any importance is absurd." Review, of *Democracy and the Organization of Political Parties*, p. 334; and Professor Macmahon's conclusion that "despite the apparent sophistication involved in [Ostrogorski's] method of observation . . . the core of his thinking was a vast naivete, which indeed was the ardent spirit of the man himself" in *Encyclopaedia of the Social Sciences*, VI, 504.

such an answer. Nor did he ever inquire whether the Constitution of the United States, with its numerous patently undemocratic features, might provide a more convincing explanation of some of the undemocratic aspects of American life than the "national character" in terms of which he sought to explain them.[61] Nor, finally, does Ostrogorski appear to have asked himself at any time whether he was working from doctrinaire assumptions regarding "democracy" that were uniquely his own, and thus unlikely to be accepted as standards by his prospective readers.

Most of the difficulties in Ostrogorski's general position, moreover, clearly derive from his atomistic conception of democracy. Democracy, for Ostrogorski, was inconceivable save as a society of isolated individuals, all prepared to devote much of their time and energy to rational discussion of public affairs, all eager to form an association with others who hold identical views on a given issue, and all ready to dissolve that association as soon as the issue is settled. Popular *control* of government was not, in itself, Ostrogorski's goal, but rather popular control carried on in a particular way and utilized exclusively for certain enumerated purposes. Ostrogorski was, moreover, unwilling to see the word "democracy" applied to any other kind of popular control.

Now, Ostrogorski's definition of democracy applies to no actual society known either to him or ourselves; and it is doubtful whether any political theorist save Ostrogorski has ever thought in terms of such a definition on any level except that of pure speculation. And, while he was aware that a society based on his conception of democracy would make unprecedented demands upon the time, the energies, the capacity, and the civic virtue of the citizens, he had no reply to offer to the question of how to produce citizens able to meet those demands except the formula: education. While he must have been aware of the chasm that separated him, intellectually and spiritually, from his readers, he took no pains to bridge that gap—as he might have done by stating the case for his objectives and making a genuine effort to convince others that they were realistic objectives. He simply assumed, instead, that those of his readers who sincerely believed in "democracy" would go along with his argument.

The point can, without injustice to Ostrogorski, be pressed still further. In the democracy he envisaged the people would be expected to decide not only (a) what their wants are, but also (b) *how* their wants should be satisfied, and (c) whether or not adequate steps are in fact being taken to satisfy those wants. People capable of deciding these questions would have to be a race of legislative experts who could be counted upon to draw up specific resolutions to society's problems after choosing among the various alternatives. Ostrogorski never really came to grips with the party-government view that the contribution

---

[61] On the contrary, for reasons to be noted below, Ostrogorski believed that the Constitution was one of the few forces in the United States operating to preserve the remnants of democracy.

of the people in a democratic government is necessarily limited to (a) and (c), and that to require them to decide questions of type (b) is to define democracy in such a way as to make it impossible. Now this may or may not be a correct view, but Ostrogorski, by merely assuming that, unless the people do in fact contribute (b), the society is undemocratic without asking (as the writers he criticized were fully prepared to do) whether within the predictable future the people would ever be able to satisfy his demands, cut himself off from those realities of politics which, in some other contexts, he understood as clearly as any of the other writers of his time.[62]

Ostrogorski's greatest failures as a critic of the party-government writers stemmed from his inability to understand that their whole position rests upon a conception of democracy which he completely repudiated. So deeply committed was he to the notions that the essence of democracy is the protection of individual and minority rights and that unrestrained power in the hands of popular majorities is therefore the greatest of all threats to democracy that he never even bothered to defend them against the party-government position that majority-rule is an essential characteristic of democracy.[63] Having already severely criticized the party-government writers for failing to see how fundamental the majority-rule conception of democracy is to their whole position, it is only fair to recognize the basic irrelevance of any criticism that, like Ostrogorski's, attacks them because the kind of party system they advocate is not calculated to provide a kind of "democracy" in which they do not believe. Had Ostrogorski met them on their own ground and argued that his conception of democracy had a better claim to the label than theirs, his consequent blasting of their notions of responsible party government would have been very effective indeed. But as it was, he did not even recognize their basic position, let alone criticize it; and in consequence much of his attack on their ideas about how American parties should be organized is simply beside the point.

---

[62] One can imagine Ostrogorski's replying to this criticism: But until you have a system that makes such demands on the people they obviously will not develop the necessary capacities; and, meantime, how can you assert that they are incapable of doing so? Insofar as this may have been what was in the back of his mind, and insofar as he was willing to accept sight unseen the social, political, and economic consequences of the experiment, this would have been a tenable position. But the point in the text still stands: in his published writings, Ostrogorski simply did not anticipate, and thus did not answer, any such objection.

[63] There is considerable evidence for this assertion, some of which has already been presented: his citation of the constitutional guarantee and judicial protection against popular majorities of individual rights as one of the few bright spots in the American system; his belief that separation of powers could be a good thing if it enabled a "good" President to check a "degenerate" Congress or vice versa; and the running fire he maintained against what he was pleased to call "truckling to the majority." And nowhere in all his writings can one find anything resembling a defence of his position that inviolable minority rights are the essence of democracy. Apparently he simply assumed that no reasonable person could hold the majority-rule conception of democracy.

As just one illustration of this fact, Ostrogorski dismissed the party-government school's notion of *party* responsibility, as embodied in the English system, as nothing more than a screen for actual *ir*responsibility. This has the sound of a damning indictment; but careful examination of the relevant passages in his writings will show that Ostrogorski was merely begging the question (as he begged the question of whether minority rights or majority-rule is the essential condition of democracy). His argument ran as follows: the English version of party responsibility fails to establish popular control over government. The reason it fails is that where you have party responsibility individual responsibility disappears. Why is this important? Because individual responsibility is the only sort that has any meaning. This simply assumes away the question at issue. Unable as he was to conceive of any kind of responsibility other than that of the individual member of parliament to his constituents, he did not hesitate to conclude that the Wilson-Ford idea of party responsibility was sheer nonsense. The point is further complicated by the fact that Ostrogorski moved back and forth, quite uncritically, between two very different meanings of the word "responsibility." In some places he appears to have meant by it direct popular control of accountable public officials, i.e., exactly what the party-government writers meant by it. But in other places he was obviously talking about a sense of self-restraint, an unwillingness of public officers and/or the majority to oppress the rights of minorities and individuals. This confusion made it impossible for him to come to grips with the Wilson-Ford point of view.

Ostrogorski's atomistic picture of democracy obliged him to attack political parties from every angle he could think of, and encouraged him to deny that they had accomplished anything worthwhile. His zeal of advocacy, in the context of his assumption that whatever parties touched they tainted, sometimes tricked him into patent inconsistencies and errors of judgment.[64] He was, for example, capable of criticizing American parties in one place for having the caucus dictate how legislators should vote, and thus debilitating their judgment and conscience, only to argue in another place that American parties had no discipline on matters of public policy, and were interested only in spoils. Clearly, he could not have it both ways. A further example is his attempted refutation of the Ford-Goodnow argument that parties had constituted the one agency making separation of powers workable, and that they had therefore made an invaluable contribution to the operation of American government. Only a zealot would have replied in terms so wide of the mark as Ostrogorski's insistence

---

[64] Ostrogorski's tendency to abandon the judicious, impartial attitude of the scholar and replace it with that of the prosecuting attorney, seizing charges wherever he could find them, was noted and deplored by two contemporary scholars who otherwise were his great admirers. See Jesse Macy's review of *Democracy and the Party System in the United States,* pp. 473-74; and A. W. Small's review of *Democracy and the Organization of Political Parties* in *American Journal of Sociology,* VIII (January, 1903), 565.

that, since the executive and legislative agencies had for many years been in the hands of different parties, the influence of parties was therefore really to widen rather than bridge the gap between the two branches. Ford's and Goodnow's point was that except for the services of parties American government would always be the helpless prisoner of separation of powers, and that split control in the off-years was the result of the staggered terms provided for in the Constitution—the result, that is to say, not of party but of a constitutional framework that made it next to impossible for parties to perform this function all the time. Ostrogorski, who did not understand their position, was thus unable to join issue with them.

Despite its broad scope and wealth of learning, therefore, Ostrogorski's indictment of American parties and his attack upon the party-government point of view cannot withstand close analysis. He assigned to "democracy" an arbitrary definition under which no political parties mankind has ever seen could have any place, and sought to prove, by means of arguments derived from that definition, that parties as he observed them could not possibly be democratic institutions. He therefore had won his battle against parties even before the commencement of hostilities. But it is quite as accurate to say that, from any point of view save his own, he lost the battle.

CHAPTER EIGHT

Herbert Croly

Between 1870 and 1915 a number of American writers were contending that democracy is unattainable in the United States so long as political parties continue to dominate its governmental system. Among the more prominent spokesmen of this point of view were Charles C. P. Clark, Albert Stickney, Samuel E. Moffett, and James S. Brown.[1] Although there were differences among them, they all agreed upon these essential points: Democracy requires the widest possible *direct* popular participation in government, which is impossible where parties interpose themselves between the sovereign citizen and his government. Parties hamper rational popular discussion of public issues, make impossible the meaningful expression of public opinion, and in general corrupt whatever part of the national life they touch. The only way to achieve democracy in the American system, these writers concluded, is to destroy the influence of party. To this end they made a number of proposals for reform, ranging from the plans put forward by Clark and Stickney for government by a pyramidal series of "town meetings" to Brown's proposals that any candidate nominated by a political party be declared legally ineligible.

By far the ablest of the writers taking this general position was Herbert Croly. Originally an architecture critic and editor of the *Architectural Record*, Croly resigned in 1906 to devote the rest of his life to the study of social and political questions. He helped to found the *New Republic* in 1914, and was its editor until his death in 1930.[2]

The bulk of Croly's political thought was contained in his two major works,

---

[1] Their principal works were: Clark, *The Commonwealth Reconstructed* (New York: A. S. Barnes and Company, 1878) and *The "Machine" Abolished and the People Restored to Power* (1900); Stickney, *A True Republic* (New York: Harper and Brothers, 1879), *Democratic Government* (1885), *The Political Problem* (1890), and *Organized Democracy* (Boston: Houghton, Mifflin and Company, 1906); Moffett, *Suggestions on Government* (1894); and Brown, *Partisan Politics: The Evil and Remedy* (Philadelphia: J. B. Lippincott Company, 1897).

[2] A short but useful biography of Croly by George Soule may be found in the *Encyclopaedia of the Social Sciences* (New York: The Macmillan Company, 1937), II, 603. For further biographical information and a number of eulogies on Croly, see the memorial edition of the *New Republic*, LXIII (July 16, 1930), 243-71.

The Promise of American Life and *Progressive Democracy*.[3] In both he proceeded from a fundamental conviction that "the American nation is committed
to a purpose which is not merely of historical manufacture. It is committed to
the realization of the democratic ideal; and if its Promise is to be fulfilled, it
must be prepared to follow whithersoever that ideal may lead." [4] This democratic ideal can be fulfilled, he pointed out, only under certain conditions. For
one thing, Americans must abandon their purely sectional and local loyalties,
and realize that "only by faith in an efficient national organization and by an
exclusive and aggressive devotion to the *national* welfare, can the American
democratic ideal be made good." [5] He labeled this combination of the Jeffer-
sonian democratic ideal with the Hamilton nationalistic ideal "the New Nation-
alism," a phrase which became the battle cry of Theodore Roosevelt and the
Progressive party in 1912.

Croly also recognized that Americans can realize their democratic ideal only
if they (a) fully understand the nature of democracy, and, (b) in the context
of a full understanding, give thought to the problem of what institutions will
achieve it. He was clearly dissatisfied with the state of knowledge and opinion
on both of these problems, and emphasized that no progress can be made in
realizing the democratic ideal until (a) has been accomplished, the relation
between (a) and (b) made clear, and (b) begun. These are the terms in which
he conceived his own task as a political theorist.

THE NATURE OF DEMOCRACY

Croly's conception of democracy was carefully worked out and painstakingly
presented. It represented, as he fully realized, a considerable departure from
the ideas of most of his contemporaries. He was unable to accept their view of
democracy, for, he argued, it was essentially negativistic, and too exclusively
political to be of much value:

One of the great weaknesses of professional democrats in this country has been
their tendency to conceive democracy as essentially a matter of popular political
machinery. From their point of view the way to assure the preservation of a democratic social system was to enable the people to vote upon the qualifications of
the maximum number of public measures. . . . This conception of democracy,
precisely because it fails to associate democracy with the *conscious realization of a
social ideal*, always assumes a negative emphasis. Its dominant object is not to

---

[3] *The Promise of American Life* (New York: The Macmillan Company, 1909), and
Progressive Democracy (1914). Other works by Croly which contain comments relevant
to his ideas about political parties are: *Marcus Alonzo Hanna: His Life and Work* (New
York: The Macmillan Company, 1912) ; "Democratic Factions and Insurgent Republicans,"
North American Review, CXCI (May, 1910), 626-35; "State Political Reorganization,"
American Political Science Review, VI, Supplement (February, 1912), 122-35; and "Test
of Faith in Democracy," *American Magazine*, LXXV (November, 1912), 21-23.
[4] *The Promise of American Life*, p. 6.
[5] *Ibid.*, p. 270. The emphasis is added.

give positive momentum and direction to popular rule. It seeks, above all, to prevent the people from being betrayed—from being imposed upon by unpopular policies and unrepresentative officials. But to indoctrinate and organize one's life chiefly for the purpose of avoiding betrayal is to invite sterility and distintegration.[6]

Croly therefore believed that to equate democracy merely with control of the government by the popular majority is misleading, and that "such a conception of democracy contains only part of the truth." [7] His general position on majority-rule was, therefore, carefully qualified. He stated in general terms his belief that "every popular government should in the end, and after a necessarily prolonged [sic] deliberation, possess the power of taking any action, which, in the opinion of a decisive [sic] majority of the people, is demanded by the public welfare." [8] He denied, however, that there is anything sacred about majority-rule:

Majority-rule, under certain prescribed conditions, is a necessary constituent of any practicable democratic organization; but the actions or decisions of a majority need not have any binding moral and national authority. Majority-rule is merely one means to an extremely difficult, remote, and complicated end; and it is a piece of machinery which is peculiarly liable to get out of order. Its arbitrary and dangerous tendencies can, as a matter of fact, be checked in many effectual and legitimate ways, of which the most effectual is the cherishing of a tradition, partly expressed in some body of fundamental law, that the true people are, as Bismarck declared, in some measure an invisible multitude of spirits—the nation of yesterday and tomorrow, organized for its national historical mission.[9]

Croly's doubts about unfettered majority-rule are intimately related to his conviction that any purely *political* definition of democracy, i.e., any definition of it solely in terms of the location and method of exercise of the ultimate power over government, is inadequate. There must be something in addition: "The assertion of the doctrine of popular Sovereignty is . . . rather the beginning than the end of democracy. There can be no democracy where the people do not rule; but government by the people is not necessarily democratic. The popular will in a democratic state must be expressed somehow in the interest of democracy itself; and we have not traveled very far towards a satisfactory conception of democracy until this democratic purpose has received some definition." [10]

Croly therefore conceived of truly democratic government as popularly controlled governmental machinery *used for a certain purpose*. The distinctively democratic purpose, he believed, is "that of bestowing a share of the responsi-

---

[6] *Progressive Democracy*, pp. 213-14. The emphasis is added. See also *ibid.*, pp. 212-13; and *The Promise of American Life*, pp. 12-17.

[7] *The Promise of American Life*, p. 33.

[8] *Ibid.*, pp. 35-36. See also *ibid.*, pp. 197-98.

[9] *Ibid.*, p. 280.

[10] *Ibid.*, p. 179.

bility and the benefits, derived from political and economic association, upon the whole community." [11] Or, as he put it in another passage, "the salutary and formative democratic purpose consists in using the democratic organization for the joint benefit of individual distinction and social improvement." [12]

Croly was fully aware that the achievement of such a democracy will be by no means easy, and that the discovery and subsequent erection of the appropriate institutions will call for careful thought and unflagging effort. He was, nevertheless, ready with a set of standards by which to evaluate, at least provisionally, any institutions claiming to be democratic:

A democracy, like any other active and progressive community, must have organs for the consideration and the realization of its policy. If it seeks to convert the ballot-box into the chief instrument of democratic action, it will most assuredly disintegrate. It needs an efficient method of representation, but its agents should not represent districts or parties or an elusive and remote public reason. They should represent, first, the essential function of determinate action; secondly, the various vital popular interests and classes; and, finally, the effective popular ideals and aspirations. A system of this kind would enable a democracy at once to act, to deliberate and, most of all, to learn.[13]

It was upon these scales that Croly proceeded to weigh the political parties in the American system.

EVALUATION OF AMERICAN PARTIES

Most American writers of the "anti-party" school, like Ostrogorski, condemned political parties without qualification. Clark, Stickney, Brown, and the rest argued that parties corrupt whatever they touch, and that their persistence in the American system can be explained only in terms of the sloth and ignorance of the masses and the reluctance of the "better people" to lead reform movements against the bosses. Croly, by contrast, felt free to argue that political parties have no place in a genuinely democratic system without first showing that parties have never done anything but harm. He believed, rather, that parties have in fact performed some valuable functions in the American system, particularly on the national level, and that the United States is greatly in their debt: "The two-party system has an extraordinary record of achievement. . . . It has proved to be the one practically effective method of organizing majority-rule and of adapting the exigencies of a complicated and responsible political system to the realities and frailties of human nature." [14]

Croly was convinced, however, that the parties have, despite their past record, outlived their usefulness—perhaps not entirely on the national level, where

[11] *Ibid.*, p. 194.

[12] *Ibid.*, p. 207.

[13] *Progressive Democracy*, p. 528.

[14] *Ibid.*, p. 330. See also *The Promise of American Life*, pp. 125-26, 323.

democracy has by no means been achieved, but certainly in the states, which he regarded as well along toward democracy. Parties, in short, are devices for rendering undemocratic governments somewhat more amenable to the popular will, and should be eliminated as soon as amenability to the popular will can be taken for granted.[15]

Croly was prepared to present a bill of particulars on the unfitness of parties to participate in democratic government. For one thing, he argued, the consequence of the growth of parties anywhere in the American system has always been

a separation of actual political power from official political responsibility. The public officers are still technically responsible for the good government of the states, even if, as individuals, they have not been granted the necessary authority effectively to perform their task. But their actual power is even smaller than their official authority. They are almost completely controlled by the machine which secures their election or appointment. The leader or leaders of that machine are the rulers of the community, even though they occupy no offices and cannot be held in any way publicly responsible.[16]

It was, in other words, inconceivable to him that democratic government can exist so long as institutions like parties contrive the separation of actual power from official responsibility.

Then, too, in what Croly termed a "progressive democracy," the administrative agencies would be called upon to bear the enormous burden of faithfully converting the expressed will of the people into a workable program of governmental action. It would therefore be urgently necessary, he said, for those agencies to be as expert, efficient, and economical as they could possibly be.[17] But observation of the effect of political parties upon the various levels of American administration convinced him that

the overthrow of the two-party system [is] indispensable to the success of progressive democracy, because, under American conditions, the vitality of the two-party system has been purchased and must continue to be purchased at the expense of administrative independence and efficiency. Party government has interfered with genuine popular government both by a mischievous, artificial and irresponsible method of representation, and by an enfeeblement of the administration in the interest of partisan subsistence.[18]

Croly contended, in the third place, that parties undermine the allegiance which the democratic state must command from its citizens, and thus militate against the habits appropriate to such a government:

---

[15] *Progressive Democracy*, pp. 331-33.
[16] *The Promise of American Life*, p. 125.
[17] *Progressive Democracy*, pp. 350-58, 370-77.
[18] *Ibid.*, p. 349. See also *ibid.*, pp. 347-49.

The two-party system, like other forms of representative democracy [*sic*], proposes to accomplish for the people a fundamental political task which they ought to accomplish for themselves. It seeks to interpose two authoritative partisan organizations between the people and their government. It demands of them that they act and think in politics not under the influence of their natural class or personal convictions, but according to the necessities of an artificial partisan classification. In this way it demands and obtains for a party an amount of loyal service and personal sacrifice which a public-spirited democrat should lavish only on the state. The unity of purpose and the effective power of joint action which results from the action of partisan discipline and patriotism should accrue to the benefit not of Republicanism or Democracy, but to that of the nation and of the really significant social ingredients which enter into the national composition.[19]

The essential character of Croly's attack upon parties emerges clearly from these arguments. He had no quarrel with the party-government school's proposition that "representative government is party government." [20] His thesis was, rather, that representative government is itself incompatible with real democracy. The only kind of representative government that has ever existed, Croly pointed out, is that based upon the representation of geographical districts in a legislature which possesses most of the governmental power. The result of such a system has never been the faithful expression of the *national* popular will. On the contrary: "recent political experience has conclusively proved that the executives, elected by the whole constituency, are much more representative of public opinion than are the delegates of petty districts. One hundred district agents represent only one hundred districts and not the whole state, or the state insofar as it is whole." [21]

The universal result of representative government, he believed, is the dominance of politics by the clash of petty localisms, and the exclusion of any real consideration of the general interest.[22]

Croly saw two alternatives between which a non-despotic society must choose: representative government organized by political parties, or direct democracy plus executive power and responsibility. His preference lay with the latter, primarily because, as the above form of wording suggests, he was convinced that political parties, though inseparable from representative government, intensify rather than alleviate the evils attendant upon it. He had, besides those already noted, this further reason for that conviction: political parties, as he understood them, can make representative government work only by develop-

---

[19] *Ibid.*, p. 341. It should here be noted that the parties Croly decided were unfit for democratic government were the *existing American* parties. He said nothing about the Wilsonian double-use of the term, and apparently assumed that all parties are in essence like the American parties he observed. The significance of this view for the value of his criticism will be discussed below.

[20] *Ibid.*, pp. 311-12.

[21] *The Promise of American Life*, pp. 331-32.

[22] *Ibid.*, p. 69. See also "Democratic Factions and Insurgent Republicans," p. 635.

ing strong organizations and by engendering a passionate partisan spirit; but in the process these things tend to become more important than the *official* organization and *public* spirit they are supposed to serve.[23] Thus he could believe that

the partisan organizations, which were created to be the safe, sensitive and efficient agents of popular rule and which were to mediate between the people and their alien government, had ceased to perform any such work. Instead of using the parties to democratize the government, it was becoming necessary to use the government to democratize the parties—to force upon them obedience to the will of their own members. Thus the feeling of mutual confidence which had justified the primitive system of partisan representation, and which contrasted so curiously with the entire lack of confidence in official representations and leadership, faded away. . . . The partisan leaders justified the opposition which the theoretical enemies of any effective concentration of political power have always offered to such concentration. They betrayed their trust.[24]

And Croly did not shrink from the clear implication that democracy cannot survive this reversal of the role of parties.

This, then, is the gist of Herbert Croly's evaluation of political parties in the American system: Parties are indeed necessary to make representative government work, particularly in the United States; representative government without parties has certainly been unworkable in the past, and so the parties that have come into existence to make it work have undeniably performed valuable services. But this does not dispose of the fact that under any conditions representative government tends irresistibly towards government dominated by petty local interests, and thus towards government incompatible with a genuinely democratic order. Moreover, representative government cannot be expected to outgrow its need for the services of political parties; and in the United States the parties are clearly destined to become, under representative government, so overbearing as to convert themselves into masters of the people. On the national level, where real democracy is unlikely for some time to come, there is no alternative but to accept representative government, and to recognize that the parties will continue to play their traditional role. On the state level, however, the situation is ripe for genuinely democratic government, and rapid progress is being made toward its achievement. But in the states, as in any community seeking a democratic system, this will involve destroying the influence of party.

EXPLANATION OF AMERICAN PARTIES

In seeking to explain the nature of American parties, Croly posed two main questions: Why have political parties in fact assumed such an important role

[23] *Progressive Democracy,* pp. 79-80.
[24] *Ibid.,* p. 99.

in the American system of representative government? And why are they unable to provide the kind of "party government" which Wilson, Goodnow, and the others said they should provide? His answer to the first question was similar to that suggested by the party-government writers: Parties are made necessary by the deficiencies of the formal government:

The political system was based on the assumption that the individualism it encouraged could be persuaded merely by the power of words to respect the public interest, that public officials could be deprived of independence and authority for the real benefit of the "plain people," and that the "plain people" would ask nothing from the government but their legal rights. These assumptions were all erroneous; and when associated action and specialized leadership became necessary in local American politics, the leaders and their machine took advantage of the defective official system to build up an unofficial system, better suited to actual popular needs.[25]

Our formal government, in short, is entirely unsuited to the needs of democracy in a non-laissez faire age, particularly at the national level, and political parties have arisen in response to the need for an agency for making the government to some extent amenable to the popular will.

The second question, however, presented more difficulty. Croly began by rejecting as an answer a notion he believed to be current among many reformers: That parties and therefore the government are being run by "bad" men, and that the solution lies in replacing them with "good" men. "When a large number of individuals to whom authority is delegated exercise that authority improperly," Croly commented, "one may assume that the system is at fault as much as the individuals." [26]

In the last analysis, he argued, "party government" on the Wilsonian model cannot be achieved in the United States because the whole idea is self-defeating, and because it calls for a kind of responsibility that cannot be established. The final proof of these contentions, he believed, was provided by the failure of the unique attempt of Woodrow Wilson, the leading exponent of the party-government view, to put the theory into practice in the course of his activities as President. He had nothing but praise for Wilson's "significant, intelligent and gallant attempt to give renewed vitality to partisan government and to convert it into an agency of what he understands by progressivism." [27] The irony of Wilson's attempt, he pointed out, was that its very success was in fact a blow to the party-government theory—a weakening of *party* responsibility and *party* strength. His administration was proving again that in the American system unified party action can apparently be achieved only by strong and able *presidential*

---

[25] *The Promise of American Life*, pp. 124-25. See also *ibid.*, pp. 105-26.

[26] *Ibid.*, p. 321.

[27] *Progressive Democracy*, p. 337.

leadership of the Wilsonian variety. Such leadership, however, not only is not *party* leadership but actually results in weakening it. A strong President, determined to lead his party,

can, of course, hide behind the fiction of partisan responsibility, whenever he wants to avoid speaking to his party about a legislative proposal upon which he is likely to encounter serious resistance; but no suavity of manner and no amount of wise self-restraint in the employment of his power can obscure the real facts of the situation. At the final test the responsibility is his rather than that of his party. The party which submits to such a dictatorship, however benevolent, cannot play its own proper part in a system of partisan government. It will either cease to have any independent life or its independence will eventually assume the form of a revolt.[28]

At the same time, however, nothing resembling "party responsibility" can be achieved without strong presidential leadership; it is clear, therefore, that "the necessity of such leadership is itself an evidence of the decrepitude of the two-party system." [29]

Fundamentally, Croly concluded, American parties exist only because they can render our undemocratic government somewhat less undemocratic. If the government *itself* were made more democratic, parties would no longer have any valid reason to exist:

The organization of a strong official government would not only render the Constitution of less importance, it would also tend to dethrone the party machines. It would imply that the government itself was by way of being democratized, and that the democracy no longer needed to depend upon partisan organizations to represent popular purposes. . . . Such a government could not be controlled by party organizations whose strength depended on the weakness of the official mechanism and which were bound to be weakened just in proportion as the government itself is strengthened.[30]

On this foundation, then, Croly rested his plans for achieving democracy in the American system.

ACHIEVING DEMOCRACY IN THE AMERICAN SYSTEM

If the evils associated with political parties are indeed ultimately due to deficiencies inherent in representative government, Croly contended, some of the reforms then being proposed would prove worse than useless. Any attempt to "restore its purity" to the American system was idle because, for example, the system had in fact never possessed the assumed purity.[31] Many such reforms

---

[28] *Ibid.*, pp. 345-46. See also *ibid.*, pp. 337-46.

[29] *Ibid.*, p. 345.

[30] *Ibid.*, p. 124.

[31] *The Promise of American Life*, pp. 147-50.

—the Australian ballot and the direct primary, for example—actually would, he believed, increase rather than diminish the bosses' power.[32]

The essential point to keep in mind, Croly declared, is that there is *no* way to make an undemocratic government behave in a genuinely democratic manner—whether by "party government" or through some other panacea. Thus democracy cannot be achieved in the American system through any peripheral reforms practiced on the political parties themselves: "If the two-party system is breaking down as an agency for democratizing an undemocratic government, the remedy is not to democratize the party, which was organized to democratize the government, but to democratize the government itself. Just in proportion as the official organization becomes genuinely democratic, it can dispense with the services of national parties."[33]

The goal of reform, Croly affirmed, should be to replace representative government with direct democracy; and the place to begin, for reasons pointed out above, is in the states rather than at the national level.[34] Such a government might well be constructed along the following lines: The policy-suggesting and administration-directing power would be concentrated in the office of the governor.[35] This would, he felt, enable a powerful governor to provide a focal point for public opinion, and the governor would thus become "an able and indispensable instrument of formulation and of collective action."[36] Such an instrument is vital to democratic government, Croly continued, because "public opinion requires to be aroused, elicited, informed, developed, concentrated and brought to an understanding of its own dominant purposes. The value of executive leadership consists in its peculiar serviceability not merely as the agent of a prevailing public opinion, but also as the invigorator and concentrator of such opinion."[37] Croly disagreed with Lowell's view that parties can do this important job better than a strong executive: "Strong individual leadership supplies popular opinion with a needed mental and moral tonic. A vague popular aspiration or a crude and groping popular interest often requires incarnation in a single man, in order to reach a preliminary understanding of its own meaning and purposes. . . . No program is likely to be

---

[32] *Ibid.*, pp. 341-43. Croly believed the Australian ballot helps the boss by removing the publicity and therefore the onus of being one of the boss's paid voters. The direct primary also helps the boss by increasing the number of elections and thus the need for professional election-organizers.

[33] *Progressive Democracy*, pp. 324-25.

[34] *Ibid.*, pp. 267-80.

[35] *Ibid.*, pp. 304-08.

[36] *Ibid.*, p. 304.

[37] *Ibid.*

politically effective unless it is temporarily associated with an effective personality." [38]

The governor must, however, control the full power of the government in order to perform this function effectively; for full responsibility, Croly agreed with Wilson, is possible only where full power is vested.[39]

In the kind of government Croly envisaged the sole function of the legislators would be that of translating the broad policies commanded by the governor and/or the people into workable pieces of legislation. They would be "an experienced body of legal, administrative, and financial experts, comparatively limited in numbers, and selected in a manner to make them solicitous of the whole state."[40] They would, in short, be legislative councils rather than legislatures.

In addition to these devices, the new governments should provide for the full and unfettered operation of direct democracy—the initiative, referendum, and recall: "The essential political responsibility in such a plan of government falls upon the electorate. . . . The electorate reserves for itself an effective immediate or proximate control. At present the powers reserved to the people are accessible only at long intervals and under rare conditions. According to the proposed plan, these powers would always remain in a state of incipient activity." [41] Not only the ultimate power but the ultimate *responsibility* would therefore reside in the people themselves; and that, said Croly, is where it should reside: "The salutary aspect of the agitation in favor of direct legislation consists in its readiness to trust somebody with effective political responsibility. . . . The watchword of the 'progressives,' has become 'trust in the people' and such a trust constitutes manifestly the only possible foundation on which a democracy can erect an enduring superstructure of political institutions." [42] It is precisely this location of ultimate responsibility in the people, Croly declared, that constitutes the fundamental reason why direct rather than representative government is the way to achieve genuine democracy.

Croly was fully aware that he was proposing basic changes in the American system. He did not feel, however, that his scheme was therefore utopian, or incapable of immediate achievement. At any time, he said, "a decisive and resolute popular majority has the power to alter American institutions." [43]

Croly was not so fond of his proposals as to insist that they are the only reforms worth considering. Rather he stressed the need for remaining alert to

---

[38] *Ibid.*, pp. 313-14.

[39] *The Promise of American Life*, p. 324.

[40] *Ibid.*, pp. 327-80. Croly did not make any concrete proposals as to the "manner" of selecting legislators to this end.

[41] *Progressive Democracy*, p. 324.

[42] "State Political Reorganization," p. 128.

[43] *The Promise of American Life*, pp. 24-25. See also *ibid.*, p. 316; and *Progressive Democracy*, pp. 235-37.

new proposals that might embody better means for achieving the substitution of direct democracy for representative government.[44] The main thing, he concluded, is to develop a "decisive and resolute popular majority" convinced that only direct government and executive responsibility can bring democracy to the American system. The development of such a majority is, he believed, the only indispensable reform.

APPRAISAL

There are several reasons for describing Croly as the ablest of the writers of this period who took the position that political parties are the enemy of democracy. Perhaps the most compelling reason lies in the fact that Croly made a much greater effort than the others to approach the parties sympathetically. This resulted in his understanding parties better than they, and the arguments he directed against parties are more telling than those of writers who, like Ostrogorski, spoke as prosecutors, armed with moral righteousness, willing to employ any forensic devices they could lay hands on, and interested in verdicts of guilty rather than in justice. Croly alone gives evidence of having tried to understand the party-government position of men like Woodrow Wilson, and to analyze it instead of dismissing it as preposterous. Naturally, therefore, his evaluation of American parties and his explanation of why they are as they are showed a genuine comprehension of their nature and function that is entirely absent from the elaborate but always tendentious expositions of Ostrogorski and his American counterparts.

There are, however, at least two fundamental aspects of Croly's attack on parties that make it impossible to accompany him all the way to his conclusions. In the first place, Croly, like Ostrogorski, moved from a definition of democracy which necessarily affected the nature of his analysis, colored his judgments, and, in a real sense, begged the question as to whether parties should be excluded from a truly democratic system. As pointed out above, Croly refused to give democracy a strictly political definition, but rather insisted that it must be thought of as something over and above popular control of government; it must be popular control *employed for certain ends*—particularly the diffusion of social benefits through meliorative legislation. Thus, while both Croly and Ostrogorski professed, in general terms, a belief in majority-rule, both of them believed that such rule is truly democratic only if the majority behaves in a certain way.[45]

---

[44] *Progressive Democracy*, pp. 327-29.

[45] Despite their agreement on this basic point, they disagreed as to just *how* the majority should act. Ostrogorski, as pointed out in the preceding chapter, believed that the majority should operate under a strong sense of self-restraint, and that if it should violate individual and minority rights democracy could not be said to exist. Croly, on the other hand, believed that the majority would be behaving democratically only if it positively provided for social welfare.

Now the question of whether democracy is most usefully thought of as a purely political concept (that is, as a certain *way of making decisions*) or whether democracy, as Croly believed, requires also that *certain kinds of decisions be made* is widely debated today no less than in Croly's time.[46] It is not necessary, for present purposes, to take sides in this debate in order to point out that Croly never really defended his position but only made a series of assertions to the effect that the purely political idea of democracy on which the party-government writers build their case "always assumes a negative emphasis" and has not "traveled very far towards a satisfactory conception of democracy." Croly's failure to make any serious effort to establish the validity of his major premise greatly weakens his entire criticism of the party-government school; for he founded his assessment of political parties upon a definition of democracy under which parties (or any other instrument) designed only to implement majority-rule, and without regard to what the majority might do with its power, must be as a matter of course considered undemocratic. In this respect his forensic victory over the party-government school was as hollow as Ostrogorski's.

In the second place, Croly's two-point attack upon the Wilsonian theory of party government was weakened by certain marginal misapprehensions regarding the doctrine he was trying to refute. Granting the contention that representative government must be party government, Croly's first criticism was that representative government itself, no matter how it is organized, is necessarily dominated by the clash of rival localisms, and that the national interest can therefore never really be considered by such a government. He cited the notorious localism of American legislatures as his proof. Wilson and Lowell, while admitting the localism of the existing American legislatures, had contended that there is nothing *necessary*, in Croly's sense, about the relationship between that characteristic and the fact that they are representative governments. Their proof was the absence of localism in the English system of representative government—a system which was in fact the major source of their ideas about what American government and parties might become. Croly, however, never mentioned the English system, either as a possible exception to his generalizations about representative government or as the source for much of the Wilsonian view. For one who was making a serious attempt to understand that view in order more fully to expose its deficiencies, this was a curious omission.

Croly's second major criticism of the party-government writers was designed to show the futility of their hopes for unified and responsible party action. American experience indicates, he pointed out, that such action can be obtained only by strong presidential leadership; and not only does this fail to provide

---

[46] For a brief summary of both points of view, see Ranney and Kendall, "Democracy: Confusion and Agreement," pp. 430-39.

party responsibility, but it actually reduces the possibilities of such responsibility. We should therefore recognize, he concluded, that party responsibility is impossible to achieve and that executive responsibility is the only sort that can be established. This was certainly an acute criticism of the rather uncritical acceptance of "presidential leadership" by men like Wilson and Ford as the way to establish party government in the American system; [47] but here also Croly's failure to recognize and deal with the English model as the source of the Wilsonian view rendered much of his argument beside the point.

In this connection Croly, ironically, failed to perceive one of the weakest points in the Wilsonian position: its tendency to use the term "party" in two interchangeable but quite different senses: (a) the existing American parties, and (b) the organizations they believed those parties might become if certain reforms were instituted—that is to say, parties on the English model. Now, the Wilsonians agreed with Croly that American parties—in sense (a)—cannot exhibit the unified action required by party government. Croly, however, seems to have assumed that parties in this sense are the only things to be considered. He seems further to have believed that the party-government writers were using the term, as he was, only in sense (a). Thus he again ignored the Wilsonians' frequent citation of the English system as an example of how parties—in sense (b)—can assume genuine *party* responsibility, and how, in such organizations, executive leadership can be made identical with party leadership. He passed over their whole major contention that the existing American parties behave unlike parties in sense (b) less because of their inherent deficiencies than because of the hostile environment within which they are forced to operate. He also ignored their suggestions for changing that environment so as to convert the existing parties into agencies capable of carrying on party government on the English model.

Thus Croly not only missed a chance to censure the Wilsonians for confusing the argument with their double use of the term "party," but he also, by failing to consider either the English model on which they relied so heavily or their various proposals for importing it into the American system, missed the real point of much of the party-government position. It therefore seems fair to conclude that, although it was a considerable improvement upon the efforts of men like Clark, Stickney, Brown, and even Ostrogorski, Croly's attack upon that position failed in its purpose.

---

[47] Presidential leadership, once so much in vogue among party-government writers as *the* way to make the existing parties more responsible, seems now to be falling from favor with them. In this connection, see particularly "Toward a More Responsible Two-party System," pp. 93-95.

Part Four

Conclusions

CHAPTER NINE

Agreements and Disagreements

The primary purpose of this study, as stated in its initial chapter, is to inquire whether present-day political scientists who concern themselves with the function of political parties in the American system can learn anything from the considerable body of literature produced on that problem between 1870 and 1915. This concluding section will be devoted to the attempt to draw together such answers to that question as the study may have justified—first, by summarizing the areas of agreement and disagreement among the writers of the period, and second, by drawing such lessons from their writings for the present-day discussion of the problem as seem to be justified.

Before we can attempt either of these final tasks, however, it is first necessary to ask: Are these writings now so outdated as to give them little relevance to the party problems of our own time? After all, the most recent of the works considered in the foregoing chapters is over thirty-five years old, and the least recent is nearly seventy-five years old.[1] The nation and its government have changed a great deal since then, and the reader might well ask whether the parties have not also changed sufficiently to make writings based on what they were like from 1870 to 1915 simply irrelevant to any serious consideration of what they are like today. For methodological reasons, therefore, it is important to determine the answer to this question.

We must remember that one may approach the American party system from at least three different angles: (1) the *theoretical* approach, which is concerned with developing a picture of the essential nature of democracy and its institutional requirements among which an ideal or model party system may or may not take its place; (2) the *organizational* approach, which is concerned with such things as the internal structure of the parties, their methods of leader-selection and leader-control, member-discipline, finance, and power-getting techniques; and (3) the *group-alignment* approach, which is concerned with identifying which major elements in the electorate support which of the parties in any given election.

If these are legitimate distinctions, it is clear that no discussion of American parties employing the first, or theoretical approach *can* be outdated. It may be

---

[1] Respectively, Croly's *Progressive Democracy* (1914) and Wilson's article, "Committee or Cabinet Government?" (1879).

mistaken or foolish, but it cannot be outmoded; for such basic questions as the nature of democracy and its institutional requirements do not change from age to age, although the prevailing answers to them can and do change. And so what the writers from 1870 to 1915 had to say on these theoretical questions can be examined by us exactly as though it had been written yesterday. The validity (or lack of it) of their ideas is not affected by the time those ideas were expressed.

There is also considerable reason to believe that what these writers had to say about American parties from the second, or organizational, approach is not noticeably out of date. The surest evidence of this is the fact that the characteristics of the existing parties on which they all (excepting, in some respects, Goodnow) agreed—decentralization, boss-control weakness of party-lines on matters of public policy, vagueness of platforms, tendency to corruption—are substantially the same characteristics that most present-day writers, as we saw in Chapter Two, say are true of the parties today. This would suggest that the nature of the American party system, at least in its organizational aspect, has not materially changed in the interim; and we may therefore conclude that what these older writers had to say about the nature of American parties is of far more than merely historic interest.

It is only when one adopts the third, or group-alignment, approach to the study of American parties that he can observe any major differences between the parties of the 1870-1915 period and those of our own time. These changes have been ably identified by such writers as Binkley, Holcombe, and Lubell.[2] The present study, however, is concerned with American parties only from the theoretical and organizational angles; and so these changes do not in any material way affect the question of relevance to our party situation of today. It therefore seems reasonable to conclude that in those aspects of the American party system with which this study is concerned, the literature of the period from 1870 to 1915 is not outdated and is quite relevant to the present-day discussion of the party system of our own time.

AREAS OF AGREEMENT

Despite their many disagreements upon a variety of issues, there was considerable common ground among the writers discussed in this study. For one thing, they all reacted strongly against the formalistic, legalistic approach which had dominated American political science for so long, and founded their analyses upon the explicit assumption that in order to understand the real nature of

[2] W. E. Binkley, *American Political Parties: Their Natural History;* A. N. Holcombe, *The Political Parties of Today* (New York: Harper and Brothers, 1924), *The New Party Politics* (New York: W. W. Norton and Company, 1933), and *The Middle Classes in American Politics* (Cambridge: Harvard University Press, 1940); and Samuel Lubell, *The Future of American Politics* (New York: Harper and Brothers, 1952).

the American system, it is necessary, in Goodnow's words, "to get back of the formal governmental organization and examine the real political life of the people." [3] They also believed that, since political parties are in fact the most important non-formal institutions in the American system, the study of their nature and function is a proper starting point for such an investigation.[4] Again, all of these writers were guilty, in varying degrees, of the interchangeable use of different meanings for the terms "parties" and "function" referred to above.[5]

In describing the nature of the existing American parties, all of the writers considered, with the exception of Goodnow, pointed to the same characteristics: decentralization, boss-control, lack of discipline and unity on matters of public policy, and a consequent general irresponsibility that makes them incapable of accurately expressing the popular will and faithfully translating it into governmental action. They all accepted the notion that a party's membership consists of all those voters who customarily support its ticket; and they all accepted the judgment, consequent upon this notion of party membership, that the existing parties were actually controlled by a very small percentage of their members. With the exception of Ostrogorski, they all believed that American parties have, at some time, performed valuable functions. And they all, again excepting Ostrogorski, accounted for the nature of the existing parties primarily in terms of the formal governmental structure within which they are forced to operate.

The analyses of these writers, finally, had in common one great deficiency. Although the final position of each one upon the question of what kind of party system (if any) must be developed if America is to achieve genuine democratic government was basically determined by his conception of the nature and institutional requirements of an ideal or model democracy, none of them ever very carefully or at any length dealt with the questions: What *is* democratic government, and what does it require? Most of the difficulties of most of these writers stem from their slighting of these fundamental questions.

AREAS OF DISAGREEMENT

The most important difference among the writers considered in this study arose over the question of whether the existing party system, or some possible future variant of it, could have a place in a truly democratic America. The position of each writer on this question, of course, depended upon his conception of what would constitute a "truly democratic" America. Wilson, Lowell, Ford, and Goodnow held that parties not only could but must play a significant role

[3] *Politics and Administration*, p. 1.

[4] Herbert Croly alone of these writers made no such explicit statement. He clearly employed such an approach, however; and it seems reasonable to explain his silence as indicative of his belief that the approach is so self-evidently the proper one that it requires no explicit defense.

[5] *Supra*, pp. 8-9.

in such an America; and each of them based his argument in this respect upon the definition of democracy, in purely *political* terms, as popular control over government.[6] They were convinced, moreover, that popular "control" does not mean popular participation in the day-to-day activities of government, but rather popular choice between and control over alternate sets of accountable rulers. Believing this, they concluded that political parties, in the sense of the parties that would exist if certain reforms were instituted, would have to play an important role in a democratic America; for only such parties, they believed, could provide the alternate sets of responsible rulers which democracy demands.

Ostrogorski and Croly, on the other hand, argued that no kind of political party could have any place in a genuinely democratic government. Both of them believed that a democratic society is more than merely one in which the majority rules; the majority must also, they believed, rule in a certain way and for certain specified ends. And both of them believed that the very existence of political parties would preclude majority-rule in that certain way and for those specified ends.

Thus the opposing positions taken by these two sets of writers on the viability of parties as democratic agencies were the products of their opposing conceptions of democracy; and the question of the nature of democracy, while it received from none of them the attention they devoted to various other issues, was the most important single area of disagreement between the two groups.

---

[6] For the sense in which the term "purely political" is here employed, see *supra*, pp. 11, 136, 146.

CHAPTER TEN

Party Government Reconsidered

The most obvious conclusion to be drawn from the present study is that anyone seriously concerned with the problem of the proper organization and function of political parties in the American system would do well to ponder the analyses by the writers considered in the foregoing chapters. There is very little indeed in the present-day discussion of the doctrine of responsible party government that they did not consider and, in some respects, consider more thoroughly and satisfactorily than any of the writers of our own time are doing. And, as suggested in the preceding chapter, the relevance of their writings has not been materially affected by the passage of time.

This is not to say, of course, that we can learn from these writers (any more than from the writers of today) the answer to this difficult and important question. What we can learn from them, however, are some of the tasks we must accomplish before we can reasonably hope to get nearer to an answer. In the present writer's judgment, contemporary political scientists, whether advocates or critics of the party-government doctrine, are little if any nearer to a satisfactory solution of the problem than were these older writers; and it is also his opinion that they were dogged by the same difficulties, the same confusions and unanswered questions, that make our own discussion of the problem as unsatisfactory as it is. In short, in considering their difficulties we are considering our own. And the purpose of this final chapter is to make clear the nature of some of the most important of those difficulties.

PARTY MEMBERSHIP AND INTRAPARTY DEMOCRACY

Elementary though it may sound, one of the first tasks of contemporary students of American political parties is to decide who should be considered a member of a political party. For example, should any citizen who merely supports a particular party at the polls be regarded as one of its members? This, as we saw in Chapter Two, is apparently what the Committee on Political Parties of the American Political Science Association believes. And this was also the idea of party membership assumed by the six writers covered in this study. Or, as Professor Schattschneider believes, should only those who actively work for a party and assume some real obligation to it be regarded as members?

Clarity on this point is highly desirable for any debate between those who believe that American parties should be more tightly organized and disciplined and those who prefer them as they are now—for at least each group should know what the other side means by the "members" whose organizational relationship to each other is being debated. But it is absolutely essential that the partisans of responsible party government come to a much clearer understanding on this point than they have yet achieved.

Nowhere is this necessity more evident than in the party-government writers' little civil war about "intraparty democracy"—a war that began in the period of this study and has persisted ever since. The Parties Committee believes that party leaders must be made more responsible to party members through improved direct primaries and more "representative" conventions, and that this kind of responsibility is every bit as important as the responsibility of the parties themselves to the electorate at large.[1] As noted in Chapter Six, their position was even more strongly stated and more fully developed by Goodnow fifty years ago when he argued that only parties which are "democratic" internally can be part of a genuine democratic government.[2]

In our own time Professor Schattschneider has defended the parties against the charge of "oligarchy" by arguing that the ticket-voter conception of party membership on which that indictment is based is mistaken and misleading.[3] Henry Jones Ford, however, made a more fundamental attack upon the whole notion of intraparty democracy: If what we want most is parties that are sufficiently organized and well disciplined for them to assume real responsibility *as parties* for how the government is run, we most certainly had better shun any ideas—such as "intraparty democracy"—that will tend to disintegrate the parties and thereby render them incapable of assuming any real responsibility to the electorate.[4]

In the conflict between Goodnow and Ford on the problem of intraparty democracy, we can quite clearly identify the questions which the advocates of responsible party government must settle before they can make out even a clear case—let alone a convincing one—about what kind of parties we should have in America: (1) What kind of party organization does "democracy *between* the parties" require? (2) What kind of party organization does "democracy *within* the parties" mean? (3) What is the relationship between the two kinds of democracy—that is, is (2) likely to make (1) more difficult to achieve? The Parties Committee and Goodnow answered "No" to this last question; but their

---

[1] *Supra,* pp. 17-18.

[2] *Supra,* pp. 99-100, 102-03.

[3] *Supra,* pp. 18-19.

[4] *Supra,* pp. 78-79, 85-86.

simple assertion of this answer without any serious attempt to defend it is, to this reader at least, far less convincing than Ford's and Schattschneider's carefully developed argument that success in achieving "democracy within the parties" is likely to prevent the achievement of "democracy between the parties." In any case, the responsible party government case would be a great deal sounder and more convincing if the relationship between these two kinds of democracy were made more clear, and if the question of their relative priority were settled.

THE DOUBLE MEANINGS OF "PARTIES" AND "FUNCTIONS"

A more serious barrier to fruitful discussion of the party system, however, is the common practice, noted above,[5] of slipping back and forth between two quite different meanings for each of the terms "parties" and their "functions." We have observed how most writers, both advocates and opponents of responsible party government, are guilty of this "shell game." Consequently, in much of the debate, then and now, about the value of the functions American parties perform, there is far too seldom a clear joining of the issue between the opposing sides. All too often the opponents of party government attack the advocates' claims for the desirability of the parties' functions (in the sense of the functions they would perform if they were reorganized) by pointing to the less savory aspects of the role that the parties, as they now exist, are actually performing. And the advocates defend their conception of responsible parties (again the sense of what the parties would be like if they were reformed) by pointing to the general popular acceptance of the party system as it now exists.[6]

The result is that neither question—the nature and merits of the party-government school's ideal party system, and the nature and merits of the party system as it exists today—ever gets the clear and sharply focused debate it deserves. Few defenders of our present parties ever discuss the validity of the party-government school's ideal; and the reforming zeal of most party-government advocates seems to make them uninterested in exploring very thoroughly the nature and merits of the party system as it now exists, and keeps them from asking whether the kind of party system they propose might not remove the good effects of our present parties as well as the effects which they consider bad.

Clarity by both sides in this debate on just what meanings of "parties" and "functions" they have in mind at each point in their respective briefs would not, by itself, resolve all the confusions and misunderstandings that have marked the discussion both in the period of this study and in our own day; but surely it is an indispensable first step toward such resolution.

[5] *Supra*, pp. 8-10.

[6] *Supra*, p. 9.

THE IMPORTANCE OF DEFINING THE NATURE
AND REQUIREMENTS OF DEMOCRACY

If one thing is clear from our examination of the writers on the American party system from 1870 to 1915, it is surely the conclusion that one's position upon the kind of party system he would like to see established in the United States stems directly from and is determined by the picture he carries in his mind of the nature and the institutional requirements of democratic government. All the writers we have considered and all their present-day successors proclaim their devotion to democracy, and assert that their sole criterion for assessing the value of any party system, whether now existing or yet to be achieved, is its appropriateness to democratic government.

Yet we have seen what a great deal of real disagreement is masked by this apparently general agreement on "democracy" as the standard for measuring party systems; for what Wilson, Lowell, Ford, and Goodnow regarded as the most democratic party system was denounced by Ostrogorski and Croly as quite the opposite of democratic. When we pursued this disagreement further, we discovered that the latter two writers held quite a different notion of the nature of democracy from that to which the former four were committed. The party-government advocates took the position that democracy is a purely political matter—a certain *way* of making governmental decisions—and that the requirements of democracy are satisfied so long as decisions are made by the democratic process, regardless of the content of those decisions. Ostrogorski and Croly, on the other hand, believed that democracy exists only when the decisions themselves are of a certain nature, and that democracy disappears when those decisions, regardless of *how* they are made, no longer have the required content. We further observed that most of the disagreements between the two groups upon the question of what kind of party system America should have was the direct result of their disagreement upon the nature and institutional requirements of democracy. And finally, we noted that despite the fact that this disagreement was really the basic issue between them, not all of the six thoroughly and carefully expounded their conceptions of what is involved in democracy, and not one defended his conception's superior claim to the label. Consequently, the most important issue of all in the whole party-government debate was one of the least discussed.

Have the present-day writers on the problem of party advanced beyond these older writers in this respect? The answer, it would appear, is that they have not. Although the leading contemporary critic of the party-government school, E. Pendleton Herring, does make a more serious effort than can be found elsewhere in the contemporary literature to expound and defend his conception of democracy,[7] we hear little from the party-government partisans on such issues

---

[7] In his *Politics of Democracy.*

as these: Should democracy be thought of as a purely political concept, or does it also necessarily include social and economic factors? Is unlimited majority-rule or inviolable minority rights the basic political characteristic of democracy? Just how much and what kind of contribution must the ordinary citizen make to the formulating of governmental decisions in a democracy? The party-government advocates, of course, *have* a position on each of these issues; but one rarely finds in their writings a clear statement of their position, and never finds anything like a full defense of it.[8]

This is surely at least as grave a deficiency in the party-government writers of today as it was in their predecessors at the beginning of the century. And the silence of the contemporary writers on these fundamental and determining questions appears to be the result of the conception they seem to hold of their job as political scientists—a conception which, in the present writer's judgment, is a most serious and fundamental mistake, and one which underlies all the others.

THE JOB OF THE POLITICAL SCIENTIST

Confronted with the charges we have made above against the advocates of responsible party government—that they have neither carefully examined nor clearly stated the basic conception of democracy upon which their whole position rests, and that they have not bothered to defend the claim of their ideal party system to be considered as *the* model which the existing party system should be made to resemble more closely—it seems reasonable to suppose that the contemporary party-government writers would reply in some such fashion as this:[9] "We have not bothered with these theoretical problems because it is not our job to do so. We are not political theorists, but political scientists—specialists in political parties. And as such, our job is not to play about with theoretical model party systems, but rather to suggest practical ways and means for making our party system *more* responsible than it is now. We believe that the American people want a more effective and democratic government, and we believe that a more responsible two-party system will give them such a government. So our job as political scientists is to show the people *how* to get what they want, not tell them *what* they should want." And so most of the report of the Committee on Political Parties, which is widely regarded as the most authoritative present-

---

[8] It is significant, in this regard, that in a recent survey of the leading statements by present-day writers of the various positions held on these issues, the name of not one of the writers identified with the party-government school appears. Austin Ranney and Willmore Kendall, "Democracy: Confusion and Agreement," pp. 430-39.

[9] What follows is not entirely the product of the present writer's imagination. Certainly the position taken in this hypothetical statement is the same as that taken by the Committee on Political Parties, as noted above, p. 9. And in personal conversation with one of the most distinguished members of the Committee, the author received just such a defense of their report.

day statement of the party-government position, is devoted to the presentation of a large number of proposed technical changes in party machinery, all designed to make the existing parties more responsible.

The present writer has elsewhere attempted to point out why such an approach to selling the American people on making their party system more responsible is not likely to meet (as in fact it has not met) with any great success.[10] Briefly stated, the argument is this: Despite the fact that a number of eminent political scientists for over seventy years have been urging that American parties be made more responsible, the parties themselves have changed very little. Why is this so? There is little reason to believe that the explanation lies, as the Parties Committee apparently believe, in popular ignorance of the party-government case; for that case has certainly received a larger audience than most academic proposals enjoy.[11] A far more likely explanation is suggested by Lowell's argument that responsible and disciplined parties will appeal only to a people committed to the desirability of unlimited majority-rule, and that the American people, far from believing in majority-rule, are devoted to the preservation of minority rights *against* majority-rule. Our formal governmental system is therefore designed to inhibit majority-rule, and to such a system American parties, decentralized and irresponsible as they are, are entirely appropriate.[12] Thus, so long as the people reject the idea of unlimited majority-rule, they will continue to regard "independence" as a virtue in their public figures and will be unmoved by any program, such as that devised by the party-government writers, to destroy that independence in favor of adherence to strict party lines.

Now it may or may not be true, as Lowell claimed, that the American people have made a clear and irrevocable choice of inviolable minority rights over unlimited majority-rule. What *is* clear, however, is that they are not clearly committed to the idea of majoritarian democracy. In any event, the point is that when dealing with a problem like the proper organization and function of political parties in the American system the political scientist *must* be a political theorist, whether he recognizes it or not. After all, the party-government advocates' conception of a responsible party system is not something that already exists in the United States; it is rather a *model*—a theory of what the party system should be. And no proposals to make the existing parties more closely resemble the model are likely to be greeted enthusiastically by a populace unconvinced that the model is a desirable one. Only when there is general consensus

---

[10] In "Toward a More Responsible Two-party System: A Commentary," pp. 488-99. What follows here is largely drawn from this essay.

[11] Note, for example, the facts that Wilson's *Congressional Government* went through no less than twenty-five impressions from 1885 to 1925, and that Wilson continued to expound the party-government thesis from the platform of the Presidency of the United States.

[12] *Supra*, pp. 63-65.

among Americans on such theoretical questions as the nature of democracy and the model party system most appropriate to it can the political scientist profitably concentrate upon technical ways and means of realizing the model. Wilson, Lowell, Ford, and Goodnow understood this, and, in varying degrees, did attempt to make the nature of their model explicit and to defend its desirability. Their present-day successors would do well to copy them in this respect.

One unfortunate result of the contemporary party-government writers' reluctance to examine carefully the nature of their model is their failure to understand the full implications of their position—primarily because they have never faced the touchy theoretical question of majority-rule versus minority rights. This is clearly shown by their silence on the question: How should dissident minorities within a responsible party be treated? In the Parties Committee's discussion of "intraparty democracy" and the proper nature and sources of party discipline, the whole emphasis is upon the "generally binding" [sic] nature of party platforms and caucus decisions; and for the most part their explanation of the proper nature of party discipline consists of showing how fine it would be if party members would argue themselves into agreement on program and candidates so that there would be few, if any, dissidents.[13] Their proposals for creating party unity are thus designed to build it up, not by any system of forcing members of party minorities to choose (as they must, for example, in England) between going along with the decisions of the party majority or getting out of the party, but by a series of "positive measures" for discussion, by which the Committee apparently hopes that factions in the party will argue themselves into agreement and minorities seldom need arise.[14] Their report, however, never tells us how a "democratically organized" party should handle a situation in which the party majority has decided to do something with which a party minority cannot "conscientiously" agree.

Perhaps the most serious result of the contemporary party-government writers' failure to understand that they cannot avoid being model-makers is their calm assumption that the American constitutional system represents no great barrier to the achievement of responsible parties.[15] To Lowell's argument that a majoritarian party system is not likely to flourish in an anti-majoritarian governmental system like our own, they reply only that when we get the right kind of party system, the formal government will be no barrier. But to Lowell's further argument that a majoritarian party system will not be acclaimed by a people which is not sure that majority-rule democracy is what it wants, these writers have no reply whatever, probably because they do not recognize the question.

[13] "Toward a More Responsible Two-party System," pp. 52-53, 61.
[14] Ibid., pp. 20-22.
[15] Supra, pp. 21-22.

In short, those writers who wish to see a more responsible party system achieved in the United States must, however "impractical" it may seem to them, work for popular acceptance of the *whole* package of majority-rule democracy. It *is* highly impractical to plead only for a responsible party system, which after all is just one part of the total majoritarian package, and one which logically comes rather late in the argument. No matter how much the President and Congress may wish to cooperate within the present anti-majoritarian constitutional system, responsible parties can hardly flourish when it is possible for a small bloc of senators to filibuster to death any part of the winning party's program, when it is impossible, because of the staggered calendar of elections, to replace the *entire* government at any one election, and when, most important of all, a Supreme Court selected for life and largely beyond the reach of bare party majorities can, for all practical purposes, declare any of the majority-party's leading measures null and void.

The problem is not, as the party-government advocates appear to think of it, one of deciding which should be changed first—the constitutional system or the parties. The point is that the same popular beliefs about government which sustain our present anti-majoritarian constitutional system will continue to sustain (as they have for a very long time) our anti-majoritarian party system. Only when the American people have fully accepted the doctrine of majority-rule democracy can the doctrine of responsible party government expect to receive the popular acclaim which, in Lowell's time and in our own, it has so far been denied.

UNFINISHED BUSINESS

The writers considered in this study had, by 1915, accomplished an impressive and valuable exploration of the problem of the proper organization and function of political parties in the American system—a problem which is surely an important aspect of the larger questions: Do we want a more democratic America, and, if so, how do we get it? The doctrine of responsible party government which they developed and criticized remains one of the most important contributions yet made to the discussion of that problem. The political scientists of our own time, who since 1942 have re-engaged in the debate over that doctrine, have done the Republic a valuable service; but, as this study has attempted to demonstrate, neither the advocates nor the critics of responsible party government have in any significant way advanced the discussion beyond the point where their predecessors had left it in 1915.

In the present writer's opinion, no significant further advance can be made toward the solution of the problem of parties until political scientists abandon, at least temporarily, their present concentration upon technical reforms of party organization and address themselves to the task of answering these three basic questions upon which, as this study has attempted to show, the whole discussion of the proper function of parties turns: (1) What is the nature of democracy? (2) What are its institutional requirements? (3) What model party system is most appropriate to the kind of government envisioned in the answers to (1) and (2)? Only when we have achieved consensus upon the answers to these three basic questions can we fruitfully deal with the derivative problem of the ways and means for establishing such a party system in the United States. Political scientists who understand the problem of parties in these terms can attack it with high confidence that they carry on the work so excellently begun at the beginning of the century by Woodrow Wilson, A. Lawrence Lowell, Henry Jones Ford, Frank J. Goodnow, M. I. Ostrogorski, and Herbert Croly.

Bibliography

Abbott, Lyman. *The Rights of Man*. Boston: Houghton Mifflin Company, 1901.

Alden, Joseph. *The Science of Government in Connection with American Institutions*. New York: Sheldon and Company, 1876.

American Political Science Association, Committee on Political Parties, "Toward a More Responsible Two-party System," *American Political Science Review*, XLIV, Supplement (September, 1950); New York: Rinehart and Company, 1950.

Andrews, Israel W. *Manual of the Constitution of the United States*. New York: Wilson, Hinkle and Company, 1874.

Appleby, Paul H. *Big Democracy*. New York: Alfred A. Knopf, 1945.

Ashley, Roscoe L. *The American Federal State*. New York: The Macmillan Company, 1902.

Bagehot, Walter. *The English Constitution, and Other Political Essays*. Rev. American ed. New York: D. Appleton and Company, 1877.

Baker, Ray Stannard. *Woodrow Wilson: Life and Letters*. 4 vols. Garden City, N. Y.: Doubleday, Page and Company, 1927-39.

Baldwin, Simeon E. *Modern Political Institutions*. Boston: Little, Brown and Company, 1898.

Barker, Ernest. *Reflections on Government*. London: Oxford University Press, 1942.

Barnes, Harry Elmer. *Sociology and Political Theory*. New York: Alfred A. Knopf, 1924.

———. "Some Contributions of Sociology to Modern Political Theory," in Charles E. Merriam and Harry Elmer Barnes (eds.), *A History of Political Theories*. New York: The Macmillan Company, 1924.

Bentley, Arthur F. *The Process of Government*. Chicago: The University of Chicago Press, 1908.

Berdahl, Clarence A. "Party Membership in the United States," *American Political Science Review*, XXXVI (February and April, 1942), 16-50, 241-62.

Binkley, Wilfred E. *American Political Parties: Their Natural History*. New York: Alfred A. Knopf, 1943.

Blanchard, Rufus. *The Rise and Fall of Political Parties in the United States*. Chicago: The National School Furnishing Company, 1892.

Bradford, Gamaliel. *The Lesson of Popular Government*. 2 vols. New York: The Macmillan Company, 1899.

Brooks, Noah. *How the Republic is Governed*. New York: Charles Scribner's Sons, 1895.

———. *Short Studies in Party Politics*. New York: Charles Scribner's Sons, 1895.

Brooks, Robert C. *Corruption in American Life and Politics*. New York: Dodd, Mead and Company, 1910.

Brown, James Sayles. *Partisan Politics: The Evil and Remedy*. Philadelphia: J. B. Lippincott Company, 1897.

Bryce, James. *The American Commonwealth*. 2 vols. London: Macmillan and Company, 1889.

Burgess, John W. *Political Science and Comparative Constitutional Law*. 2 vols. Boston: Ginn and Company, 1891.

Burke, Edmund. *Thoughts on the Cause of the Present Discontents*. 2d ed. London: Printed for J. Dodsley in Pall Mall, 1770.

Burnham, James. *The Machiavellians, Defenders of Freedom*. New York: The John Day Company, 1943.

Burns, James M. *Congress on Trial*. New York: Harper and Brothers, 1949.

Butler, Nicholas Murray. *True and False Democracy*. New York: The Macmillan Company, 1907.

Clark, Charles C. P. *The Commonwealth Reconstructed*. New York: A. S. Barnes and Company, 1878.

———. *The "Machine" Abolished and the People Restored to Power*. New York: G. P. Putnam's Sons, 1900.

Cocker, William J. *The Government of the United States*. New York: Harper and Brothers, 1889.

Cooley, Thomas M. *The General Principles of Constitutional Law in the United States of America*. Boston: Little, Brown and Company, 1880.

Corwin, Edward S. "Henry Jones Ford," in *The Dictionary of American Biography*, edited by Allen Johnson and Dumas Malone. New York: Charles Scribner's Sons, 1931, VI, 515.

Crane, William W. and Moses, Bernard. *Politics: An Introduction to the Study of Comparative Constitutional Law*. New York: G. P. Putnam's Sons, 1884.

Croly, Herbert. *The Promise of American Life*. New York: The Macmillan Company, 1909.

———. "Democratic Factions and Insurgent Republicans," *North American Review*, CXCI (May, 1910), 626-35.

———. *Marcus Alonzo Hanna: His Life and Work*. New York: The Macmillan Company, 1912.

———. "State Political Reorganization," *American Political Science Review*, VI, Supplement (February, 1912), 122-35.

———. "Test of Faith in Democracy," *American Magazine*, LXXV (November, 1912), 21-23.

———. *Progressive Democracy*. New York: The Macmillan Company, 1914.

Dallinger, Frederick W. *Nominations for Elective Office in the United States*. New York: Longmans, Green and Company, 1897.

Dawes, Anna L. *How We Are Governed*. Chicago: The Interstate Publishing Company, 1885.

Dole, Charles F. *The American Citizen*. Boston: D. C. Heath and Company, 1892.

———. *The Spirit of Democracy*. New York: Thomas Y. Crowell Company, 1906.

Emery, Henry C. *Politician, Party and People*. New Haven: Yale University Press, 1913.

Fess, Simeon D. *The History of Political Theory and Party Organization in the United States*. New York: Ginn and Company, 1910.

Finer, Herman. *The Theory and Practice of Modern Government*. 2 vols. London: Methuen and Company, 1932; Rev. ed. New York: Henry Holt and Company, 1949.

Finletter, Thomas K. *Can Representative Government Do the Job?* New York: Reynal and Hitchcock, 1945.

Finley, John H. Review of Moisei I. Ostrogorski's *Democracy and the Organization of Political Parties*, in *Atlantic Monthly*, XCI (March, 1903), 422-25.

Fiske, John. *Civil Government in the United States Considered with Some Reference to Its Origins.* Boston: Houghton Mifflin and Company, 1890.

Ford, Henry Jones. *The Rise and Growth of American Politics.* New York: The Macmillan Company, 1898.

———. "Political Evolution and Civil Service Reform," *Annals of the American Academy of Political and Social Science*, XV (March, 1900), 145-59.

———. Review of Frank J. Goodnow's *Politics and Administration*, in *Annals of the American Academy of Political and Social Science*, XVI (September, 1900), 177-88.

———. "The Results of Reform," *Annals of the American Academy of Political and Social Science*, XXI (March, 1903), 221-37.

———. "Principles of Municipal Organization," *Annals of the American Academy of Political and Social Science*, XXIII (March, 1904), 195-222.

———. "Municipal Corruption," *Political Science Quarterly*, XIX (December, 1904), 673-86.

———. Review of J. Allen Smith's *The Spirit of American Government*, in *American Political Science Review*, III (February, 1909), 137-38.

———. "The Direct Primary," *North American Review*, CXC (July, 1909), 1-14.

———. *The Cost of Our National Government.* New York: Columbia University Press, 1910.

———. "The Cause of Political Corruption," *Scribner's Magazine*, XLIX (January, 1911), 54-61.

———. "American and Canadian Political Methods," *North American Review*, CXCIV (November, 1911), 685-96.

———. "Woodrow Wilson—A Character Sketch," *Review of Reviews*, XLVI (August, 1912), 177-84.

———. "Direct Legislation and the Recall," *Annals of the American Academy of Political and Social Science*, XLIII (September, 1912), 65-77.

———. *Woodrow Wilson: The Man and His Work.* New York: D. Appleton and Company, 1916.

———. *The Cleveland Era.* New Haven: Yale University Press, 1919.

———. *Representative Government.* New York: Henry Holt and Company, 1924.

Ford, Worthington C. *The American Citizen's Manual.* New York: G. P. Putnam's Sons, 1882.

Fuller, Robert H. *Government by the People.* New York: The Macmillan Company, 1908.

Galloway, George B. *Congress at the Crossroads.* New York: Thomas Y. Crowell Company, 1946.

Giddings, Franklin H. *The Principles of Sociology.* New York: The Macmillan Company, 1896.

———. *Democracy and Empire.* New York: The Macmillan Company, 1900.

Goodnow, Frank J. "The Tweed Ring in New York City," in James Bryce, *The American Commonwealth* (cited above), Chapter LXXXVIII.

———. *Municipal Home Rule.* New York: The Macmillan Company, 1895.

————. *Comparative Administrative Law.* 2 vols. New York: G. P. Putnam's Sons, 1897.

————. *Politics and Administration.* New York: The Macmillan Company, 1900.

————. "Political Parties and City Government," *The International Monthly,* I (June, 1900), 618-31.

————. Review of Moisei I. Ostrogorski's *Democracy and the Organization of Political Parties,* in *Political Science Quarterly,* XVIII (June, 1902), 332-34.

————. *Municipal Problems.* New York: Published for the Columbia University Press by the Macmillan Company, 1907.

————. *Municipal Government.* New York: The Century Company, 1909.

————. *City Government in the United States.* New York: The Century Company, 1910.

————. *Social Reform and the Constitution.* New York: The Macmillan Company, 1911.

Haddow, Anna. *Political Science in American Colleges and Universities, 1636-1900.* New York: D. Appleton-Century Company, 1939.

Hadley, Arthur T. *Standards of Public Morality.* New York: The Macmillan Company, 1907.

Hart, Albert Bushnell. *Actual Government.* New York: Longmans, Green and Company, 1903.

Hedges, Job E. *Common Sense in Politics.* 7th ed. New York: Moffat, Yard and Company, 1912.

Herring, E. Pendleton. *The Politics of Democracy.* New York: W. W. Norton and Company, 1940.

————. *Presidential Leadership.* New York: Farrar and Rinehart, 1940.

Hinsdale, B. A. *The American Government.* Ann Arbor: The Register Publishing Company, 1891.

Holcombe, Arthur N. *The Political Parties of Today.* New York: Harper and Brothers, 1924.

————. *The New Party Politics.* New York: W. W. Norton and Company, 1933.

————. *The Middle Classes in American Politics.* Cambridge: Harvard University Press, 1940.

Hollingsworth, William W. *Woodrow Wilson's Political Ideals.* Princeton: Princeton University Press, 1918.

Hook, Sidney. *Reason, Social Myths and Democracy.* New York: The John Day Company, 1940.

Hyslop, James H. *Democracy: A Study of Government.* New York: Charles Scribner's Sons, 1899.

James, James A. and Sanford, A. H. *Government in State and Nation.* New York: Charles Scribner's Sons, 1901.

Jennings, W. Ivor. *Cabinet Government.* Cambridge: Cambridge University Press, 1936.

Johnson, Allen. "The Nationalizing Influence of Party," *Yale Review,* XV (November, 1906), 283-92.

Jones, Chester L. (ed.). *Readings on Parties and Elections in the United States.* New York: The Macmillan Company, 1912.

Kales, Albert M. *Unpopular Government in the United States.* Chicago: The University of Chicago Press, 1914.

Kendall, Willmoore. *John Locke and the Doctrine of Majority Rule.* Urbana: The University of Illinois Press, 1941.

Key, V. O. *Politics, Parties and Pressure Groups.* 2d ed. New York: Thomas Y. Crowell Company, 1947.

Lewis, Edward R. *A History of American Political Thought from the Civil War to the World War.* New York: The Macmillan Company, 1937.

Lieber, Francis. *Manual of Political Ethics.* 2 vols. Boston: Charles C. Little and James Brown, 1838.

———. *Civil Liberty and Self-Government.* 2 vols. Philadelphia: Lippincott, Grambo and Company, 1853.

Lindsay, A. D. *The Essentials of Democracy.* Philadelphia: University of Pennsylvania Press, 1929.

Lowell, A. Lawrence. *Essays on Government.* Boston: Houghton Mifflin Company, 1889.

———. *Governments and Parties in Continental Europe.* 2 vols. Boston: Houghton Mifflin Company, 1896.

———. "Oscillations in Politics," *Annals of the American Academy of Political and Social Science,* XII (July, 1898), 69-97.

———. "The Influence of Party upon Legislation in England and America," *Annual Report of the American Historical Association for the Year 1901.* Washington, D. C.: Government Printing Office, 1902, I, 321-542.

———. *The Government of England.* 2 vols. New York: The Macmillan Company, 1908.

———. *Public Opinion and Popular Government.* New York: Longmans, Green and Company, 1913.

———. *Public Opinion in War and Peace.* Cambridge: Harvard University Press, 1923.

Lubell, Samuel. *The Future of American Politics.* New York: Harper and Brothers, 1952.

McLaughlin, Andrew C. *The Courts, the Constitution, and Parties.* Chicago: The University of Chicago Press, 1912.

Macmahon, Arthur W. "M. I. Ostrogorski," in *Encyclopaedia of the Social Sciences* (New York: The Macmillan Company, 1937), VI, 503-04.

MacIver, Robert M. *The Web of Government.* New York: The Macmillan Company, 1947.

Macy, Jesse. *Our Government.* Rev. ed. Boston: Ginn and Company, 1891.

———. *Party Organization and Machinery.* New York: The Century Company, 1904.

———. Review of Moisei I. Ostrogorski's *Democracy and the Party System in the United States,* in *American Political Science Review,* V (August, 1911), 472-74.

Mencken, Henry L. *Notes on Democracy.* New York: Alfred A. Knopf, 1926.

Merriam, Charles E. *A History of American Political Theories.* New York: The Macmillan Company, 1903.

———. *American Political Ideas.* New York: The Macmillan Company, 1920.

——— and Gosnell, Harold F. *The American Party System.* Rev. ed. New York: The Macmillan Company, 1933; 3d ed. New York: The Macmillan Company, 1947.

Michels, Robert. *Political Parties: A Sociological Study of the Oligarchical Tendencies of Modern Democracy.* Translated by Eden and Cedar Paul. London: Jarrold and Sons, 1915.

Moffett, Samuel E. *Suggestions on Government.* New York: Rand, McNally and Company, 1894.

Morse, Anson D. "The Place of Party in the Political System," *Annals of the American Academy of Political and Social Science,* II (November, 1891), 300-08.

————. "Our Two Great Parties, Their Origin and Tasks: the Democratic Party," *Political Science Quarterly,* VI (December, 1891), 593-612; VII (September, 1892), 522-35.

————. "What is a Party?" *Political Science Quarterly,* XI (March, 1896), 68-81.

Mosca, Gaetano. *The Ruling Class.* Translated by Hannah D. Kahn, edited and revised by Arthur Livingston. New York: The McGraw-Hill Book Company, 1939.

Mowry, William A. *Studies in Civil Government.* Boston: Silver, Burdett and Company, 1888.

Nordhoff, Charles. *Politics for Young Americans.* New York: Harper and Brothers, 1882.

Odegard, Peter H. and Helms, E. Allen. *American Politics.* 2d ed. New York: Harper and Brothers, 1947.

Ostrogorski, Moisei I. *Democracy and the Organization of Political Parties.* Translated from the French by Frederick Clarke. 2 vols. New York: The Macmillan Company, 1902.

————. *Democracy and the Party System in the United States.* New York: The Macmillan Company, 1910.

Padover, Saul K. (ed.). *Wilson's Ideals.* Washington, D. C.: American Council on Public Affairs, 1942.

Pareto, Vilfredo. *The Mind and Society.* Translated by Andrew Bongiorno and Arthur Livingston, edited by Arthur Livingston. New York: Harcourt, Brace and Company, 1935.

Patton, Jacob H. *Political Parties in the United States: Their History and Influence.* New York: New Amsterdam Book Company, 1896.

Penniman, Howard R. *Sait's American Parties and Elections.* 4th ed. New York: Appleton-Century-Crofts, 1948.

Peterman, Alexander L. *Elements of Civil Government.* New York: American Book Company, 1891.

Ranney, Austin. "Goodnow's Theory of Politics," *Southwestern Social Science Quarterly,* XXX (March, 1950), 268-76.

————. "Toward a More Responsible Two-party System: A Commentary," *American Political Science Review,* XLV (June, 1951), 488-99.

————. "The Reception of Political Parties into American Political Science," *Southwestern Social Science Quarterly,* XXXII (December, 1951), 183-91.

———— and Kendall, Willmoore. "Democracy: Confusion and Agreement," *Western Political Quarterly,* IV (September, 1951), 430-39.

Richardson, Charles. *Party Government.* Philadelphia: American Academy of Political and Social Science, 1892.

Roady, Elston E. "Party Regularity in Congress, 1913-1921," Unpublished doctoral dissertation, University of Illinois, 1951.

Robinson, Edgar E. *The Evolution of American Political Parties.* New York: Harcourt, Brace and Company, 1924.

Sait, Edward M. *American Parties and Elections*. 3d ed. New York: D. Appleton-Century Company, 1942.

Schattschneider, E. E. *Party Government*. New York: Farrar and Rinehart, 1942.

———. *The Struggle for Party Government*. College Park, Md.: The University of Maryland Press, 1948.

Schouler, James. *Ideals of the Republic*. Boston: Little, Brown and Company, 1908.

Sedgwick, Arthur G. *The Democratic Mistake*. New York: Charles Scribner's Sons, 1912.

Shaler, Nathaniel S. *The Citizen*. New York: A. S. Barnes and Company, 1904.

Shaw, Albert. *Political Problems of American Development*. New York: The Columbia University Press, 1907.

Sloane, William M. *Party Government in the United States of America*. New York: Harper and Brothers, 1914.

Small, Albion W. Review of Moisei I. Ostrogorski's *Democracy and the Organization of Political Parties*, in *American Journal of Sociology*, VIII (January, 1903), 563-65.

———. *General Sociology*. Chicago: The University of Chicago Press, 1905.

Smith, J. Allen. *The Spirit of American Government*. New York: The Macmillan Company, 1907.

Smith, Joseph W. *Training for Citizenship*. New York: Longmans, Green and Company, 1902.

Soule, George. "Herbert Croly," in *Encyclopaedia of the Social Sciences* (New York: The Macmillan Company, 1937), II, 603.

Stickney, Albert. *A True Republic*. New York: Harper and Brothers, 1879.

———. *Democratic Government*. New York: Harper and Brothers, 1885.

———. *The Political Problem*. New York: Harper and Brothers, 1890.

———. *Organized Democracy*. Boston: Houghton Mifflin and Company, 1906.

Sumner, William Graham. *What Social Classes Owe to Each Other*. New York: Harper and Brothers, 1883.

———. *Collected Essays in Political and Social Science*. New York: Henry Holt and Company, 1885.

———. *Folkways*. New York: Ginn and Company, 1906.

———. *The Challenge of Facts and Other Essays*. Edited by A. G. Keller. New Haven: Yale University Press, 1914.

Thompson, Daniel G. *Politics in a Democracy*. New York: Longmans, Green and Company, 1893.

Tiedeman, Christopher G. *The Unwritten Constitution of the United States*. New York: G. P. Putnam's Sons, 1890.

Townsend, Calvin. *Analysis of Civil Government*. New York: Ivison, Phinney, Blakeman and Company, 1870.

Turner, Julius. "Responsible Parties: A Dissent from the Floor," *American Political Science Review*, XLV (March, 1951), 143-52.

Tyler, Lyon Gardiner. *Parties and Patronage in the United States*. New York: G. P. Putnam's Sons, 1891.

Waldo, Dwight. *The Administrative State*. New York: The Ronald Press, 1948.

Ward, Lester F. *Dynamic Sociology*. 2 vols. New York: D. Appleton and Company, 1883.

———. *Applied Sociology*. New York: Ginn and Company, 1906.

———. *The Psychic Factors of Civilization.* 2d ed. New York: Ginn and Company, 1906.

———. "The Sociology of Political Parties," *American Journal of Sociology,* XIII (January, 1908), 439-54.

Wilson, Francis G. *Elements of Modern Politics.* New York: McGraw-Hill Book Company, 1936.

Wilson, Woodrow. "Cabinet Government in the United States," *International Review,* VII (August, 1879), 146-63.

———. "Committee or Cabinet Government?" in *Public Papers* (cited below), I, 95-129; Orig. publ.: *Overland Monthly,* series 2, III (January, 1884), 17-33.

———. *Congressional Government* (Boston: Houghton Mifflin and Company, 1885).

———. "The Study of Administration," *Political Science Quarterly,* II (June, 1887), 197-222.

———. Review of John W. Burgess' *Political Science and Comparative Constitutional Law,* in *Atlantic Monthly,* LXVII (May, 1891), 692-99.

———. "Mr. Cleveland's Cabinet," in *Public Papers,* I, 198-222; Orig. publ.: *Review of Reviews,* VII (April, 1893), 286-97.

———. *An Old Master, and Other Political Essays.* New York: Charles Scribner's Sons, 1893.

———. *Mere Literature, and Other Essays.* Boston: Houghton Mifflin and Company, 1896.

———. "Leaderless Government," an address before the Virginia Bar Association, August 4, 1897, in *Public Papers,* I, 336-59; Orig. publ.: Richmond: James E. Goode Printing Company, 1897.

———. "Democracy and Efficiency," *Atlantic Monthly,* LXXXVII (March, 1901), 289-99.

———. *The State.* Rev. ed. Boston: D. C. Heath and Company, 1902.

———. *Constitutional Government in the United States.* New York: Columbia University Press, 1908.

———. "Hide-and-Seek Politics," *North American Review,* CXCI (May, 1910), 585-601.

———. "Political Reform," an address before the City Club of Philadelphia, November 18, 1909, in *Public Papers,* II, 188-92.

———. *The New Freedom.* Garden City, N. Y.: Doubleday, Page and Company, 1913.

———. *The Public Papers of Woodrow Wilson: College and State.* Edited by Ray Stannard Baker and William E. Dodd. 2 vols. New York and London: Harper and Brothers, 1925.

Woolsey, Theodore Dwight. *Political Science, or the State Theoretically and Practically Considered.* 2 vols. New York: Scribner, Armstrong and Company, 1877.

Wright, A. O. and Kuhn, W. D. *Civil Government in the United States.* Topeka: Crane and Company, 1897.

Young, Roland. *This is Congress.* New York: Alfred A. Knopf, 1943.

Index